DATE DUE

DEMCO 38-296

MUSIC ON RECORD 1

Brass Bands

edited by Peter Gammond
and Raymond Horricks

MUSIC ON RECORD 1

Brass Bands

edited by Peter Gammond
and Raymond Horricks

 Patrick Stephens, Cambridge

First published 1980

British Library Cataloguing in Publication Data

Music on record.
  1: Brass bands
  1. Music—Discography
  I. Gammond, Peter
  II. Horricks, Raymond
  016.7899'12   ML156.2

  ISBN 0 85059 366 2

Text photoset in 9 on 10 pt and 10 on 11 pt Plantin
by Manuset Limited, Baldock, Herts.
Printed and bound in Great Britain, on 100 gsm
Five Star Velvet, by The Garden City Press,
Letchworth, Herts, for the publishers
Patrick Stephens Limited, Bar Hill, Cambridge,
CB3 8EL, England.

Contents

Introduction by E. Vaughan Morris
Organiser of the National Championships 1945-71

It is a century and a half since the first brass bands were formed in the factories and mining communities of the North of England. This has been a period of tremendous change—a period of wars and peace, of great industrial and technological achievements, together with far-reaching social progress. Through it all the brass band movement has marched forward until it has now become one of the great influences on the cultural and social life of the people.

Loyalty and devotion in the face of bitter struggles and sacrifices, true tenacity and a love of music-making, have brought brass bands through to the heights of achievement which must command the respect of any thinking musician.

Furthermore, the introduction of the competition element into amateur music-making is no new thing. This has long been a means towards perfection much favoured by British bands and, in turn, by those in Europe and all countries settled by Europeans. But Britain has continued to lead in the development and projection of brass music and the resultant competition. Musicians and fans throughout the world still look to us as the pacesetters in this, their chosen field.

The influx of bandswomen taking an active playing role is also welcome, together with the infusion of young, bright-thinking players into the ranks of our bands. These developments owe much to the foresight of educational authorities in providing facilities, along with highly qualified tutors in brass instrumentation at British schools.

Brass bands today are a living force, and their cultural value is of the utmost importance. They render a priceless service to the community from which they spring and describe. Long may they flourish, bringing delight and inspiration to the people of Britain.

A book such as this was long overdue. It has been prepared by a respected music-critic and by the most active working record producer of brass bands. I welcome it; and I feel sure that anyone who reads it will find it both informative and enjoyable.

Contributors

Peter Gammond was born in Northwich, Cheshire in 1925. Educated at Sir John Deane's Grammar School, Northwich and Wadham College, Oxford. Served in the Royal Armoured Corps 1942-7. Played the trombone for a time in jazz and brass bands and theatre orchestras; now sticks to the piano and a little composing. Joined the Decca Record Company in 1952 and left in 1960 to become a freelance writer and journalist. Edited *Audio Record Review* from 1966 to 1970 and then became Music Editor of *Hi-Fi News & Record Review* 1970-9. Wide ranging tastes in music and has published over 20 books on classical music, jazz, ragtime, musical instruments, music hall and a variety of subjects. Occasional broadcaster and prolific record sleeve-note writer. **Books** *The Decca Book of Jazz* (ed) (1958); *Duke Ellington: His Life and Music* (ed) (1958); *Terms Used in Music* (1959); *101 Things* (with Peter Clayton) (1959); *A Guide to Popular Music* (with Peter Clayton) (1960); *Jazz on Record* (with Charles Fox & Alun Morgan) (ed) (1960); *Music on Record*, 4 vols (with Burnett James) (ed) (1962/4); *14 Miles on a Clear Night* (with Peter Clayton) (1966); *Bluff Your Way in Music* (1966); *The Meaning and Magic of Music* (1969); *Your Own, Your Very Own* (music-hall) (1971); *One Man's Music* (1971); *Music Hall Songbook* (ed) (1975); *Musical Instruments in Colour* (1975); *Scott Joplin and the Ragtime Era* (1975); *The Music Goes Round and Round* (with Raymond Horricks) (1979); *The Illustrated Encyclopedia of Opera* (ed) (1979); *The Magic Flute* (1979); *The Good Old Days* (ed) (1980).

Raymond Horricks was born in 1933 at Withington. Educated at the Xaverian College, Manchester. 1951-3 in France and Egypt. Co-author with Alun Morgan of *Modern Jazz: a Survey of Developments Since 1939*, the first book of its subject, author of *Count Basie and His Orchestra*—for which he received a fellowship and which was described in the American press recently as 'still the only authentic account of the band'; editor and part-writer of *Jazzmen of Our Time* and author of *The Jazz Century* as well as two monographs about Rudyard Kipling in India. For the past 20 years has worked as a record producer of music ranging from Bach and Stravinsky to Frank Sinatra, rock and progressive folk; and including the Decca *Sounds of Brass* series and other brass recordings for Pye and Warwick. With Peter Gammond recently finished editing and writing *The Music Goes Round and Round: a Cool Look at the Record Industry*. **Books** *Count Basie and his Orchestra* (1957); *Modern Jazz* (with Alun Morgan) (1959); *These Jazzmen of Our Time* (ed) (1959); *The Music Goes Round and Round* (with Peter Gammond) (1979); *The Jazz Century* (1979).

William Arthur Chislett was born in Rotherham in 1895 into a modestly musical family, his main contacts with music at an early age being via brass and military band concerts, and an early present of a phonograph and a lot of cylinders helped to set him on the road. Legal studies were interrupted by the first World War. Completed his studies after the war and settled in Halifax where he took a leading part in the musical life of the town and contributed what were possibly the first record reviews in a Provincial paper to the *Halifax Courier*. Joined the panel of *The Gramophone* in 1925 where he has since reviewed all the brass band recordings and other music in the light classical field. Settled in Lancashire, awarded the OBE in the second World War and shortly after gave up his law practice to concentrate on music in Oxford. Was chief music critic of the *Oxford Mail* for more than 20 years and received an honorary degree from Oxford University.

John Knight attended Eggars Grammar School. He started piano lessons at the age of five. Served as a musician for five years with the RAF and was solo cornet and band sergeant of the Fighter Command Band. Afterwards studied at the London College of Music for four years. Has been a teacher of brass-playing in Hampshire since 1946 and supervises all brass band activities for the Hampshire Education Authority, as head of the Brass Teaching Department and Director of County Brass Bands. Formed the Hampshire Youth Concert Band in 1965. In 1977 he received the Queens Jubilee Medal in recognition of his work.

James Scott, like many brass band conductors, started his career as a cornet player and by the age of 16 had appeared as soloist in many concerts and on the radio. But it was from 1947 onwards, when he joined Munn & Felton's Band (later known as GUS) that he came to prominence and earned a reputation which was crowned in 1959 and 1960 with the Cammell Laird Band with whom he enjoyed some notable successes. He also gained valuable musical experience at the time by playing cornet and trumpet with the leading symphony orchestra in the North. In 1973 he was appointed professional conductor of the Brighouse & Rastrick Band and led them to victory in the same year in the National Championships. Under his direction in 1975 they won the Granada TV Band of the Year Contest. In October 1975 he accepted the post of Director of Music of Fodens Motor Works Band with whom he won the BBC TV contest *Champion Brass* in 1978. In 1979 he became musical director of the Rochdale-Wilsons band.

James Watson—see section on 'Who's who in brass band music'.

The brass band world and the story of the National Championships
by Raymond Horricks

A few years back, all the members of the renowned Black Dyke Mills Band were returning to their native Queensbury after one of their victories in the National Championships at the Royal Albert Hall. The mood in the coach was naturally euphoric: a heady mixture of knowing they had played well, feeling superior to their old rivals Fairey and Brighouse & Rastrick, the downing of a little champagne and a rather more sizeable quantity of best bitter. And when they got to Queensbury one of the bandsmen piped up with the suggestion that they walk through the streets playing their winning test-piece. 'Just to let everyone know we've won again . . . .'

'Don't be daft', the conductor snapped at him. 'Nobody's going to thank us for waking them up in the early hours of the morning.' But the wit was not easily silenced. 'All right then', he called back down the coach. 'Let's take us boots off an' tie t'laces 'round us necks and walk through t'streets playing test-piece in us stocking-feet!'

Another old brass band story originates from further north still; Scotland in fact. A small-town band—one of hundreds in the brass movement—had been struggling to keep going with the help of a generous local businessman. When suddenly their benefactor died, the band's members felt it was right and proper that they offer their services to play a piece of music at his graveside; an offer the family were pleased to accept. Came the day, the musicians mingled with the mourners and then, at the end of the ceremonial part and to everyone else's surprise, they launched forth with a spirited rendition of *Will Ye No Come Back Again?* 'Sounding off regrets at there being no more subsidies', as someone murmured darkly.

The daughter of the house chose to think the best of them. But later, handing around the refreshments, she did comment to the bandmaster on his selection of the item. 'Well, ye see, Miss, it's like this', he replied. 'It's so difficult to get a full rehearsal these days. What wi' half the lads doing shift-work and so on. So we thought it wisest to do something we all knew. That way at least we could send him off wi' a bitty music really well-played . . . .' One suspects that following such an explanation his daughter continued to subsidise the band.

To return to Black Dyke Mills though. In 1975 I was invited by Roy Newsome, at that time the band's professional conductor, and by Major Peter Parkes, their principal guest conductor, to attend a rehearsal in what is certainly one of the brass band world's holy-of-holies: Dyke's practice-room at Queensbury. This was an honour indeed, especially since they were rehearsing the test-piece for that year's National Championships, Robert Farnon's *Une Vie De Matelot*. However I had worked with Roy before; and with Peter too in his other capacity as Director of Music, Grenadier Guards. Also I was about to produce a long-playing album with the band, including—I hoped—the Farnon test-piece as a suitable memorial to yet another of their victories.

The latter subsequently came to pass. (The first of a whole series of wins Peter

Parkes has had with the band.) But I was totally unprepared for Dyke's practice-room. At first glance it reminded me of my 'basic training' barrack-room at Catterick Camp (which, when I was incarcerated there in 1951, had already been condemned since 1916). It would probably have interested Dickens, certainly Mayhew and more recently and for very different reasons, George Orwell and Henry Livings. There were a couple of floor-boards missing, what paint had not actually peeled off the walls was of an unidentifiable colour, and the night I was there the rain came in. The only attempt at any form of decoration had been to hang the photographs of former band-master/conductors around the walls. All very solemn and severe, with one or two of the earlier faces heavily moustachioed, they looked down upon the latest generation of music-makers as if critics in aspic, each of them self-righteous and beyond argument. But a typical touch of Dyke had been added to these portraits. Underneath the visage, in immaculate script, were details of the actual prize money the man had won.

Worst of all though was the sound in the room. Being so cramped, it was hardly possible for the players to sit in their competition formation, and the noises coming from their instruments banged and bounced around the place like a musical can-nonade. There was no escape, no real reverberation, nothing to give the sections a decent blend and no respite for my ears either! Fortunately Peter Parkes had been with the band some time by this date; he had grown 'acclimatised', if that is the right word to use. Quite clearly he was well on top of things that night, both musically and in coping with Dyke's committee-style 'democracy'. (There are immediate post-mortems and usually heads roll if they fail to win.) Also, as Peter pointed out to me later: with such awful acoustics in the room, once he can get the band sounding even reasonably good in there, then he knows it is going to sound a whole lot better at the Albert Hall and, of course, this is precisely what happened. A few days later they sallied forth from their 'hole in the wall', not in the least bit overawed by going to London—where they won with a handsome margin, fully avenging their defeats by Cory in 1974 and Brighouse the year before that.

Now Dyke are by no means a band short of money. Apart from the prizes they pick up each year, they do many successful concerts and the band is permanently supported by the Queensbury textile manufacturers, John Foster and Son. But then, over an immense, piled-high Yorkshire supper with Roy Newsome and his wife, I discovered another interesting feature about the band. This very gifted, hard-headed (even ruthless, when it comes to competing) ensemble of musicians is acutely superstitious. Mature men, nevertheless they believe that if once they have to leave that practice-room they will *never, never* win another competition. John Foster and Son have offered to build a new one for them, much larger, with professionally-supervised acoustics and the chance to rehearse there with fully-accredited soloists from all spheres of music. But Dyke will not budge. The band's committee will not budge. And so they play through each winter with the snow melting all around their feet. It is marvellous; as well as being their own, vital, still being lived-in epitaph!

Readers must forgive me this somewhat unconventional preamble. It has come about because I had contracted to do a book about the record industry called *The Music Goes Round and Round* and asked Peter Gammond to be my co-editor. He in turn then asked me to join him for a book about brass bands, since as he pointed out, for *Hi-Fi News* he always seems to be reviewing brass LPs which I have produced. Moreover we had both grown up within a few miles of one another in Cheshire: not far over the great, green wet plain from the sounds of Fodens and Fairey.

In addition though, what I have been trying my hardest to get down on paper here are a number of reasons why brass bands are unique. Unique because there has been no precedent in the whole history of music for men, or boys (and now a few girls) remaining essentially amateur in their financial status and yet creating music of such a high standard. At least I do not think there has since the choristers and instrumentalists of the Renaissance.

Enthusiasm has been the real common denominator. Brass bandsmen in the cause of 'banding' (ie, travelling to and taking part in competitions) can be bad-tempered, back-stabbing and often as downright awkward as it is possible to be; but they are also—at their best—the most human and *humane* of music-makers. Warm, generous, outward-going, outspoken; far from modest in victory, but at the same time critically honest (and self-critical) in adversity: the brass bandsman is the one species of musician who has never truly surrendered to Mammon. By and large, for instance, he still sticks up two fingers at the Musicians' Union. He is not averse to making money (for the band); but the perfection of his art comes first—and in any case he is the last person in the world to hold any degree of respect for union officials who either cannot, or no longer, play musical instruments. Tennis-players, footballers and now even cricketers, all originally amateur 'folk' heroes, have reached out for gold; likewise most musicians, whether it is an agent for a famous conductor demanding that he should get a bigger fee than another famous conductor, or a session trumpet-player charging 25 per cent above his basic fee because the arrangement has required him to play eight bars on flugelhorn.

But while all this has been going on the brass bandsman has become a kind of musical aristocrat of his day. A man professional in his executive standards while still amateur in his enthusiasm and dedication. A genuine love for music is now often suspect among prominent figures on the international and even the national scene but it is still there with brass band players. Love for music and the embryonic fires of competition.

Nor must one forget the remarkable way in which the brass band background has upholstered the wider world of music which lies beyond it. It has become a well-known cliché (although true) that Mozart was a child prodigy; and Mendelssohn not far behind him. But how many people who have not actually worked with him know that James Watson was playing cornet with the Desford Colliery Band at the age of nine, was the youngest-ever principal trumpet with the Royal Philharmonic Orchestra at 22 and has been a Full Professor of Trumpet at the Royal Academy of Music from the age of 26? However, as Josephine Tey, once put it: 'The Daughter of Time is the truth'. Fortunately—in the end—history generally manages to sort out its own anomalies.

★   ★   ★

It all began 'up north' of course; since when it has spread throughout the world, exciting peoples as diverse as the Canadians and Australians, the Belgians and even the normally phlegmatic Swiss. And it began with the essential inner caucus of northern counties: Northumberland and Durham, Cumberland, Yorkshire and Lancashire. Soon afterwards it spread to Cheshire; while there were 'sideswipe' invasions of Derby and Lincolnshire. But by the time it had reached into Nottinghamshire and Leicestershire the other northerners were already competing against one another; and the Yorkshiremen clearly regarded themselves as the pacesetters. (They still do!) In 1974, when Cory won the National Championship for Wales for the first time, psychological sackcloth and ashes were worn in various townships of Yorkshire for the whole of the next year. Certainly Yorkshire, even ahead of the north-west, is the most fiercely competitive of all the regional areas in the National Championships. It is harder to get through from these parts than from any other heat; somewhat similar to Western Europe's position in the World Cup at soccer. In fact, sport perhaps provides the clue here. Yorkshire bandsmen have very much the attitude of their own county's Cricketing Board: 'If you weren't born here then you don't belong. And if you *were* born here and we select you to play, then don't think you're going to find it easy . . . .'

Only comparatively recently have the leisure pursuits of working-class people become the subject of sociological studies; and due to this lack of firm documentary evidence the origins and reasons for 'banding' are hazardous for any writer to try to pinpoint. One thing is clear, however. By the time of Great Britain's involvement in the Napoleonic wars, a wide variety of brass and other musical instruments had found their way into the hands of workers in certain 'key' industrial areas of the north. From which date, and as musical proficiency increased, the workers' own community sense and fellow-feeling drew them together into small units of players and then into the creation of whole bands. They became very popular in their towns and villages. Let's face it: there was precious little else to relieve the grinding poverty and the hardship of life down the pit or in the smoke-belching, overcrowded factories during this period.

A good case can, and has been made out for a Durham band being the first of its kind. It was founded in 1808, when a few employees of the local colliery got together and called themselves the Coxlodge Institute Band, later known as the Coxlodge and Hazelrigg Band. Just a few years after this, in 1816 and with Napoleon now finally toppled and in exile on Saint Helena, the famous Black Dyke Mills Band was founded; with Besses o' th' Barn very soon afterwards. (Although Besses lay claim to having started out as a string band as early as the 1790s; which then became a brass and reed band about 1818, financed by the Clegg Brothers, Lancashire cotton manufacturers.)

Dyke too started out as a reed band and was known first of all—after the name of its leader—as Peter Wharton's Band. Wharton, landlord of the Old Dolphin in Queensbury, apparently used to travel to Manchester and buy music from the military bands garrisoned there. A number of the band's musicians though were workers in the mills of the first Mr Foster of Queensbury, near Bradford; and their employer was himself an enthusiastic member of the band, playing French horn. People claimed that there were still a number of reeds in the line-up as late as 1833 but then the band was continually breaking up and reforming. However, in the 1850s, during yet another economic crisis, the company of John Foster and Son stepped in. They connected the band—officially and legally—with their mills, found employment for all of its members, purchased new instruments and uniforms, and engaged as its trainer and conductor a Mr Samuel Longbottom of Mixenden. (Later on Alexander Owen, the most famous cornet soloist and teacher of the 19th century, would direct both Dyke and Besses and win some quite substantial prizes with them.)

Meanwhile other bands had also come into being. The Stalybridge Old Band, which soon called itself the New Band, were actually booked to play at St Peter's Fields, Manchester on that fateful day in August 1819 which would turn into the Peterloo Massacre. While the radical politician and orator Henry Hunt was addressing the crowds, the local magistrates, in a panic, unleashed the King's cavalry. At this precise moment the Stalybridge Band, just prior to playing, were refreshing themselves at the Union Rooms in Ancoats. Suddenly, one John Cotterill rushed in, white-faced, to tell them of the attack. Collecting their precious instruments, the bandsmen ran. They thought of ducking into the George and Dragon at Pin Mill

Brow, but then they met a man whose hat had been sliced in two by a cavalry-sabre and so they ran on—at one point crouching down behind a hedgerow while a troop of horsemen rode by. It was a lucky escape, because as bandsmen and in working-clothes they were directly associated with Hunt's cause.

Another important band of the period was the New Mills Prize Band. They too had begun as a brass-and-reed group, and in marked contrast to their Stalybridge colleagues, they seem to have had some support from the local gentry. At least in the purchasing of their instruments—and with their uniforms, which consisted of 'a swallow-tailed coat, blue tunic with epaulettes and grey tall hats'. Their first conductor was a Mr Timothy Beard.

Once England had settled back into peace, so the number of bands grew along with the stories and legends attached to them. Some of them, like the Bolton Band, consisted of discharged military musicians—which accounted for them playing clarinets and piccolos and even bassoons and serpents at the outset. The Chorlton Band, so we are informed, had 'twenty-four members . . . who played a variety of brass instruments, clarionets and piccolos'. And one James Axon made a big bass drum for it which, unfortunately, proved too large to go through the door! By the 1920s Denton Original, the Ecclesfield Silver Prize, the Slaithwaite Brass Band and over in Yorkshire the Bramley Band had been formed.

In July 1821 it was considered a great honour indeed when Besses and several other bands were invited down to London to take part in the celebrations for the coronation of George IV. The crowd's attention was firmly focused upon the spectacle of Queen Caroline, the estranged wife of 'Prinny', being turned away from the great portals of Westminster Abbey. But afterwards there was a general relaxation; and much appreciation for the music. Joseph Hampson, a later chronicler of Besses, tells us that 'Mr. William Johnson, a very prominent leader of bands at that time, in order to while away the time during the marshalling of the people, drew the various bands together and made a subscription to form a prize for the band that should play the best piece of its own selection. At the close of the contest the prize, amidst the general acclamation of the public, was awarded to Besses o' th' Barn, who for their test-piece played *God Save The King*.' The first 'unofficial' brass band championship competition?

However an event of even greater importance occurred in 1836—near the time when Queen Victoria ascended the throne. On the occasion of William IV's coronation, so their chronicler William Hesling records, the Bramley Band, or Bramley Old Reed Band, had played at Woodhouse Moor with an instrumentation of four clarinets, a 'keyed' bugle, two trumpets, two French horns, serpent, bassoon, two trombones, bass trombone and drum, the latter weighing 75 lbs! (Oh yes, and the serpent player travelled with wax plasters 'for repairs', because 'in those days, fighting was part of a bandsman's duty'.) But in 1836—after considerable internal debate—the Bramley players voted to sign the pledge; and to switch to an all-brass instrumentation. Not only did they become the first Temperance Band; in addition they were paving the way towards the brass band combination that we know today.

It must have been very shortly after this that the concept of a general brass band movement took its hold upon the imagination of the proletarian communities of the North. Brass bands were springing into being nearly everywhere (they were turned to for entertainment) and before another quarter of a century had elapsed the idea of formal brass band contests—so great and pronounced a feature of the movement today—had also taken hold.

On Victoria's coronation day in 1838 Besses o' th' Barn won another triumph. But the first 'formal' contest on record was held at Burton Constable, near Hull, in 1845.

A loosely-organised contest apparently took place in Sheffield as early as 1818 and there were other unofficial contests in the intervening years. But Burton Constable had the stamp of a proper championship about it, inspired by the Ladies Chichester, who persuaded their brother-in-law, Sir Clifford Constable to arrange a competition like those they had seen between town-bands in the South of France. It took place during an 'olde English' Magdalen Feast and was organised by George Leng, Sir Clifford's bandmaster. Five bands, each comprising 12 bandsmen, took part and there was a total prize money of £20. No percussion was allowed and the adjudication was by Richard Hall, a Hull organist. The bands were allowed to play a piece of music of their own choice and the compositions ranged from the *Hallelujah Chorus* to *Hail Smiling Morn*. Eventually the Wold Band led by James Walker, a famous D soprano cornetist, were declared the winners. (Black Dyke under Mr Longbottom did not win at Hull until 1856. A delay which considerably niggled the band's members!)

Following this the contest side of things really got into its stride; leading on towards the great competition held at the Belle Vue Gardens and Amusement Centre, Manchester in 1853. Eight bands took part, and the staging of this event proved so popular that contests have been held there every year since—except in war-time and just once (1859) when there were insufficient entries. In 1860, the first contest was held at the Crystal Palace, London, when no less than 170 bands were entered!

Although subsequently the events at Hull, and even those at Belle Vue have appeared less important than the National Championships at the Royal Albert Hall in London, nevertheless there are one or two interesting items worth recording here from those early years. In connection with Hull, most probably the advent of the contests being moved to the Zoological Gardens and organised there by Enderby Jackson, who would later play a significant role in the earliest contests (and forerunners of the National Championships) at Crystal Palace. Jackson had been an impressionable 18-year-old flautist with the Quadrille Band at Burton Constable and had grown 'considerably excited' by the brass groups he heard there. He was a man of great energies and it was widely acknowledged that his Hull bandings were 'very well-supervised affairs'.

Belle Vue in its turn saw the introduction of giving instruments as prizes at contests and these were donated variously by Joseph Higham of Manchester, Antoine Courtois of Paris (through his agent, Arthur Chappell of London) and Messrs F. Besson and Company of London. Another feature of Belle Vue was the over-subscription of bands eager to compete, despite the black year of 1859, when only Dewsbury, Black Dyke and the Holmfirth Band entered. In 1886 the managers, Messrs Jennison, were forced to inaugurate a July contest, open only to bands not gaining any prizes at the September contests of the previous four years. They decided to limit the new contest to 20 bands. Immediately there were 30 applications! Clearly Belle Vue had come to stay. (Even today a win there, in the Open Championships, is considered not far short of a win at the Albert Hall; while to pull off the double is decidedly every dedicated bandsman's dream.)

Obviously there would be no going back now. Literally hundreds of bands were in existence—and spread all over the kingdom; from the Scottish coaling communities in the far north down to Wales and the Cornish tin-mining towns in the west. Musical orchestration was improving too; and new, original compositions were being written for brass bands, many of them intended for use as test-pieces at the more important contests.

A further 'key' figure emerges at this point. Richard Smith, a successful bandmaster who would later been publishing brass band music in London; as well as editing the *Champion Brass Band Journal*, which he had founded in Hull in 1859.

He continued to conduct at contests, most notably with his Saltaire Band ('consisting of workmen in the employment of Sir [then Mister] Titus Salt'). After their 1861 win at the Crystal Palace *The Illustrated News of the World* hailed Smith as 'the champion teacher of Yorkshire'. In all he took 19 bands to prize-winning positions, beginning with the Leeds Railway Foundry Band at Belle Vue in 1854. But it was as its first dedicated and respectable publisher and editor that the brass band world would have the greatest reason to thank him. He made brass band scores readily available, and at much more reasonable prices, to anyone who wanted to buy them; and the publishing house he founded is still in existence today.

Meanwhile the energetic Enderby Jackson had moved south; and with him the brass band movement's aspirations towards having a showcase in the capital; with (hopefully) some truly National Championships. Jackson first of all had to prove his organising abilities to the management at Crystal Palace by putting on a handbell ringing contest, which he did with 12 teams from the north: from both sides of the Pennines. Crystal Palace were impressed and offered him the site for the following year to bring the brass bands south. As Jackson himself recalls: 'The previous few years were ones of endless anxiety and hard work, rarely going to bed before three o'clock and up again ready for the early postman. But my name had become a household word in the homes of the British working man, and as I found the quality of the bands most wonderfully improved, I determined upon displaying their proficiency before the critics of London'. The series of contests held at the Crystal Palace, Sydenham in the years 1860, 1861 and 1862 under Jackson's overall direction are now rightly regarded as landmarks in the history of banding. Happily too the occasions were reasonably well documented.

Prior to July 10 and 11 1860, the *Daily Telegraph* drew the attention of its readers to 'the first contest of brass bands ever held in the South of England'. The reporter went on: 'This will serve to illustrate their character, and will show the interest they have created by drawing together from all parts of the country the best bands now existing'.

Seventy-two bands entered for the first day's contest, 98 for the second and 44 bands came forward on the first day. They were divided into six groups and then played before their appointed judges. There were 18 of these judges and they presided as follows: Platform No 1, Henry Nicholson, bandmaster to the Duke of Rutland; J. Smythe, Royal Artillery, Woolwich; Mr Hanson, late of the 39th Infantry. No 2, Wellington Guernsey; George Loder; H. Rogers, Waterford Artillery. No 3, Dan Godfrey, Director of Music, Grenadier Guards; H. Schallehn, late of the Crystal Palace Band; J.A. Kappey, Royal Marines, Chatham Division. No 4, Charles Godfrey Senior, Coldstream Guards; Charles Godfrey Junior, now of the Royal Horse Guards (The Blues); William Miller, 1st Battalion Rifle Brigade. No 5, Herr Koenig, Norfolk Artillery—a brother of the celebrated cornet soloist; William Money, 5th Lancers; M. Hartmann, 10th Hussars. No 6, C. Boose, Royal Horse Guards (The Blues); George Leng, late of the Hull Harmonic Society; H. Basket, 58th Regiment. Final Referee: Mr Enderby Jackson.

The contesting got under way at ten o'clock in the morning, and by three in the afternoon all the members of the 44 bands were assembling as The Handel Orchestra to give the public a musical entertainment. (While the judges deliberated, selecting the 12 bands, two from each platform, who would compete in the final section.) The Handel Orchestra was claimed to be the largest in Britain's musical history. It consisted of 1,390 players; arranged in rows according to their instruments. It was made up with '144 soprano cornets, 184 cornets *primo*, 210 cornets *secundo*, 83 E flat althorns, 71 D flat althorns *primo*, 51 D flat althorns *secundo*, 100 B flat baritones, 74 tenor trombones, 75 bass trombones, 80 euphoniums, 133 ophicleides, 155 E flat contre-basses, 2 B flat basses, 26 side drums, monster gong drums and the great organ'.

This mass of instrumentalists was conducted by—guess who? Yes, Mr Enderby Jackson. They played *Rule Britannia, Hallelujah* (Handel), Mendelssohn's *Wedding March*, a part of Haydn's *The Creation (The Heavens Are Telling)* and *God Save the Queen*. The following morning *The Times* commented: 'The effect of the combined legion of blowers was tremendous. The organ, which accompanied them, and which on less exceptional occasions is apt to drown everything, was scaracely audible in the midst of the brazen tempest. Nothing less than the new *monstre* gong drum manufactured by Mr. Henry Distin—to wield the thunder of which required the united efforts of Messrs. Charles Thompson, of the Crystal Palace Band, and Middleditch, of the London Fire Brigade—could prevail against it. The pieces that pleased the most (perhaps because they were best executed) were Mendelssohn's *Wedding March* and the National Anthem, both of which were unanimously encored. The whole performance was conducted with wonderful vigour and precision by Mr. Enderby Jackson, of Hull, a sort of Delaporte in his way, who has exerted himself in forwarding the brass band movement among the mechanics, artisans, petty tradesmen, manufacturers and labourers of the northern and midland counties with almost as much energy and unremitting zeal as Monsieur Delaporte the Orpheonist movement in the provinces of France'.

At the end of this impressive performance the 12 selected bands engaged in their final struggle before the 18 judges. These bands were Black Dyke Mills Band, conducted by Samuel Longbottom; the Saltaire Band, R. Smith; Cyfarthfa Band, H. Livesey (and including the celebrated ophicleide player, Mr Hughes); Darlington Saxhorn Band, H. Hoggett; Dewsbury Band, J. Peel; Deighton Mills Band, P. Robinson; Witney Band, J. Crawford; Stanhope Band, R. de Lacy; Chesterfield Band, H. Slack; Stalybridge Band, J. Melling; Accrington Band, R. Barnes; and Holmfirth Temperance Band, W. Roberts. Prizes were awarded to the first five listed here. The proceedings at the next day's contest were very similar, except that the Black Dyke and Saltaire bands were barred from contending, being already first and second-place winners.

Enderby Jackson's organisation and publicity had been brilliant. He had arranged with the railway companies that the bandsmen could travel to London free of charge. And in each individual town in the north he had arranged that the band most local should 'parade' at least twice in public before they left for the south. Meanwhile at the Crystal Palace itself half-a-crown was charged for the first day's banding and one shilling for the second. The first day's winners received £40 (a lot of money in those days), a silver cup and an instrument, a contre-bass worth 35 guineas—presented by Henry Distin of Newport Street. The second prize was £25: one in the eye for Belle Vue, who were still paying their outright winners this amount.

The following year, 1861, Jackson added a competition for bass players to the year's events: the prize being a sonorophone contre-bass in E flat, with rotary valves. Each competitor had to play an air with variations, especially arranged to include band accompaniment. Five players entered the lists on this occasion, and the prize was eventually carried off by a bass player from the Keighley Band, playing a double B flat trombone of his own invention. (Second was the ophicleide player of the Heckmondwike Albion Band and third was a trombone player from the Civil Service.) *The Manchester Guardian* duly commented: 'This portion of the competition greatly excited the risible faculties of the assembly. The unwieldy instruments, the gruff and deep tones they emitted, the elephantine gambols they were made to execute, and the earnestness of the players, made the scene irresistibly comic'. Obviously the reporter was not dedicated to banding . . ..

Contests continued to be intermittent at the Crystal Palace though. At least until the end of the century. Enderby Jackson went to Australia, turning his drive and enthusiasm to the variety theatre. Belle Vue reasserted itself as the banding capital, and there, for the next 30 years or so three great musical figures battled it out. John Gladney, professional conductor of Meltham Mills Band, who won more medals at Belle Vue than anyone before or since. Alex Owen, the conductor of Black Dyke Mills, who brought that band to its first real peak and Edwin Swift, perhaps the hardest working of the three, who conducted Linthwaite, Littleborough Public, Lindley and at least 12 other bands! As regards Crystal Palace and the south, well, there was very little doing. There was a contest at Crystal Palace in 1871, when the famous band of the Mounted Artillery, then a brass band under its well-known conductor James Lawrence, took the first prize of £50. But a proposal to hold another at the Inventions Exhibition in 1885 fell through. The dismal Jimmies said there was a lack of interest. But was there? Apparently not. No, rather more a case of brass bands and bandsmen awaiting the coming of a John Henry Iles to give new impetus and direction to the movement. Which is precisely how things turned out. By the close of the 1800s the contests were back at the Crystal Palace on a regular basis and the crowds who flocked to hear the bands were greater than ever.

Iles was young, ambitious, but above all 'mad about banding'. Moreover a remarkable *entrepreneur*, capable of achieving well-nigh everything he set out to do. By 1900 the National Brass Band Festival had been founded, with headquarters actually inside the great glass Palace. The National Championships, their mentor told everyone, were now under way for real and accompanied by a good deal of entertainment and invention at the Festival concerts afterwards . . . 'to relieve the stresses and strains of the players' day-long competing'. Iles also managed to interest Sir Arthur Sullivan in brass band affairs. Sullivan was a director of the Crystal Palace complex, and he was quick to spot the dedicated craftsmanship of the bands taking part in the National Festival there. It led to him being the first composer/conductor of world stature to stand in front of massed brass bands at the Royal Albert Hall. Keen as mustard, Iles persuaded Lord Northcliffe, then the proprietor of *The Daily Mail*, to lend his support to the idea. Northcliffe was assisting in the raising of funds for the benefit of relatives of soldiers engaged in the Boer War. Ever the super-salesman, Iles jumped at the opportunity to bring a number of prize-winning bands to London with Northcliffe promising to finance their travel and also recompense Sullivan if he would conduct them. The latter declared himself equally enthusiastic over the venture, and in the end the concert at the Albert Hall made a profit of £2,000, a staggering sum in those days.

However, I am digressing from the real story of the National Championships. This remarkably successful state of affairs under Iles then slalomed on without interruption for 38 years. In fact, it did genuinely begin to seem as if 'the yard went on forever'. Not even the burning down of the Crystal Palace in 1937 could deter Iles from his overriding purpose to give the bands their own national showcase. The following year he simply moved everything northwards to Alexandra Palace.

It took a second World War to put an end to his longstanding activities, *temporarily*. But when he came to pick up the pieces afterwards he needed help, and knew it. Massive financial help; of the kind he recognised would demand a big say in the structure of command. No matter. He judged the continuation of the bands being able to go on competing with one another of supreme importance. And so a new phase was reached in brass band history following Germany's surrender in 1945.

The Daily Herald *Brass Band Contest of 1946 in the Albert Hall* (Daily Herald).

Especially as regards the Championships. For in that year (with Iles' encouragement and co-operation) *The Daily Herald* took over the financing, organisation and presentation of the National Brass Band Championships and the accompanying Festival concerts. The *Herald* installed their own man to take over the actual running of these events, the capable and extremely vigorous Edwin Vaughan Morris, who was destined to remain on as overall director of the Championships until the 1970s.

Meanwhile bands were becoming popular with an increasingly larger audience due to frequent broadcasts over the BBC. And another attractive feature of their music was the revived public interest in massed bands concerts in addition to the one held each year at the National Festival. The great seal of authority had been stamped upon the idea of massed bands when Sir Henry Wood conducted Denis Wright's arrangement of Tchaikovsky's *1812 Overture* in his Jubilee Year at the Royal Albert Hall. Topped by row upon row of gleaming cornets and with five percussionists and three sets of tubular bells, Sir Henry was given a standing ovation afterwards. Massed bands concerts around the country were now definitely 'on'. Since then probably their most distinguished conductor has been the well-known, and frequently honoured, Harry Mortimer. Actually all of the Mortimers—Father Fred and his three sons, Harry, Alex and Rex—have held 'starring' positions in the brass band world; and to mention them at this point is in no way a diversion.

If any one band could be said to have dominated the later inter-war years then it was Fodens, or Fodens Motor Works Band of Sandbach, Cheshire to give them their full title. Which in turn came to mean Fred Mortimer. William Halliwell had built Fodens into a good band by the 1920s, in the 1930s Fred Mortimer, Halliwell's former bandmaster, lifted them to be a great one. With E.R. Foden himself (son of the firm's founder) puffing away at a big cigar through most rehearsals and, more importantly, guaranteeing the men's jobs during a period of economic depression, Fred could afford to behave like a martinet—and did. Woe betide anyone who arrived late for practice, or then played a wrong note. (In fact an old putty medal used to be given to the offender!) Nevertheless he set new, high musical standards with the band. In 1926, under William Halliwell, Fodens had notched up a hat-trick of wins at Belle Vue. Under Fred Mortimer they won at the Albert Hall in 1930, 1932, 1933, 1934 and again in 1936, 1937 and 1938. It even became something of a joke in the 1930s that Fodens' players, on their way to London in the coach, would lay bets between themselves on who would come *second*.

On the other hand, they were very good for the brass band movement because their improved standards of sound, internal balance, dynamics and individual musicianship caused other bands to strive for greater performances. Their closest rivals, Dyke, Callender's Cable Works from Kent, Grimethorpe Colliery Band, Brighouse & Rastrick, GUS Footwear, Besses and later Fairey Aviation all *knew* that in order to win they had to have the beating of Fodens, and so their level of playing was raised too.

Each of Fred Mortimer's sons became involved with Fodens. Alex as solo euphonium (although he then went on to conduct CWS, Manchester), Rex as a later conductor and, of course, Harry as principal cornet and then conductor. Harry (who as a young man made his name with the Hallé Orchestra and as the recording soloist on Purcell's *The Trumpet Voluntary*) proved to be more than just a fine player. He

Sir Malcolm Sargent conducting the 1946 Festival Concert in the Albert Hall (Daily Herald).

became a supreme trainer of bands and, through the war and immediate post-war years, the brass movement's most charismatic conductor: a master of colour, flourish and the dramatic gesture. He had a series of championship wins with the brilliant new Fairey Aviation Works Band and then went on to put several bands together and so dominate this particular area of brass entertainment.

But to continue with the story of the National Championships because more and more these have come to be the major story of the brass band movement itself. Competing is the very life-blood of bands—and the annual pilgrimage to the Royal Albert Hall every October remains the grand climax to the brass player's year.

First of all a note on instrumentation. Over the Crystal Palace years this had gradually stabilised itself into a band which at the Albert Hall contests was limited to a maximum of 25 players, not counting the musical director. Rule No 6 at the Albert Hall stated: 'Only 32 Registered Member Bandsmen shall be selected by a Band as Contest Bandsmen from which the band may choose, on the day of the Contest, a maximum of 25 playing Bandsmen to compete'. A majority of bands who competed settled—and still do—for ten or 11 cornets (including soprano, repiano and flugelhorn), two tenor and one bass trombone, three tenor horns, two euphoniums, two baritone horns, two B flat basses and two E flat basses.

However, this was essentially to give a standard size at contests. On the ordinary concert-platform, playing a programme purely to entertain, bands would, and again still do, enlarge the cornet section and sometimes add as many as three percussion. Apart from giving the band a bigger sound this has had the added advantage of 'blooding' many talented youngsters within the atmosphere and the exigencies of public music-making. For many years percussion was deliberately excluded from the competing side of things, but in his years as director of the National Championships Vaughan Morris would have the commissioned composers of his test-pieces add percussion parts for when the music was later featured on the concert-platform or gramophone records. On the whole this system worked well, and percussion is now a respected part of brass band playing.

As already mentioned, it was the ebullient John Henry Iles who had reached agreement with *The Daily Herald* about re-establishing the National Championships and the National Festival after the war. In 1945 this super-showman (who in later years always wore his OBE and black-tailed coat) was 74 years of age. Moreover Great Britain was still facing the devastation of the conflict years, costs were rising sharply and Iles had come to terms with the problems of endeavouring to mount the championships again all on his own. Hence his initial negotiations with Fleet Street.

Clearly it must be hard to imagine two people more diverse than Iles and Vaughan Morris. Whereas the former was flamboyant and dramatic, Vaughan Morris was essentially a skilled administrator, although he had the experience of a number of promotions for Odhams to his credit and had a natural love of music, going back to his Holyhead boyhood as a chorister. Anyway, the two men got on well. They became firm friends; with a basis of trust to cement their revival of the championships. Their first joint effort took the form of a Championship Section contest, based on invitations extended to 20 selected bands, with a massed bands concert as the culmination to the day's proceedings. But holding the contest at the Royal Albert Hall gave to brass bands a dignity they had never quite achieved before. Denis Wright had been commissioned to write an original work for the occasion, aptly titled *Overture For An Epic Occasion*. Fairey Aviation conducted by Harry Mortimer were declared National Champions, and at the Festival Concert afterwards Sir Adrian Boult conducted the massed players of Black Dyke, Cresswell Colliery, Fairey Aviation, Fodens Motor Works band and the Scottish CWS. A large choir under the

Sir Adrian Boult conducts the 1954 Daily Herald *Brass Band Contest* (Daily Herald).

direction of Charles Proctor was there to lend support. Other principal guests were Eva Turner (soprano), Frank Titterton (tenor), Jack Mackintosh and Harry Mortimer (cornet duets), Reginald Foort (organ) and Frank Phillips (announcer), the latter beginning a long and close association with the championships.

The old Crystal Palace Festival, involving as it did a series of varying sections, had enabled a large number of bands to compete. But the very nature of its one-day presentation had brought about a discriminating and restrictive procedure. Vaughan Morris and the *Herald* believed it was right to encourage *every* band to compete. And so a new competing format was established. Eight regions of the British Isles were defined purely geographically, following which local committees—comprising qualified and long-standing enthusiasts—were formed to assist in organising the Area Qualifying Finals: Championship, Second, Third and Fourth. These eight area boundaries have remained unchanged. They are Scotland, Northern (Northumberland and Durham), North-East (Yorkshire), Midlands (Notts, Derby, Staffs, Warwickshire and Salop), North-West (Lancs, Cheshire, North Wales and Cumbria), London and Southern Counties, West of England, South and West Wales. Bands gaining the first and second prizes in each of their Area Qualifying Finals are then invited to the National Finals in London.

Each year following 1945 was marked by the inception of some fresh measure, either in organisation, presentation or procedure, designed to ensure an unquestioned basis for fair-play allied to an acceptance of the necessity for progressive development, uniformity of conditions and good operative practices throughout the regions and in turn the bands gave the organisers their wholehearted support. In 1945 the

Officials stand guard outside the judge's box at the brass band contest that was held at Central Hall, Westminster. The judge inside the box can hear the music but cannot see the band that is performing (BBC Hulton Picture Library).

number of bands competing was 214, in 1946, 320, by 1947 it was 399 and in 1948 it had reached 423. Looking back over those years and the ones which followed, certain landmarks become very clear. In 1946 the policy of staging the heats in concert halls was initiated. Also, the National Brass Band Contesting Rules and Conditions had been formulated to govern the procedure applicable to all qualifying events. These rules were allied to the National Registry of Brass Bandsmen, which, for the first time, gave the brass movement a national system of registration. Thus a bandsman's registration card was issued to cover every player registered by a band. The holder had to produce this documentary evidence to certify he was a *bona fide* member of the band before he could compete at any contest. In 1947, the National Registry totalled well over 15,000 bandsmen; by 1948 it had reached 22,000.

Another note here about adjudication. From the inception of the new contests it became the practice to screen competing bands from the view of their adjudicators. The paramount reason for this was—and continues to be—the natural and inevitable relationships between bands. Family ties, longstanding loyalties, prejudices, temperaments and the need to provide facilities conducive to undisturbed concentration on the job in hand; all made their contribution to this procedure. Adjudicators are invariably well-versed in brass band music from knowledge acquired either as composers, conductors or tutors. They might be drawn in from other forms of musical life, such as Colonel Rodney Bashford and other officers from Kneller Hall. But they have a real relationship with brass bands in general and are chosen for their genuine impartiality. Screening them from the bands removes any possibility of embarrassment and confirms their impartiality to both bands and public. The late Frank Wright, one of the movement's most respected adjudicators, made a number of pertinent comments about screening—well-worth repeating here. 'Once inside the box incarceration is complete. No visitors are allowed, except the small committee elected by the bands on the day who inspect the box shortly after the adjudicators enter it. Their duty is to see that there are no crevices or holes in the fabric—particular care being taken to examine the side of the box facing the stage—through which the wandering eye of an adjudicator might chance to peer.'

By 'box' he was, of course, referring to the special one introduced at the Albert Hall by Vaughan Morris and his team. It has become known as 'the refrigerator' because of its colour and size; but, according to Wright, 'is a great improvement on the old. Well-lighted, with a noiseless air-changer at work, it provides for ample desk-room not only for writing but also for the tea and coffee flasks and plates of sand-wiches—usually chicken. (Other promoters please copy!) Most important of all, audibility is perfect. Separated by only about twenty feet from the stage, there can be few sounds that fail to reach it'. The organisers had even installed an outsize *pot de chambre . . ..* Even so, he felt compelled to add: 'It's unwise to cherish any great hopes of pleasing all the bands and their devoted supporters all of the time. If the good Lord himself came down to judge a brass band contest there would still be that unmistakable element of disgruntled surprise at the decision!'

Championship winners over a long period of time have come from many different localities. For Yorkshire, as previously noted, Black Dyke Mills won the first-ever National Contest at the Crystal Palace in 1860; for the Midlands, the Chesterfield Rifle Corps Band won the 1862 contest; for the West Country the Blandford (Dorset) Band won in 1863; and for Wales, the first band to win a National award was Cyfarthfa, third prize-winners in 1860. In our own century the record-book shows that Lancashire triumphed in 1900 when the Denton Original Band won at the Crystal Palace. And since then, the first County Durham band to win the National title was Hebburn Colliery (1904); the first Cheshire band to win Fodens (1910, and they did the 'double' that year); while the first southern area band to win was Luton (1923). The first Scottish band to compete at the National events was the Milnwood, Mossend and Clydesdale Band, formed at Milnwood Colliery, Belshill in 1879, which took part in 1900.

Moreover—and this persisted under Iles and Vaughan Morris after the second World War—the maximum attention has been paid to ensuring that brass band players retain their amateur status. No musicians active in any professional musical capacity are allowed to play at competitions; otherwise it would give the better-off bands an unfair advantage over their opponents. To form a band can involve an expenditure of many thousands of pounds on the purchase of instruments, music and uniforms. Then it requires rehearsal facilities and a big outlay on travel. Players give their own time to perfecting musicianship, yet only after their daylight hours have been taken up earning their livings in some other way. It often involves a great deal of personal sacrifice. The more attractive 'name' bands like Dyke, Fairey and Fodens can earn money at concerts; which goes into the band fund. Their members still have day-jobs and so can compete with one another as amateurs at the different contests. It remains a world where the Musicians' Union would like, but rarely manages, to tread.

The great success which accompanied the Regional Qualifying Finals throughout the country meant that the Royal Albert Hall was filled to capacity with all those who wanted to be present at the National Championships. A similar position existed at the massed bands concert in the evening, while the town halls of Kensington, Fulham and Hammersmith were also filled to capacity during the day, when bands and their supporters concerned with the Second, Third and Fourth graded bands competed for

Princess Elizabeth attends the 1949 Festival Concert (Daily Herald).

National honours in their own class. London was literally 'taken over' for the day's banding.

Following an approach he made to Buckingham Palace Vaughan Morris was informed that HRH The Princess Elizabeth would attend the 1949 Festival Concert at the Albert Hall and present the awards to the successful Championship bands. This recognition of the work and service provided by brass bands was a gracious act which reached out to tens of thousands of amateur musicians and the movement was greatly encouraged by it. Since then, and with her accession as Queen Elizabeth II, never a year goes by without the Championships receiving their 'good luck' telegram from the Palace.

During these years brass bands have consolidated a national image which is as familiar to us today as athletics, ballroom dancing, Formula 1 racing, show-jumping and other leisure pursuits. Much of the credit for this must go first to Iles, then to Vaughan Morris and the National Council which the latter had organised. Also to other dedicated bodies such as the National Brass Band Club (formed in 1925 to further the welfare of brass players), the National Association of Brass Band Conductors, the Coal Industry Social Welfare Organisation and the National Schools Brass Band Association. The unbiased service to the movement by the men serving on these various committees has earned the respect of the great majority of bandsmen throughout Great Britain as well as in other parts of the world where an enthusiasm for this kind of music has now taken hold. As regards the National Championships themselves, these even survived successfully the various Fleet Street upheavals of the 1960s.

Odhams Press (and with it *The Daily Herald*) was acquired by *The Daily Mirror* group in 1961 and Hugh Cudlipp (now Lord Cudlipp) became its chairman. Cudlipp had worked with Vaughan Morris many years before on the old *Sunday Chronicle*, but before very long the latter was informed that the *Herald* could no longer shoulder the costs and operational responsibilities of the National Championships. 'Man is born into trouble', says the Book of Job and this decision by the *Herald* appeared to be trouble of disastrous proportions. An unremitting effort had been made, during the previous 16 years, to establish a structure both responsible and above suspicion. Involved in this structure were the National Finals, National Festival, National Brass Band Championship Regional Finals, National Registry of Brass Bandsmen, National Grading Register and so on.

Fortunately though it became possible for Vaughan Morris, backed by the National Council, to reach a financial accommodation with *The People*; and this helped bridge the gap until the National Championships became completely independent under Vaughan Morris' direction in 1966. From this date too one particular anomaly was removed from the championships. The Finals comprised four graded sections. In operation, it was not unlike the promotion and relegation which goes on in the Football League. The band in the Championship Section (top grade) which emerged as the current winners at the Finals, was not called upon to compete at the qualifying stage in the following year's contests. It was given a 'bye' to the Finals to defend its title. The bands securing comparable honours in the Second, Third and Fourth Sections had been required to compete at the qualifying point in the following year. This discrimination seemed to be genuinely unfair, particularly as the Champions in these

Festival poster outside the Albert Hall, 1967 (London Press Photos).

three lower grades were upgraded to the next higher section as a mark of their standards. To give equal recognition to the success achieved by the Champion bands, in each of the four graded sections of the National Finals, it was announced that the principal of giving a 'bye' to the following year's finals would apply equally to the four sections in future. This proved to be a very popular measure. Likewise the award each year of 'The Insignia of Honour' to one particularly deserving soloist or important figure in the movement. On the other hand, the experiment of elevating a number of successful and well-known bands to a separate 'World Championship' Section, proved to be lacking in general popularity and was promptly dumped. These are just one or two examples of the brass band movement's continually seeking to keep its own house neat and tidy.

'Remember please', Lawrence Durrell wrote in one of his poems, 'time has no joints, pours over the great sills of thought, not clogging nor resisting but yawning to inherit the year's quarters'. In 1971 Edwin Vaughan Morris, by this time himself an OBE, finally gave up overall direction of the National Championships (although he was to continue as a journalist and a consultant for gramophone records.) Iles had been dead for some years. But what they had set in motion and developed is still going on. The championships have been controlled since then by Geoffrey Brand with Peter Wilson, and now by Robert Alexander, while such distinguished musical figures as Sir Charles Groves and Dr Malcolm Arnold have added their names to the honourable company of conductors and composers and we have witnessed exciting new phenomena in the movement like the James Shepherd Versatile Brass.

The brass band world has overcome the early struggles for its very existence and is now a musical force to be reckoned with. It has even been represented in the hit-parade with Brighouse & Rastrick's *Cornish Floral Dance* and Peter Skellern's singles. More importantly though it is constantly renewing itself; and at the time of writing perhaps the most heartening thing of all is the staggering number of youngsters in schools who are blowing their first faltering notes of music through cornets and trombones, tenor horns, basses and euphoniums. We must guard them well. One day they will be the inheritors, in turn continuing the grand tradition.

Nothing can deter dedication. On November 16 1943 Coventry was blitzed. The City of Coventry Band (only formed in 1939) were broadcasting from Birmingham at 10 o'clock that night. Subsequently they were bombed out of five different practice-rooms. But the band *never* ceased its activities. This is just one example of what I mean.

British Open Championships, 1853-1979 (Belle Vue)

1853	Mossley Temperance Saxhorn (William Taylor)—(2 individual choices).
1854	Leeds Railway Foundry (Richard Smith)—(2 individual choices).
1855	Accrington (Radcliffe Barnes)—*Orynthia* (Melling) & individual choice (until 1866).
1856	Leeds Railway Foundry (Richard Smith)—*Stradella* overture (Flotow).
1857	Leeds (Smith's) (Richard Smith)—*Il Trovatore* (Verdi).
1858	Accrington (Radcliffe Barnes)—*The Creation*, excerpts (Haydn).
1859	No contest.
1860	Halifax (4th West Yorkshire Rifles)—*Zampa* overture (Hérold).
1861	Halifax (4th West Yorkshire Rifles)—*Satanella* (Balfe).
1862	Black Dyke Mills (Samuel Longbottom)—*Muette de Portici* (Auber).
1863	Black Dyke Mills (Samuel Longbottom)—*Faust* (Gounod).
1864	Bacup (John Lord)—*Reminiscences of Auber.*
1865	Bacup (John Lord)—*Un ballo in maschera* (Verdi).
1866	Dewsbury Old (John Peel)—*L'Africaine* (Meyerbeer).
1867	Clay Cross (3rd Battalion Rifles) (John Naylor)—*Der Freischütz* (Weber) (single choice from this year).
1868	Burnley 17th Lancashire Rifle Volunteers—*Robert le Diable* (Meyerbeer).
1869	Bacup (John Lord)—*Le Prophète* (Meyerbeer).
1870	Bacup (John Lord)—*Ernani* (Verdi).
1871	Black Dyke Mills (Samuel Longbottom)—*Il Barbiere di Siviglia*—overture (Rossini).
1872	Robin Hood Rifles (H. Leverton)—*Souvenir de Mozart.*
1873	Meltham Mills (John Gladney)—*Dinorah* (Meyerbeer).
1874	Linthwaite (Edwin Swift)—*Faust* (Spohr).
1875	Kingston Mills (John Gladney)—*Il Talismano* (Balfe).
1876	Meltham Mills (John Gladney)—*Aida* (Verdi).
1877	Meltham Mills (John Gladney)—*Jessonda* (Spohr).
1878	Meltham Mills (John Bladney)—*Romeo e Giulietta* (Gounod).
1879	Black Dyke Mills (J. Fawcett)—*The Last Judgment* (Spohr).
1880	Black Dyke Mills (Alexander Owen)—*I Vespri Siciliani* (Verdi).
1881	Black Dyke Mills (Alexander Owen)—*Cinq-Mars* (Gounod).
1882	Clayton-le-Moor (Alexander Owen)—*Il Seraglio* (Mozart).
1883	Littleborough Public (Edwin Swift)—*Il Giuramento* (Mercadante).
1884	Honley (John Gladney)—*La Gazza Ladra* (Rossini).
1885	Kingston Mills (John Gladney)—*Nabucco* (Verdi).
1886	Kingston Mills (John Gladney)—*La Favorita* (Donizeti).
1887	Kingston Mills (John Gladney)—*L'Étoile du Nord* (Meyerbeer).
1888	Wyke Temperance (Edwin Swift)—*Der Fliegende Holländer* (Wagner).
1889	Wyke Temperance (Edwin Swift)—*La Reine de Saba* (Gounod).

1890   Batley Old (John Gladney)—*Euryanthe* (Weber).
1891   Black Dyke Mills (John Gladney)—*Das Nachtlager in Granada* (Kreutzer).
1892   Besses o' th' Barn (Alexander Owen)—*Zar und Zimmermann* (Lortzing).
1893   Kingston Mills (John Gladney)—*Elaine* (Bemberg).
1894   Besses o' th' Barn (Alexander Owen)—*The Golden Web* (Goring Thomas).
1895   Black Dyke Mills (John Gladney)—*Hansel und Gretel* (Humperdinck).
1896   Black Dyke Mills (John Gladney)—*Gabriella* (Pizzi).
1897   Mossley (Alexander Owen)—*Moses in Egypt* (Rossini).
1898   Wyke Temperance (Edwin Swift)—*Mendelssohn Fantasia.*
1899   Black Dyke Mills (John Gladney)—*Aroldo* (Verdi).
1900   Lindley (John Gladney)—*La Gioconda* (Ponchielli).
1901   Kingston Mills (John Gladney)—*Mirella* (Gounod).
1902   Black Dyke Mills (John Gladney)—*L'Ebreo* (Appolini).
1903   Pemberton Old (John Gladney)—*Caractacus* (Elgar).
1904   Black Dyke Mills (John Gladney)—*Semiramide* (Rosinni).
1905   Irwell Springs (William Rimmer)—*Così fan tutte* (Mozart).
1906   Wingates Temperance (William Rimmer)—*Les Huguenots* (Meyerbeer).
1907   Wingates Temperance (William Rimmer)—*Robin Hood* (MacFarren).
1908   Black Dyke Mills (William Rimmer)—*A Souvenir of Grieg.*
1909   Fodens Motor Works (William Rimmer)—*Il Bravo* (Marliani).
1910   Fodens Motor Works (William Halliwell)—*Acis and Galatea* (Handel).
1911   Hebden Bridge (William Halliwell)—*Eugene Onegin* (Tchaikovsky).
1912   Fodens Motor Works (William Halliwell)—*Les Diamants de la Couronne* (Auber).
1913   Fodens Motor Works (William Halliwell—*A Souvenir of Gounod.*
1914   Black Dyke Mills (John Greenwood)—*Joseph und seine Bruder* (Méhul).
1915   Fodens Motor Works (William Halliwell)—*Il Furioso* (Donizetti).
1916   Horwich RMI (John Greenwood)—*La Traviata* (Verdi).
1917   Horwich RMI (John Greenwood)—*La Pré aux Clercs* (Hérold).
1918   Wingates Temperance (William Halliwell)—*Il Bravo* (Marliani).
1919   Harton Colliery (G. Hawkins)—*The Lily of Killarney* (Bendedict).
1920   Besses o' th' Barn (W. Wood)—*I Lombardi* (Verdi).
1921   Wingates Temperance (William Halliwell)—*Maritana* (Vincent Wallace).
1922   South Elmsall & Frickley Colliery (Noel Thorpe)—*Lohengrin* (Wagner).
1923   Wingates Temperance (William Halliwell)—*Dinorah* (Meyerbeer).
1924   Australia (Newcastle Steel Works) (A.H. Bailie)—*Selection from Liszt.*
1925   Creswell Colliery (John Greenwood)—*Macbeth* (Thomas Keighley).
1926   Fodens Motor Works (William Halliwell)—*A Midsummer Night's Dream* (Thomas Keighley).
1927   Fodens Motor Works (William Halliwell)—*The Merry Wives of Windsor* (Thomas Keighley).
1928   Fodens Motor Works (William Halliwell)—*Lorenzo* (Thomas Keighley).
1929   Brighouse & Rastrick (F. Berry)—*Pathetique* (Beethoven).
1930   Eccles Borough (J. Dew)—*Oriental Rhapsody* (Granville Bantock).
1931   Besses o' th' Barn (William Halliwell)—*Springtime Suite* (Haydn Morris).
1932   Brighouse & Rastrick (William Halliwell)—*The Crusaders* (Thomas Keighley).
1933   Brighouse & Rastrick (William Halliwell)—*Princess Nada* (Denis Wright).
1934   Brighouse & Rastrick (William Halliwell)—*Pageantry* (Herbert Howells).
1935   Black Dyke Mills (William Halliwell)—*A Northern Rhapsody* (Thomas Keighley).
1936   Brighouse & Rastrick (William Halliwell)—*Robin Hood* (Henry Geehl).

1937 Besses o' th' Barn (W. Wood)—*Academic Festival Overture* (Brahms; arr Denis Wright).

1938 Slaithwaite (N. Thorpe)—*Owain Glendwr* (Maldwyn Price).

1939 Wingates Temperance (W. Wood)—*A Downland Suite* (John Ireland).

1940 Bickershaw Colliery (W. Haydock)—*Clive of India* (Joseph Holbrook).

1941 Fairey Aviation Works (Harry Mortimer)—choice of *Academic Festival Overture* (Brahms; arr D. Wright), *Robin Hood* (Geehl) or *The Crusaders* (Keighley).

1942 Fairey Aviation Works (Harry Mortimer)—choice of *Lorenzo* (Keighley) or *Pageantry* (Howells).

1943 Bickershaw Colliery (W. Haydock)—*Themes from Symphony No.5* (Beethoven; arr Denis Wright).

1944 Fairey Aviation (Harry Mortimer)—*The Tempest fantasia* (Maurice Johnstone).

1945 Fairey Aviation (Harry Mortimer)—*Pride of Race* (Kenneth A Wright).

1946 Bickershaw Colliery (Harry Mortimer)—*Salute to Freedom* (Eric Ball).

1947 Fairey Aviation (Harry Mortimer)—*Henry V* (Maldwyn Price).

1948 CWS Manchester (Eric Ball)—*Music for Brass* (Denis Wright).

1949 Fairey Aviation (Harry Mortimer)—*Rhapsody in Brass* (Dean Goffin).

1950 Fairey Aviation (Harry Mortimer)—*Resurgam* (Eric Ball).

1951 Ransome & Marle's (Eric Ball)—*The Conquerors* (Eric Ball).

1952 CWS Manchester (Eric Ball)—*Scena Sinfonica* (Henry Geehl).

1953 National Band of New Zealand (K.G.L. Smith)—*The Three Musketeers* (George Hespe).

1954 Munn & Felton's (Stanley Boddington)—*Tournament for Brass* (Eric Ball).

1955 Ferodo Works (George Hespe)—*Sinfonietta for Brass Band* (Eric Leidzen).

1956 Fairey Aviation (Harry Mortimer)—*Tam o' Shanter's Ride* (Denis Wright).

1957 Black Dyke Mills (Major G.H. Willcocks)—*Carnival* (Helen Perkins).

1958 Carlton Main Frickley Colliery (Jack Atherton)—*Sunset Rhapsody* (Eric Ball).

1959 Besses o' th' Barn (W. Wood)—*The Undaunted* (Eric Ball).

1960 CWS Manchester (Alex Mortimer)—*Mozart Fantasia* (arr Malcolm Sargent).

1961 Fairey Band (Leonard Lamb)—*Main Street* (Eric Ball).

1962 Fairey Band (Leonard Lamb)—*Island Heritage* (Helen Perkins).

1963 Fairey Band (Leonard Lamb)—*Life Divine* (Cyril Jenkins).

1964 Fodens Motor Works (Rex Mortimer)—*Lorenzo* (Keighley).

1965 Fairey Band (Leonard Lamb)—*Saga of the North* (Cyril Jenkins).

1966 CWS Manchester (Alex Mortimer)—*A Downland Suite* (John Ireland).

1967 Grimethorpe Colliery (George Thompson)—*A Comedy Overture* (John Ireland).

1968 Black Dyke Mills (Geoffrey Brand)—*John O'Gaunt* (Gilbert Vinter).

1969 Grimethorpe Colliery (George Thompson)—*Spectrum* (Gilbert Vinter).

1970 Yorkshire Imperial Metals (Trevor Walmsley)—*Pageantry* (Herbert Howells).

1971 Yorkshire Imperial Metals (Trevor Walmsley)—*Festival Music* (Eric Ball).

1972 Black Dyke Mills (Geoffrey Brand)—*Sovereign Heritage* (Jack Beaver, arr Frank Wright).

1973 Black Dyke Mills (Roy Newsome)—*The Accursed Huntsman* (César Franck, arr Siebert).

1974 Black Dyke Mills (Roy Newsome)—*James Cook—Circumnavigator* (Vinter).

1975 Wingates Temperance (Richard Evans)—*Fireworks* (Elgar Howarth).

1976 Black Dyke Mills (Major Peter Parkes)—*An Epic Symphony* (Percy Fletcher).

1977 Black Dyke Mills (Major Peter Parkes)—*Diadem of Gold* (Balay; arr Frank Wright).

1978   Brighouse & Rastrick (Geoffrey Brand)—*Benvenuto Cellini* (Berlioz, arr Frank Wright).

1979   Fairey Engineering Works (Walter Hargreaves)—*Le Carnaval Romain* (Berlioz; arr Frank Wright).

National Championships, 1900-1979
(October—Crystal Palace, Albert Hall)

1900 Denton Original (Alexander Owen)—*Gems from Sullivan's Operas No.1* (arr J. Ord Hume).

1901 Lee Mount (W. Swingler)—*Gems from Sullivan's Operas No.3* (arr J. Ord Hume).

1902 Black Dyke Mills (John Gladney)—*Hiawatha* (Coleridge-Taylor; arr C. Godfrey).

1903 Besses o' th' Barn (Alexander Owen)—*Die Meistersinger* (Wagner; arr Shipley Douglas).

1904 Hebburn Colliery (Angus Holden)—*Gems of Mendelssohn* (arr C. Godfrey).

1905 Irwell Springs (William Rimmer)—*Roland à Roncervaux* (Auguste Mermet).

1906 Wingates Temperance (William Rimmer)—*Gems of Chopin* (arr W. Short).

1907 Wingates Temperance (William Rimmer)—*Gems of Schumann* (arr W. Short).

1908 Irwell Springs (William Rimmer)—*Rienzi* (Wagner; arr Samuel Cope).

1909 Shaw (William Rimmer)—*Flying Dutchman* (Wagner).

1910 Fodens Motor Works (William Halliwell)—*Gems of Schubert* (arr W. Rimmer).

1911 Crossfield's (Perfection) Soap Works (William Halliwell)—*Les Huguenots* (Meyerbeer; arr W. Rimmer).

1912 St Hilda Colliery (William Halliwell)—*William Tell* (Rossini).

1913 Irwell Springs (William Halliwell)—*Labour and Love* (Percy Fletcher).

(In abeyance 1914-19)

1920 St Hilda Colliery (William Halliwell)—*Coriolanus* (Cyril Jenkins).

1921 St Hilda Colliery (William Halliwell)—*Life Divine* (Cyril Jenkins).

1922 Horwich RMI (John Greenwood)—*Freedom* (Hubert Bath).

1923 Luton Red Cross (William Halliwell)—*Oliver Cromwell* (Henry Geehl).

1924 St Hilda Colliery (William Halliwell)—*On the Cornish Coast* (Henry Geehl).

1925 Marsden Colliery (John Greenwood)—*Joan of Arc* (Denis Wright).

1926 St Hilda Colliery (James Oliver)—*An Epic Symphony* (Percy Fletcher).

1927 Carlisle St Stephens (William Lowes)—*The White Rider* (Denis Wright).

1928 Black Dyke Mills (William Halliwell)—*A Moorside Suite* (Gustav Holst).

1929 Carlisle St Stephens (William Lowes)—*Victory* (Cyril Jenkins).

1930 Fodens Motor Works (Fred Mortimer)—*Severn Suite Op. 87* (Edward Elgar).

1931 Wingates Temperance (Harold Moss)—*Honour and Glory* (Hubert Bath).

1932 Fodens Motor Works (Fred Mortimer)—*A Downland Suite* (John Ireland).

1933 Fodens Motor Works (Fred Mortimer)—*Prometheus Unbound* (Granville Bantock).

1934 Fodens Motor Works (Fred Mortimer)—*Comedy Overture* (John Ireland).

1935 Munn & Felton's Works (William Halliwell)—*Pride of Race* (Kenneth A. Wright).

1936 Fodens Motor Works (Fred Mortimer)—*Kenilworth* (Arthur Bliss).

1937 Fodens Motor Works (Fred Mortimer)—*Pageantry* (Herbert Howells).

1938 Fodens Motor Works (Fred Mortimer)—*An Epic Symphony* (Percy Fletcher).
(In abeyance 1939-44)
1945 Fairey Aviation Works (Harry Mortimer)—*Overture for an Epic Occasion* (Denis Wright).
1946 Brighouse & Rastrick (Eric Ball)—*Oliver Cromwell* (Henry Geehl).
1947 Black Dyke Mills (Harry Mortimer)—*Freedom* (Hubert Bath).
1948 Black Dyke Mills (Harry Mortimer)—*On the Cornish Coast* (Henry Geehl).
1949 Black Dyke Mills (Harry Mortimer)—*Comedy Overture* (John Ireland).
1950 Fodens Motor Works (Harry Mortimer)—*Pageantry* (Herbert Howells).
1951 Black Dyke Mills (Alex Mortimer)—*Epic Symphony* (Percy Fletcher).
1952 Fairey Aviation Works (Harry Mortimer)—*The Frogs of Aristophanes* (Sir Granville Bantock; arr Frank Wright).
1953 Fodens Motor Works (Harry Mortimer)—*Diadem of Gold* (Balay, arr Frank Wright).
1954 Fairey Aviation Works (Harry Mortimer)—*Sovereign Heritage* (J. Beaver; arr Frank Wright).
1955 Munn & Felton's Works (Harry Mortimer)—*Blackfriars* (Eric Cundell; arr Frank Wright).
1956 Fairey Aviation Works (Major George Willcocks)—*Festival Music* (Eric Ball).
1957 Munn & Felton's Works (Stanley Boddington)—*Variations for Brass Band* (R. Vaughan Williams).
1958 Fodens Motor Works (Rex Mortimer)—*Variations on The Shining River* (Edmund Rubbra).
1959 Black Dyke Mills (Major George Willcocks)—*The King of Ys* (Lalo; arr Frank Wright).
1960 Munn & Felton's (Footwear) (Stanley Boddington)—*Three Figures* (Henry Howells).
1961 Black Dyke Mills (Major George Willcocks)—*Les Francs Juges* (Berlioz; arr Frank Wright).
1962 CWS (Manchester) (Alex Mortimer)—*The Force of Destiny* (Verdi; arr Frank Wright).
1963 CWS (Manchester) (Alex Mortimer)—*The Belmont Variations* (Sir Arthur Bliss).
1964 GUS (Footwear) (Stanley Boddington)—*Variations on a Ninth* (Gilbert Vinter).
1965 Fairey Band (Leonard Lamb)—*Triumphant Rhapsody* (Gilbert Vinter).
1966 GUS (Footwear) (Stanley Boddington)—*Le Carnaval Romain* (Berlioz; arr Frank Wright).
1967 Black Dyke Mills (Geoffrey Brand)—*Journey into Freedom* (Eric Ball).
1968 Brighouse & Rastrick (Walter Hargreaves)—*Prelude, The Mastersingers* (Wagner; arr Frank Wright).
1969 Brighouse & Rastrick (Walter Hargreaves)—*High Peak* (Eric Ball).
1970 Grimethorpe Colliery (George Thompson)—*Pride of Youth* (Gordon Jacob).
1971 Wingates Temperance (Dennis Smith)—*Le Roi d'Ys* (Lalo; arr Frank Wright).
1972 Black Dyke Mills (Geoffrey Brand)—*A Kensington Concerto* (Eric Ball).
1973 Brighouse & Rastrick (James Scott)—*Freedom* (Hubert Bath).
1974 Cory (Major H.A. Kenney)—*Fantasy for Brass Band* (Malcolm Arnold).
1975 Black Dyke Mills (Major P. Parkes)—*Une vie de Matelot* (R. Farnon).
1976 Black Dyke Mills (Major P. Parkes)—*Sinfonietta for Brass Bands*—'The Wayfarer' (Eric Ball).
1977 Black Dyke Mills (Major P. Parkes)—*Connotations for Brass Bands* (E. Gregson).

1978 The Band of Yorkshire Imperial Metals (Denis Carr)—*Dances from the Ballet Checkmate* (Sir Arthur Bliss; arr Eric Ball).

1979 Black Dyke Mills (Major P. Parkes)—*Volcano* (Robert Simpson).

Conducting brass bands

by James Scott

I wanted to be a conductor from quite an early age; although I also had in my youth a burning ambition to gain a reputation as a cornet soloist. Whether I achieved this or not, I will leave other people to decide, but this leads me to the first of my thoughts on conducting.

I consider it a definite advantage to have been a soloist in a top band, since I feel that I can begin to train my band by telling them exactly how, technically speaking, they should produce the sounds I have in mind. There have, of course, been a few very good conductors who were not particularly good performers on an instrument, but in my experience it has always been a great help. A conductor of a first class professional orchestra will expect his players to know how to achieve whatever he may be asking them to do, but we must remember that the job the conductor of a band is doing is very much more concerned with actual training, at least until conductor and band have been together for some time. Then, providing they are both of the necessary competence, a worthwhile unit with the collective understanding that time and application alone can bring should be the result. I think it is now recognised, more than ever, that the level of playing in a few bands in this country is quite up to professional standards.

One of the greatest stumbling blocks to becoming a good conductor is the inability to hear exactly what is going on around him. So many conductors stand in the middle of their band and imagine what is being produced, rather than hearing it precisely as it is. Assuming this ability, then our conductor needs to have in his mind the sound and style he wishes to produce from his players, and from there on it is all a question of painstaking attention to detail. How easy it all sounds!

But behind all this there are many hours of hard, patient work which, of course, can be very draining on the conductor! But I have found with bands I have worked with, that the higher the standard demanded, the more the players enjoy the work. Though after almost 20 years' conducting experience, I am by now well aware that after many an arduous rehearsal, my parentage has been in question! However, I have been fortunate in being able to establish a rapport between myself and bands I have worked with, without which, of course, it would be difficult to achieve anything. Indeed I look upon it as an essential part of one's job as a conductor.

If we are talking of top class bands none of the foregoing is of much use to the conductor unless he has the material to work with—to put it simply, people who can play their instruments! And it is not just a question of auditioning new players, but of finding people who will fit in, not just musically, but in every way. After all, in a top band the members spend a good deal of time together, and the ability to get on with one's colleagues seems to me to be as important as playing qualities. I have found in recent years there are a good many young men around all with potential ability, who can in the building or rebuilding of a band, bring freshness, enthusiasm, and desire and willingness to learn.

Of course, the works-sponsored band is perhaps a little better off, in that it can attract new members by offering employment in its works; but it is true to say that any successful band, whether sponsored or not, will be able to attract talented players. After all, we all like to be part of a success story! The best example of this is probably Brighouse & Rastrick, who are quite rightly proud of their unsponsored status, and to my first hand knowledge, have no trouble whatever in recruiting a new player when necessary.

Another aspect of a conductor's job that we can briefly consider is something that is, after all, the basic reason for our existence as musicians, and that is to entertain. Concert programme planning is a job to which I attach much importance and over which I spend considerable time. Naturally, it goes without saying that you cannot hope to please all your audience all the time, and I am reminded of this at many concerts, when someone will say 'I enjoyed the concert, but why didn't you play a good old brass band march?' or 'Why didn't you include a test piece?' Occasionally of course, we include both and then someone will say 'I enjoyed the concert, but I don't like that test-piece stuff!' But today we are in a much better position than in my younger days as a player, in that we have a good deal more to choose from in light and popular music arrangements and original music. I try as far as possible to include some of each of these, indeed I think it is necessary, in order to create a balanced and entertaining programme. Though I feel there is a tendency to over-emphasise 'pop' music these days with some bands. After all, if anyone is interested only in pop, they will go to a concert played by a group, they do it so much better anyway! The same applies to the big band dance music arrangements. These I avoid, unless I am sure that I can get my band to faithfully reproduce the style, which is difficult for a brass band to do. Again I would say the best dance bands do it better.

A very important part of the band scene is, of course, contesting though I must confess that this aspect of my work as a conductor appeals to me least, while still recognising the need for contesting as an essential part of the scene. It is the linchpin of the band world and has the advantage of providing a target, for most bands, at which they can aim several times annually, depending on how many such events they attend, and there can be no doubt that competition can improve performance in general. Personally, I always feel more like a football manager than a musician at a contest, though it is always a thrill to hear the name of one's own band announced as winners!

Naturally, preparing a test-piece for an important contest requires intensive rehearsal. The difficulty of the music at championship level makes this necessary, of course, but I have always made it clear to my bands that I expect contesting standards at all times and this is something that we keep very much as a standard at which to aim. In short I see my job as a conductor as one in which I spend my time wholly in the pursuit of musical excellence.

A soloist's view

by James Watson

In this short chapter I would to recount my own experiences as a player in the hope that they will help and encourage other youngsters. I began playing at the early age of five. This may seem very young indeed, but I'd better explain that all my family, uncles and cousins included, played with the local brass band; therefore as soon as I was big enough to hold an instrument, I was roped into the Desford Colliery Band as a lowly third cornet.

Each week I had one hour's tuition from the bandmaster, Mr Bernard Springett, for which my parents paid him the princely sum of five shillings. I have very fond memories of those lessons, particularly Mr Springett's phraseology. Here are two examples, with translation: 'It's as straight as a yard of pump-water' (You are playing without expression) and 'I have to take a spoke shave to that tongue o' yours me lad' (Your production is imprecise and flabby). Each day I practised for an hour, closely observed by my mother, who picked on every mistake and insisted on my correcting it. In these practice-sessions I concentrated on scales, arpeggios, studies from the Arban tutor and finally I worked on a piece to be played at a contest or concert. Apart from illness I was never allowed to miss a day's practising. I remember once going on a camping holiday to North Wales. Every morning my father and myself would climb the hills behind Conway Castle, then I would play my daily dozen while my father sat quietly smoking his pipe sitting on a pile of rocks. It is at this point that I must stress how important it was for me to have strong support from my parents. Of course, sometimes we had fights because I did not want to work, but looking back I realise I would not have made it without them.

At this time I started to enter solo competitions and, thanks to Mr Springett's expert guidance, I had a fair amount of success. Also, I was appointed principal cornet with the Bedworth silver band at the age of 11, and after the initial shock over the responsibility of leadership weighing so heavily on my shoulders, I settled down and spent four very happy years with them. When I was 14 I won the National Open Solo Championship at Oxford which proved to be a major turning-point in my career. Up to this time I had been a country boy playing with good but small bands. Suddenly, after the championship win I became a so-called 'hot property', with offers coming in from the really big-name bands. I desperately wanted to go with one or other of them, but my father very wisely insisted that I stayed at school to complete my education. However, I was bitterly disappointed at first and began to lose direction in my playing. But then Eric Pinket, the music adviser for Leicestershire schools invited me to join the schools' orchestra on a trip to Denmark. It meant playing the trumpet, and despite warnings from Mr Springett that this could ruin my position with brass bands, I decided to go. I enjoyed the trip so much that I opted to become a regular member of the orchestra. And during my period with it I performed Aaron Copland's *Quiet City* in the Berlin Philharmonic Hall. It was a marvellous experience and from this point on I decided to take up trumpet playing in all seriousness. Two of the obvious difficulties for me were learning to transpose and also learning to project my sound over a full symphony orchestra. However, as new challenges I accepted them with relish. Now I knew: I was destined to follow a professional career in music.

All of my friends in the schools' orchestra had their sights set on a place at one of the London musical institutions and I followed suit. In the spring of 1969 I travelled down to London and was auditioned by the Royal Academy of Music. I was extremely nervous and thought I had played quite badly. However, four weeks later I received a letter accepting me on a performer's course. My trumpet professor at the RAM was Sydney Ellison. During my first term Sydney was away on tour with the London Philharmonic Orchestra in Japan, so I went to the late William Overton for my first six lessons. I will never forget my opening lesson. Mr Overton was very stern. 'So you're the cornet champion are you?' he said. 'Well, let's see what you can do . . ..' He then proceeded to grill me on the 14 Arban studies for a whole hour. I suffered this treatment for the next six weeks, and although I resented it at the time I can now see that he was proving to me that I was not as good as I thought I was. Sydney Ellison then returned after half-term and we set to work, trying to lose my 'cornet' style of playing and to develop the skills of orchestral trumpet-playing.

The transition from cornet to trumpet-playing is, I am sure, a subject which will interest many young players. In my first two years at the Royal Academy I was obsessed with the idea that orchestral trumpet-playing was absolutely straight. I then realised that I was not enjoying the sound I was making and neither was anyone else. So I decided to try to warm the tone. I believe there is a difference between natural vibrance and vibrato in a sound. If one tries to play too straight one faces the danger of squeezing all of the natural vibrance and timbre from the tone. In learning to use a controlled vibrato I was greatly influenced by jazz players. Like many of them, I would start a note, holding it very straight, then using a slow, wide vibrato and gradually quickening it into a fast, tight one. I did this by careful movement of my right hand over the valves.

Another problem I had to sort out was my production. Like so many young players I made pear-shaped notes sounding 'twaa'. They start softly and balloon out. This is caused by not synchronising the push from the diaphragm with the action of the tongue. To cure this I practised scales using no tongue at all, trying to push the notes out with my diaphragm as a singer does in fast-moving passages in oratorio. I then found that I did not use my tongue as a method of spitting out notes. I had much more control and could vary the attacks and strikes. If one watches good string players one will notice how they use their bows in many ways to create different sounds and effects. A brass recital either by a soloist or by an ensemble can become very tedious for the listener unless we try to develop a way of producing different tones and attacks. For instance, in slow, quiet music I quite often use no tongue at all, just breathing the notes through the instrument.

On the subject of double- and triple-tonguing, I must say I have reservations about the old method of 'tu tuka'. This is all very well for playing loudly in a symphonic work, for example in the fourth movement of *Scheherezade*, but I personally find this too angular for use in solo playing. I prefer to use 'da da ga' in cornet solos as this produces a smoother, rolling effect.

The choice of repertoire for the soloist is most important. The temptation for many players is to play all fast music. This, of course, is very impressive, but after the initial impact of millions of notes per square inch the sound can become monotonous. It is important, therefore, to select a varied programme, always remembering that slow music is often more demanding musically than quick pieces. Many soloists tend to approach polkas and airs with variations as they would the Grand National, as obstacle-races and endeavouring to be the first past the winning post. In cornet repertoire, particularly the works of Herbert Clarke and Hartmann, one should always try to introduce poise and delicacy into the music while taking care not to over-express.

During the last five years or so I have pestered many young composers into writing new repertoire for brass soloists, especially in the medium of trumpet and band. This I feel is very important, because otherwise we could arrive in the 21st century with well-trained players and hardly any repertoire from the most recent generations.

When learning new repertoire one should never rush the fences. I work my way very slowly through a piece, correcting difficult passages as I go and trying to understand the shape of the piece. Most of the Victorian and even later cornet solos tend to be fairly predictable in that one is rarely surprised by awkward intervals and strange key changes. However, the more contemporary repertoire tends to be less straightforward. In mastering a difficult passage in a new piece I first of all learn the finger patterns. This is a great labour-saving device, in that one can practise the value progressions in a piece without the instrument and—more importantly—without using up any precious lip. I often sit on an aeroplane, in trains, buses or even sometimes at traffic-lights fingering my way through a new piece. For young players this is also a very good way to learn scales.

Nerves obviously play a great part in any performance. I am very lucky in that having played so many solos from an early age I rarely suffer from stage jitters. No one can really cure their nerves, but if one is totally prepared, has stamina enough for a performance and concentrates really hard on stage, then one can dramatically reduce the odds against a disaster occurring. Also I think it is truly important to be at the place of a performance in good time to relax. There is nothing worse than arriving at a concert hall minutes before the start and rushing breathlessly out on to the platform.

Since leaving the Royal Philharmonic Orchestra I have concentrated on solo and chamber music, playing with the Philip Jones Brass Ensemble, the London Sinfonietta and the Nash Ensemble, as well as playing regularly for TV, films and on the radio. I play the cornet and trumpet most days of my life, and in conclusion I would like to say that the most important asset of any player is to enjoy one's music and one should never forget that as a performer each of us has a duty to create an emotion from within audiences.

Brass, youth and education
by John Knight

The brass band scene has witnessed many changes in recent times, but most would agree the greatest change has taken place at the youth level. One only has to pick up the newspaper, switch on the radio or television to be aware of the importance that youth music-making and youth brass bands in particular play in present times.

In the last 20 years Educational Authorities have taken increasing interest in instrumental instruction in schools and many teachers are now employed in this specialist field. In the Hampshire Authority at the present time almost 4,000 children are receiving brass instruction and already there is some indication that much of their involvement is of a lasting nature.

The importance of the brass band in education is a success story in itself and there are many instances where schools can boast of brass groups of high quality produced often in relatively short periods of time, and these successes are not to be found in the large schools alone but often in the small Junior and Village schools.

School brass groups have probably flourished and died for many years but the school brass band really began to develop after the second World War. The advantages when forming the accepted brass band are mainly, a) nearly all the instruments use the same clef. b) Most instruments are valve instruments using the same system of fingering. c) Relative ease of movement from one part to another. d) The greatest certainty of producing a really musical result than any other instrumental group. Again the development of the school brass band was helped when brass bands adopted low pitch and co-operation with other school instrumental activities was made easier. Many of the early school bands centred on the work and enthusiasm of an individual; and this is true to some extent in school bands today.

One of the great problems in those early days was the sad lack of suitable music and because two people were concerned about the value and needs of the school brass band, the decision to form a School Brass Association was made in a boat in Christchurch harbour, Hampshire in June 1952.

The preliminaries had begun some months before when Mr Lance Caisley had written a letter to Kenneth Cook approving of an article of his deploring the shortage of suitable music for school brass bands. Kenneth Cook was then unknown to Mr Caisley although he was already well-known in the brass band world. An exchange of letters led to exchange visits between his band from the Featherstone Secondary School in Southall and the band Mr Caisley had helped to form in Portchester School, Bournemouth. The results of these visits were so valuable in showing the benefits of co-operation and in highlighting problems that they decided to form an association which would be concerned specifically with the needs of school bands. Such an association, they agreed, must be concerned with increasing the supply of suitable music, providing opportunities for bands to get together and helping music teachers to learn the skills needed to run school brass bands.

At their first (official) meeting they declared the Association formed, with their two schools bands as the initial members. It is worth recording, by the way, that these two schools are still members of the Association. Kenneth Cook, already a recognised brass band composer and conductor, was the obvious choice for Chairman and Mr Caisley was elected Secretary. In spite of protests, he was also elected Treasurer, on the casting vote of the Chairman. The book-keeping then, however, was not yet very complicated as the total assets amounted to £3, the two subscriptions from the member bands. The next step was to enlist support from useful people in the music world and find out how many school bands there were to join them. Kenneth Cook's contacts here were invaluable. Through him they were able to set up an Advisory Council with Boyd Neel as President. Most important of all, perhaps, they enlisted the support of a publisher, the late Max Hinrichsen.

It is impossible to estimate how valuable and generous his help was at this early stage. He undertook to produce music for the association even though he knew that for some time it would be impossible to make any profit and that the Association might never be big enough to bring him any financial return. However, the Hinrichsen Band Books began to appear and eventually he published Kenneth Cook's *First Band Book* which provided an excellent collection of easy pieces suitable for training school bands in their efforts to play together.

These were supplemented by producing duplicated copies of arrangements made mainly by Kenneth Cook but also by J.R. McKenna of Norfolk and Harold Greensmith of Birmingham. Mr J.R. McKenna played a very important part in the affairs of the Association until he died in 1956. It was through his enterprise that they started annual festivals. He organised the first one in 1954 at the Birmingham Town Hall. To their great relief, for they always worked on a shoe-string then, they made 8s 10d profit (45p in modern debased coinage). Most of all it showed how valuable such a festival could be in setting standards and providing valuable and exciting experiences for young bandsmen. Since then they have held festivals every year—twice a year since 1966.

After the confident—perhaps rather cheeky—formation the first task was to find out how many—or how few—school bands there were. So they wrote to every education authority in the United Kingdom, and, as a result, ended the first year with about 20 school members. It was soon realised that if more school bands were to be formed, efforts must be made to interest music teachers in this particular form of music-making. So they produced their first Handbook, *Music Through the Brass Band.* Then it became clear that a number of music teachers wanted the sort of help which only a course could provide. So a course was arranged at Oakfield Conference Centre near Worcester in 1958. This was only the first of a number of such courses, but it was one of the most important because one of the teachers attending it was Charles Sweby who became Secretary of the Association in 1963. Under his indefatiguable direction, the Association has grown, not only in membership—there are now over 150 school bands—but in its standing in the school music world. The musicianship of many of our school bands now has to be acknowledged even by those who give very grudging recognition to brass bands as musical units. Many serious composers are producing music for school bands and many publishers are now anxious to publish their music. Much of this due to Charles Sweby's musicianship, energy and personality, and to the original supporters.

A special Festival was held in 1973 to mark the 21st Anniversay of the Association; and for this Dr Malcolm Arnold was commissioned to write a work for Choir and Brass Band called *Song of Freedom.* In 1978 the Association organised its first Young Composers Competition, for which 80 scores were submitted, the winner being George Benjamin from Westminster School, London.

The school band has asserted itself. No longer is it a makeshift combination fit only for those who are not good enough to play stringed instruments, but a serious musical activity able to hold its own musically with any group of school instrumentalists, although even now there are many instances of attitudes that reflect the old prejudices.

The National Association for Brass Teachers in Education was formed in 1977. Some of their objectives are *a*) to publish the Association's own graded syllabus *b*) to co-operate with the publishers and manufacturers in the production of suitable music and instruments and *c*) to issue a seal of approval of suitable teaching material. The Association aims to represent brass teachers work in education, and has arranged inservice training courses also lecture recitals by the finest brass players.

The success of Brass teaching in schools I would suggest depends on four factors: support received from the Local Authority, a co-operative and interested Headmaster, a well organised music Department and a competent and enthusiastic Brass Teacher. Unfortunately one finds so often at least one weak link in this chain, and then much of the effective work is nullified. The system operated by Education Authorities varies tremendously, instruction in some Authorities is free and at the other end of the scale charges for instruction are closely linked with those found in the private sector.

The help received from Local Authorities varies from one extreme to the other. Some teachers have almost all they might desire, others have little or no help at all. The school band has by now proved that it can provide so much for the school, the child and the community that I quote Mr Lance Caisley writing in *The Trumpeter*, 'it costs less to produce a happy well-developed schoolchild than to keep a neglected one in an approved school'.

Many Headmasters are aware of the advantages that brass ensembles or bands give to a school and provide excellent support. So often the only available opportunities for band rehearsal is one particular lunch period when the peripatetic teacher is at the school and this clashes so frequently with sport activities. This is a situation where a Headmaster can often find a satisfactory solution. Again the often desperate need for instruments can be eased by the influence of a keen Headmaster.

The Head of a Music Department in a large Comprehensive school has a very demanding task, not the least being to organise, timetable and supervise as many as eight or nine peripatetic teachers. He is the person that makes the school's music tick. The visiting teacher finds it almost impossible to go in search of missing pupils, in a large school most of a lesson would be wasted by the time the missing pupil was located not to say a lesson spoilt for the other eagerly waiting pupils. To make the best use of the work done by the teacher, supervision and involvement in group playing is necessary during the week. Of course, many schools have well developed brass departments and are fortunate in having a considerable amount of teaching time available, this itself is a great advantage, and perhaps the most important single factor is that lessons can be arranged on a rota basis and so the disruption of normal school lessons for any particular child is kept to a minimum.

The school band is used to introduce young people to a wide range of band music, but the school band presents also opportunities for a very varied arrangement of small group playing. Trios, quartets, small ensembles, and today, with a good selection of suitable music, this is a field that can contribute a great deal to the development and pleasure of the brass player.

The availability of instrumental teaching in schools has brought its own problems. Often there is so much going on that the busy music master just has not the time or in some cases the ability to develop all the various music activities and one wonders if the wisest course would be to concentrate on one activity and do it really well.

The role of the teacher is fundamental to all that develops later and the work is both interesting and demanding. Many brass teachers may visit eight, ten, 12 or more schools each week. He is often expected to teach all the brass instruments and this is particularly essential in rural areas where it would be impossible to have the luxury of a specialist teacher for each instrument of the brass family. Often a teacher will have an hour or less to spend at a school so the complexities of accommodating a wide range of brass instruments needs careful planning and constant assessment. In many schools the teacher is responsible for brass ensembles or bands and with a changing pattern of players in each school the teacher is forever arranging and re-arranging music for the next concert or school assembly. Needless to say the end of term concerts usually provides the teacher with a very hectic time. It is usually the brass teacher who is presented with the child who has failed in his school work or perhaps the child who is causing problems in other ways and the success of teachers faced with this challenge may be measured by the number of people today who admit that the vital link between success and failure was forged within the framework of the brass band.

Selection of pupils should be a very important part of a peripatetic teacher's responsibility, consultation with teachers in the schools visited is vital. I know a junior school where they have quite a large number of brass instruments but just one tuba. The Headmaster always takes great care to select a boy who has a good recorder training, who is able academically, usually one of the brightest children in the school, also with parents who will encourage and support. Needless to say that school has produced a line of very good tuba players. This leads me to express my view that the two greatest foundations on which to build instrumental teaching of any kind is a sound recorder training in the early years of schooling coupled with good choral training.

The peripatetic teacher's lot is not always a happy one. They have been known to teach in many strange places, the potting shed, the kitchens, corridors, under the stage, even the toilets; but to be fair I think these cases are mostly in the past, although some teachers may still claim that times have not changed. Whilst some teachers (as in many other occupations) are able to take an easy level course, others find the possibilities and the challenge so stimulating that their future is fully committed to a way of life that has few free moments but at the same time offers rewards rarely found in other occupations.

The contesting field has played its part in helping to create enthusiasm and challenge for the youthful players. In 1965 E. Vaughan Morris incorporated a Youth Section in the National Brass Band Contests only to find insufficient support, with the result that the Youth Section was not again introduced until 1968, and now in 1978 a total of 43 bands participated. Most Youth Contests now allow Bands to use up to 50 players and this I think is a major factor in the support given to youth contesting. The Contesting field has provided brass composers with a valuable shop window. Particularly has the younger composer benefited, and in return the brass repertoire is the richer. This opportunity also places responsibility on Composers and Contest managements alike, as our young players deserve music of the highest level and I would add have a very discerning taste between the good and indifferent music.

A number of works have been commissioned by the organisers of the National Brass Band Championships for the Youth Section, these include such works as *County Down* (Paul Patterson); *Andalucia* (Brian Kelly), *Coliseum* (Gareth Wood) and *Metropolis* (Gordon Langford). Other pieces featured in these same contests are

Strand on the Green (Kenneth Platts) *Fanfare and Soliloquy* (Trevor Sharpe) and *Concert Prelude* (Philip Sparke). Many of these pieces are providing interesting additions to many adult bands' repertoires.

Contesting by Youth Bands is not confined to Youth Sections, and Youth Bands are to be found competing on equal terms with adult bands in the other sections. International Youth Music Festivals are now providing an increasing opportunity for travel and the privilege of meeting young people from other countries, and I think it is time to say that the Youth Brass Bands have played an important role in the noticeable improvement in standards at these festivals in recent years.

The National Youth Brass Band was formed in 1952 by Denis Wright and since that time has arranged residential courses, usually in the school holidays, and has provided young players with many wonderful opportunities. The future position perhaps may well be difficult for the National Youth Brass band as the quite dramatic development in standards and opportunity of school and County Bands, puts great pressure on the National Youth Brass Band to provide that something extra. It is not easy to find suitable music for a group of young players at this level and recently the Arts Council have commissioned works to meet the need.

The development of brass teaching in my own county of Hampshire may be similar or very different to other counties, or Education Authorities. In 1947 when I first started teaching brass in Hampshire schools there was very little brass teaching, in fact the greatest development started around 1963. At that time there were six part-time brass teachers. Now in 1978 there are 25 full-time brass teachers covering 270 schools and providing tuition for almost 4,000 children. Time is allocated to schools on the basis of six pupils each hour and the usual procedure is to have a group of three children each half hour. This rule is flexible and adjusted to meet the different school situations, although over a week about 150 pupils are taught by each teacher. Where possible we try to arrange continuity of teaching so that children have the same teacher as they progress through Junior, Middle, Comprehensive and Sixth Form College. Many authorities make provision for the more able players and in the Hampshire Authority almost 600 children have Music Awards and so have the advantage of individual lessons.

It was in 1963 that I decided to bring together children from schools in Basingstoke, Winchester and Alton to form a Brass Band, and under the name Mid Hants Schools' Band competed for the first time in 1965. In 1968 the band won the Youth Championship of Great Britain and in the space of four years progressed through the four sections to reach Championship grading. In the last ten years, now renamed Hampshire Youth Concert Band we have had many wonderful opportunities to make music through radio, television, Decca Recordings and many foreign tours.

In the early days of the band I could claim to have taught every member of the band, seeing most of the children three or four times each week. Now the situation is very different, as so much of my time is taken with administration and I rely on the work of other teachers. The regular Saturday Band rehearsals are always a thrilling experience, at the stroke of 10.00 am rehearsal starts, rarely is there a late comer or absentee and finishes without break at 12 noon. A good behaviour pattern has been established and the children themselves are keen to uphold the tradition. I am confident that the brass band situation is an ideal one to introduce and foster many of the qualities that are sadly lacking today. I try never to allow animosity to creep in between two children and I endeavour to make the band a family. I shall always endeavour for high standards but I feel that the development of the person must take priority.

The rehearsals are serious occasions but there are also many hilarious moments, some perhaps are not funny at the time. Some years ago during a rehearsal when the band was actually playing I was amazed to see one of the larger variety of licorice allsorts disappearing into the mouth of one of the young third cornet players (now a young man making his mark as a composer) I stopped the band and asked this young man what he though he was doing. The rather hurt-tones reply was, 'well sir, we had four bars rest . . ..' Although on second thoughts as a school boarder he was probably quite capable of dispensing this object in four bars at *Andante*, I am not quite so sure he would have been so successful at *Allegro*. A few months later this same young man seated in the front row of third cornets at a Schools Band Association Festival proceeded to bombard Mr Harry Mortimer, who was the guest conductor, with a level of playing he could rarely have met before, or since; all the more exasperating as I was seated in the front row of the audience and could only glare at the offender who with a nudge at his friend and the most contented of smiles continued to take full advantage of the situation.

We do not claim to be a marching band but we do spend some time rehearsing playing on the march and achieve a reasonable standard before a foreign tour, as I believe that this involvement is appreciated by our friends in other countries, and again children do enjoy the novelty. Not long ago we were in Switzerland and found ourselves in the hot mid-day sun on a three mile parade. The roads were so hot I found it painful to walk, and after two miles or so I began to worry about the children, particularly the six tuba players, all with heavy Imperials and I began to look for a convenient exit road. At that moment a British tourist stepped out of the crowds lining the route and shouted 'marvellous show kids, I'm b . . . proud to be British' needless to say we finished the course—on our knees but still playing. I almost said, on our knees and still praying!

I hope that young players, as devoted as they are, realise they are indeed fortunate, they have so many wonderful opportunities, expert instruction, good music to play, well organised activities, opportunities to play in some of the finest concert halls and chances to visit many other countries in the world. Often many of these privileges become more difficult in later years and it might well be said that some senior bands will have to look to the quality of their music and effectiveness of their organisation if the enthusiasm of our young players is to be fostered and maintained in the future.

I am sure that brass teachers are witnesses to the miracle of change that takes place in many of our children—a miracle rarely seen in our adult combinations—in the short span of 12 months a child can change almost out of recognition both as a player and as a person and so often parents with members of their families away and achieving success in a variety of occupations will say that the greatest aids to their development—perhaps not musical—were found within the association of the brass band. Obviously the brass band in education has its limitations but on the other hand the sky is the limit, and the following quotation from a foreign adjudicator about one of our Youth Bands sums up our hopes and aspirations. 'Here is what young people are capable of doing under the enlightened and intelligent guidance of a conductor serving music because it is a reality, because it brings us beauty, health, sanity and fraternisation between men, all men . . ..'

The brass band repertoire
by Peter Gammond

Long before the first stirrings of the amateur brass band movement at the beginning of the 19th century, there was music being written for brass ensemble. To trace the history of such music would be well outside the scope of this present volume nor would it have very much connection with brass band music as we know it today. The 16th century writings of Gabrieli and Monteverdi in Italy, of Matthew Locke in England and all that followed in the 17th and 18th centuries is music remote from the popular brass band tradition, and is the concern of scholarly specialists. The musical heritage of the brass band movement is more obviously to be found in military band music. The style of the mixed wind-and-brass military band and the true brass band have always remained close, with much overlapping repertoire and cross-fertilisation of musical ideas.

It is no slight on the virtuosic skills of today's brass band musicians to point out that perhaps only in the brass field could such high standards be reached by virtue of the brass instruments being the simplest to play and the soonest mastered by part-time musicians. The amateur brass band was not, however, a practical possibility until the standardised keyed instruments of today were in existence. The production of the *cornet-à-pistons* in France around 1830 and its speedy introduction into England (where it was first known as the cornopean) about 1834, where it replaced the clumsier keyed-bugle, meant that the brass band at last had an instrument capable of playing a chromatic melody with ease. The playing of such virtuosi as Hermann Koenig in the famous Jullien Promenade Concerts was a clear source of inspiration to the aspiring amateur.

The brass band got its final equipment in the 1850s when Adolphe Sax introduced his family of saxhorns which quickly joined the cornets and trombones to make up the basis of the modern brass band. The French horn, a notoriously difficult instrument, was used in early bands but soon fell out of favour. With a group of instruments of similar fingering, allowing easy adaptation from one instrument to another, common ground in the flattened keys, standardisation and availability of instruments now paved the way for the beginnings of the modern brass band tradition. The Mossley Band was one of the first to appear at Belle Vue, in 1851, completely equipped with saxhorns. They won and converted the movement to the new instruments.

The early musical repertoire was imported along with the few professionals who helped these bands on their way; the conductors, teachers, principal soloists and the bandsmasters who had retired from military or civil musical activities or been coerced from them by the prospects of a comfortable post in a provincial town. They brought with them from their various professional spheres of activity, military marches; polkas, galops and waltzes from the dance-hall world; light classics, favourite oratorios and—a favourite dish in early brass band diet—popular selections from the current operas of the day. In this respect the popular bandstand repertoire has not changed very much.

It was the keenly competitive aspect of the brass band movement that led to special music being written for brass band and instrumentalists. Gradually players evolved who could play the virtuoso pieces, many written by the great American band soloists; rather more gradually whole bands achieved the high standards that encouraged the writing of test-pieces of formidable difficulty and aspiration. Prior to the 1900s the brass band had to rely for most of its repertoire on arrangements of orchestral and operatic music generally made by their conductors and mentors. At the innumerable contests bands were often allowed to choose their own display pieces, presumably those that they played most frequently at their concerts. Such was the case at the first Belle Vue contest in 1853 when the two test-pieces were left to the band's discretion and the winners were the Mossley Temperance Band.

One of the pioneering names, still perpetuated, was that of Richard Smith who became the first publisher to specialise in brass band music. He was himself a fine cornet player, a respected teacher and a prolific composer and arranger. His publishing activities now made standard works available to all bands and he also founded the *Champion Brass Band Journal* in Hull in 1857. His company moved to London in 1878. Richard Smith died in 1890 when his magazine was taken over by Samuel Cope (then editor of *The British Bandsman*) and the company was taken over by John Henry Iles. The name R. Smith & Co is still well-known today operating from Watford. Another pioneering firm was that founded by Thomas Wright and Harry Round in Liverpool in 1875. One of the editors in their publishing firm was William Rimmer who was to become a leading figure in the brass band world. Wright & Round founded *Brass Band News* in 1881, edited at first by Thomas Round, then by William Seddon, a bandmaster of the Kettering Rifles who remained in the editorial chair until his death in 1913. Another influential figure was Samuel Cope who founded *The British Bandsman* in 1887. It became *The British Musician* in 1893 and was taken over by John Henry Iles in 1898.

A clear turning point in brass band history came in 1900 with the establishment of the National Championships. Prior to this we can get a fairly clear idea of what 19th century bands were playing by dipping into the pages of one of the periodicals that concentrated on brass band activities: At random I chose *The British Musician* for the years 1896 to 1897, firstly the Belle Vue Contest of 1896 held on September 7. The test-piece chosen was a selection from the lyric-drama *Gabriella* by Pizzi—a work and composer who have both fallen by the historical wayside, nevertheless considered then 'a composition whose difficulty offered excellent scope for comparison'. Amongst bands competing: Silverdale Town, Luton Red Cross Silver Prize, Kettering Rifles, Black Dike Mills (Queensbury), Rotherham Borough Temperance, Mossley, Goodshaw, Wyke Temperance, Pemberton Old, Linthwaite, Rushden Temperance, Heywood Old, Besses o' th' Barn, Batley Old, West Hartlepool Old Operatic, Kingston Mills, Lindley, Denton Original and Rochdale Old bands. The judges came to a quick and clear decision as follows: first—Black Dike; second—Kingston Mills; third—Batley Old; fourth—Lindley; fifth—Wyke Temperance; sixth—Besses o' th' Barn. After the result was declared 'the Black Dike Band gave a very impressive performance of a selection from *Tannhauser* which raised the audience to a high state of enthusiasm'. It was the ninth time that Dike had won at Belle Vue. Hundreds of people waited outside the Queensbury Post Office for news from Manchester and the news of victory was 'received with great cheering. Next morning the inhabitants were agreeably disturbed by hearing the band playing the popular glee *Hail, smiling morn* and *Auld Lang Syne*'.

Of incidental interest is a list of books and pamphlets available in 1896 including Rawson's *Band Primo* (Hull); Wright & Round's *Amateur Band Teacher's Guide* (Liverpool); Lodge's *The Brass Band at a Glance* (Huddersfield); Palgrave Simpson's *Bandmasters' Guide* (Boosey, London); and Griffith's *Military Band* (London). One of the most popular test-pieces chosen by bands in June 1896 was *Lucrezia Borgia* arranged by Wright & Round from the music of Donizetti's opera; others that cropped up several times were *Gems of Scotia*, a piece called *Eureka* and a selection from *Faust*.

Typical Black Dike Band programmes in June 1896, as played in the Horton and Lister parks in Bradford under Mr H. Bower were: (Horton)—*Avondale*, March (Hume); *Poet and Peasant*, overture (Suppé); *William Tell*, selection (Rossini; arr J. Gladney); *Sweet Marjorie*, waltz (Aigrette); *Beauties of Scotland*, fantasia (Hare); *Trombone*, polka (Jeffrey); *Ruy Blas*, selection (Lutz). (Lister)—*Distant Greetings*, march (Godfrey); *Halévy's Works*, selection (Round); *Cinq Mars selection* (Gounod); *Ellen Reigen*, waltz (Gung'l); *Faust*, selection (Berlioz; arr J. Gladney) and *Last Judgment*, selection (Spohr). A fair sampling of the current tastes in music. In August in Halifax at a fête organised on the occasion of the visit of the Duke and Duchess of York to open the New Royal Infirmary, the Black Dyke band played: *Washington Post march* (Sousa); *Poet and Peasant*, overture (Suppé); *Iolanthe*, selection (Sullivan); *The Breeze The Breeze is gently*, glee (Hollingworth); *Faust*, selection (Gounod); *Sur la mer*, waltz (Mitchell); *Halevy's Works* (Round); *Cavalleria Rusticana*, intermezzo (Mascagni); *Saltaire*, polka (Round); *Ruy Blas* selection (Lutz); *William Tell* selection (Rossini); *Dream on the Ocean*, waltz (Gung'l); *Patience* selection (Sullivan); *Haste, ye soft gales*, glee (Martin); *Wagner's Works* selection (Round); and *Good Night*, part song (Smart). A list which helps further to establish the most popular trends; not so very different in most respects from a typical brass band LP programme of the present day.

In October 1897 the Belle Vue contest attracted 32 entrants which were eventually thinned down to 21, the maximum allowed by the rules then being 22, the fewer the better. The test-piece was a selection from *Moses in Egypt* arranged by Charles Godfrey, lasting 12 minutes. While the audience waited for the results there was considerable excited conjecture and a great deal of money passed in bets with Black Dyke (the name seems to have been variably spelt with an 'i' or 'y' until about 1915) and the other crack bands as hot favourites. The winners turned out to be: first—Mossley; second—Kingston; third—Batley Old; fourth—Lindley; fifth—Pemberton; sixth—Luton; with Besses o' th' Barn gaining a consolation prize. 'As each winner was published there were cheers and groans, and when the whole result was known the excitement reached its climax. Disturbances were frequent amongst the various bands that expected to win, and did not; and the betting fraternity were completely thrown over. Of course the usual remarks were made about the "partiality" of the judges, etc. Mossley, who were all smiles, mounted the platform, and again replayed the test-piece, it being the only piece, evidently, of which they had the copy of the music, which may account somewhat for the suggestion that they never expected the prize'.

As reported in *The Cornet*: 'The feelings of the followers and friends of Dike, Wyke and Besses will be much better imagined than described. Those of the two first-mentioned bands emphatically declared that the judges had forgotten the first few bands completely, and when we remember that none of the first dozen bands are to be found in the prize list, it does give the assertion an appearance of truth'.

It led to some fervent discussion of what was or was not a good performance and *The British Musician* commented that while 'the playing of some of these bands was perfection, it was the perfection of machinery—there was no soul in it—the kind of performance that comes through frequent contesting'. The Black Dyke and Besses band possibly did not agree with this conclusion and took such serious umbrage at the results that they did not enter for the 1898 contest at Belle Vue. A well disposed writer suggested that they were activated by more generous motives.

The test-piece in 1898 was a fantasia entitled *Mendelssohn*, an arrangement of various pieces by the composer made by Charles Godfrey. The piece was considered interesting: 'one of the most delicate ever arranged for brass band' with a great variety of pieces 'well devised for the thorough testing of the various classes of brass, with conspicuous opportunites for success or failure for cornets and trombones'. The result: first—Wyke Temperance; second—Hucknall Temperance; third—Lea Mills; fourth—Batley Old; fifth—Kettering Rifles; sixth—Crooke; was decidedly in accord with popular judgment.

By the time John Henry Iles put the National Championships on an organised footing in 1900, contests had truly become a serious matter. Following a great concert in the Albert Hall on January 20 1900, with 11 of the best brass bands conducted by Sir Arthur Sullivan, Iles and Sullivan—then a director of Crystal Palace—agreed amongst other things, that a set test-piece was of prior importance to be played by each of the bands so that they could be properly and fairly judged. At the contest held on July 10 and 11 at Crystal Palace, the test-piece was a selection of *Gems from Sullivan's Operas* arranged by J. Ord Hume. At this time, Sullivan was seriously ill and what might have been a fruitful interest in brass band music was curtailed by his death at the age of 58 on November 22 1900. The contest that year was won by the Denton Original Band with the Black Dyke Mills Band, second and Wingates Temperance Band, third.

For the next few years test-pieces were fundamentally on the same lines: in 1901 *Gems from Sullivan's Operas No. 3* arranged by J. Ord Hume; in 1902 music from Coleridge Taylor's *Hiawatha* arranged by Lieutenant Charles Godfrey; in 1903 excerpts from Wagner's *Die Meistersinger* arranged by Shipley Douglas; in 1904 *Gems of Mendelssohn* arranged by Godfrey; in 1905 exerpts from a now forgotten Paris opera called *Roland à Roncevaux* written in 1864 by the French composer Auguste Mermet (1810-89); in 1906 *Gems of Chopin* arranged by William Short; in 1907 *Gems of Schumann* arranged by Short; in 1908 excerpts from Wagner's *Rienzi* arranged by S. Cope; in 1909 music from Wagner's *Flying Dutchman*. It is interesting to note that William Rimmer, one of the great names of the brass band movement led the Irwell Springs, Wingates Temperance and Shaw bands to victory through five years from 1905 to 1909 before being deposed by the William Halliwell reign. In 1910 the test-piece was *Gems of Schubert* arranged by William Rimmer; in 1911 music from Meyerbeer's *Les Huguenots* arranged by Rimmer; and in 1912 Rossini's *William Tell* overture.

It was a quirk of fate that the first 'commissioned' test-piece came in 1913, the last year of the contest before their discontinuation from 1914 to 1919 owing to the exigencies of war. The piece that John Iles commissioned for 1913 was called *Labour and Love* and the composer was Percy Fletcher (1878-1932), the writer of the popular *Bal masque* waltz, who also acted as one of the judges. Fletcher was obviously aware that the players had been used to pieces based on opera which gave them some foundation for characterisation. So he gave his piece a 'programme' basis and a format that included recitative and solo opportunity, instrumental duets, cadenzas and a plot, implicit in the title, that would strike a sympathetic chord in his working-class players. The father of the family groans as he toils in the pit until his anger explodes (a trombone blast) and he refuses to work any longer in such soul-destroying conditions. His wife quietens his anger and persuades him to work. His spirit revives and human nature triumphs in a happy ending. Fletcher had obviously done his homework well and produced a sample of skilled brass writing that is still held up as a model. It has remained a favourite amongst players and has survived many works of a cleverer and more demanding nature. The Irwell Springs Band won with this piece.

At least the precedent was set and when the contests were resumed in 1920 there was another original test-piece. The composer was a Welshman Cyril Jenkins (1889-1978) whose *Young Lochinvar* had been a great success at the 1911 Eisteddfod. In 1922 he was to become Director of Music for the London County Council. Jenkins (who had originally written his piece for the 1914 contest postponed by the war) took his commission seriously, first with the programmatic *Coriolanus*; and again in 1921 with a piece called *Life Divine* (originally called *Comedy of Errors*). Jenkins set out to present the players with plenty of technical difficulties to be surmounted. As such the music is an enjoyable challenge to the brass band player and calls for unstinted admiration when cleverly executed even today. *Life Divine* especially remains a piece much admired by the band fraternity but it could be criticised, as many test-pieces can be, as of more interest to the player than the listener—like much chamber-music. One critic dismissed the work as a piece of 'Lisztian bombast'. Eventually a golden period of brass-band music was to come but in the 1920s the composers tended to take the word 'test' as their guiding light.

The piece for 1922 was *Freedom* by the later prolific film composer Hubert Bath (1883-1945). *Freedom*, sub-titled 'Brass Band Symphony No 1', is in a much condensed symphonic form kept within the bounds of test-piece limits—usually around 12 minutes. Its first movement starts with a dancing subject full of dynamic contrasts. The second subject is stated by the solo cornet and then tried by the other instruments. The basses now restate the first subject. Euphoniums and basses spiral against a dotted rhythm. Now the full band refer back to the lyrical second subject before the lively dance closes the movement. An Interlude introduces a simple melody with a neat and light accompaniment. The cornet and trombone carry most of the melody backed by the whole band. The scherzo-finale is light and lively in 6/8 time. The instruments imitate one another until a broad sustained tune stops their frolics. This is now heard in various ways on trombones. The finale builds up gradually to a climax with a final reminder of the opening theme in E flat. An ambitious and interesting piece of brass writing. 1922 saw one fundamental change in band contest organisation. The traditional way for brass band players to operate was standing up in formation; in 1922 they were permitted to ape their classical brethren and to perform sitting like an orchestra with the conductor in front on a rostrum.

Two practical pieces were provided in 1923 and 1924 by Henry Geehl (1881-1961), pianist, conductor and a professor on the staff of the Trinity College of Music. He was very much a brass band specialist and one of the first English composers to write an extensive number of extended 'symphonic' works for brass band. The two pieces were *Oliver Cromwell* and *On the Cornish Coast*, both highly descriptive and technically demanding. 1923 was a remarkable year as it was the occasion on which a band from London and the Home Counties—The Luton Red Cross—managed at last to break the stranglehold that the north had maintained on the National Championships up till then. That they did it with the help of Fred and Harry Mortimer's training and under the conductorship of William Halliwell hardly diminished such an achievement and the southern supporters in the audience applauded with wild enthusiasm. Fred Mortimer leading his own band, with his sons Harry and Alex as solo cornet and euphonium respectively, ungrudgingly enjoyed the occasion. It was yet another triumph for the great William Halliwell who had won the contest for six years running from 1910 to 1921 (with a break from 1914-19) conducting the Fodens, Crossfield's, St Hilda and Irwell Springs bands—a run only broken in 1922 with John Greenwood and the Horwich RMI Band.

The respected name of Denis Wright enters the list in 1925 with *Joan of Arc*; and again in 1927 with *The White Rider*. From 1930 he was General Music Editor for Chappell and his special interest in brass and military band writing and scoring is reflected in over 1,000 pieces some 800 of them published, among them eight test-pieces. For the 1926 National Championship, Percy Fletcher was again commissioned and produced one of the most important brass band pieces so far—*An Epic Symphony*. It is actually a suite in three movements. The first, 'Recitare', is literally an instrumental recitative with solo passages interrupted with full-blooded tuttis from the band; the second, 'Elegy', is a prototype of a kind of movement lastingly popular in brass band music, opening with a solemn horn trio, offering solo passages for cornet, soprano and euphonium and, again, a thrilling combined climax. In the third movement, 'Heroic March', virtuoso passages are given to various sections of the band with a chorale-like trio for trombones offering the main melody which is given an exciting treatment by the whole band as climax. The strength of the work is its thematic unity with all the main tunes related, and it is a model test-piece in its varied opportunities for the band.

The wonderful performance that the St Hilda Colliery Band gave of *An Epic Symphony* brought to an end the reign of success of this remarkable band for after their win they were barred from the contest. They had won in 1912, 1920, 1921 and 1924 when it looked as though the Challenge Trophy almost belonged to the South Shields area. Marsden Colliery, another of the Harton Coal Company Group adjacent to St Hilda's, won it in 1925. Percy Fletcher, at that time musical director of the show *Prince Charming* at the Palace Theatre, listened to the performance of *An Epic Symphony* on a special line and expressed his astonishment that brass could sound so beautiful. So the St Hilda Band turned professional and in 1927 they played a series of engagements at London music-halls—known (because they could no longer use the word 'Colliery') as St Hilda's Professional Band or simply St Hilda's. Attempts to form another band at the colliery never materialised.

By now the high standard of brass playing; the importance of the championships and the widespread interest in the movement, meant that the most important names in British music could more easily be tempted into providing music specifically for brass band use. The coming years were to see some distinguished test-pieces.

In 1927 'Jimmy' Ord Hume (whom we have already mentioned in connection with the first Crystal Palace competitions) published a 'straight-from-the shoulder talk' in *The Melody Maker* which then ran a regular military and brass band section absorbed when it incorporated *The British Metronome*. Hume had attended the Crystal Palace events every year from 1900 (except for 1902 and 1924) when he was adjudicating in Australia) and had been an adjudicator from its earliest days to the time it arrived at the status of the Thousand Guinea Trophy Contest. He praised the capable management of Henry Iles over the years, and went on to defend the integrity of the judges, their 'unbiased and deliberate' decisions and their complete musical ability. Reflecting on the controversial history of the Belle Vue competitions he went on to analyse the unrest sometimes felt at the Crystal Palace 'slaughter-house'. He wrote:

'My own observation, based upon a solid foundation, is that much of the disappointment occasioned from year to year is through the over-confidence of the bandsmen and their teachers. Many bands are so pampered with this over-estimation, even by their supporters, that failure seems impossible. And when failure *does* result, the soreness is all the more acute. I have known brass band conductors who cannot imagine failure, and yet they very seldom get into the prize list at all! When such teachers prime their bandsmen with this empty assurance against the appointed adjudicators, it is asking for trouble. Our splendid first-class bands are as good today as they have ever been, the class of music performed is distinctly better than hitherto, and the popularity of brass band music is greater now than ever before. But in contesting, our first-class bands are not so carefully rehearsed as they were in what might be termed 'the old days'. Things have greatly altered in band contesting since the days of the giants and their 'own choice' contests, which gave out no hope to small but ambitious bands. The test-pieces of today are arranged as 'playable selections', and this is where the big bands of the day are seriously handicapped. The ambitious band settles down to hard rehearsal on a test-piece, whereas the big band of yesterday does not see enough interest in the music to rehearse it note for note, nor has it the time or inclination to become inspired in the work. Whether the big bands like the truth to be told to them or not, the fact remains that they are gradually being left behind on the contest platform while the 'small fry' are gradually climbing up to the top.'

Hume's remarks may have gone home, or some such thinking was already in the air, for certainly in the years to come the standards soared as new and important composers contributed to the music, and the competitive reign of the 'big bands' recommenced with Fodens, Black Dyke and other well-known and flourishing bands taking the competition pieces seriously and winning first place often for many years in succession.

In 1928 the test-piece was Gustav Holst's *A Moorside Suite* and it notably brought back the great name of Black Dyke Mills as the winners for the year. Elgar Howarth has written of the Holst piece: 'Perhaps the most important piece in the band repertoire. In its three movements he explores the range of the band's sonorities from the smooth texture of the opening to the mighty weight of the fortissimo in the middle movement, to the brilliance of the march and to the chamber music groupings, again of the middle movement whose final cadences demonstrate a mastery of scoring still unsurpassed. In mood it reveals an essential characteristic of the brass band, whose saxhorns have that sweet yet brooding melancholy his music so often reflects'. It is interesting to note that Holst was himself a trombone player in theatre orchestras and later in the Scottish Symphony Orchestra.

1929 had a further work by Cyril Jenkins, *Victory* and the first-prize went to the Carlisle St Stephens Band. 1930 was again a notable year when England's foremost composer, Sir Edward Elgar, agreed, after some persuasion, to write the test-piece and came up with the *Severn Suite* which he concocted from old musical ideas in his sketchbooks. Opinions have varied on this piece. Harold C. Hinds in his 'Grove's' entry considers it one of the most outstanding works written for the contests, but Elgar's biographer Michael Kennedy says rather scathingly that 'its early origins show through too plainly'. Certainly it has generally been under-rated and possibly Elgar himself was not sufficiently in touch with brass band music to understand that brass music need not be all pomp and circumstance; indeed, is often at its most effective in lyrical mood. Howarth calls it a 'flawed masterpiece—containing the greatest single movement yet written for band—the fugue, but having also a minuet which is perhaps over-long, and throughout one or two (very minor) problems of orchestration'. He conclusively finds it: 'generous in spirit, revelatory in its inward searchings—a fine gift to the band world from our greatest composer'. Elgar was unable to attend the Crystal Palace event because of an attack of sciatica. He had dedicated the work to Bernard Shaw who gracefully said that 'it will ensure my immortality when all my plays are dead and damned and forgotten'. Shaw went to Crystal Palace and sat through the piece eight times. He made several pointed suggestions—to 'drop the old Italian indications and use the language of the bandsmen' and to 'remember that a minuet is a dance and not a bloody hymn'. He found the scoring 'infallible' and enjoyed the 'curiously pleasant oboe quality of the muted flugels picking up after the cornets'. He found it 'beautiful and serious'. It has not, however, become a favourite of the brass world nor even one of Elgar's best-known works in its later orchestral guise.

1930 had seen the first of a string of victories for the great Fodens Motor Works Band under Fred Mortimer. In 1931 Wingates Temperance Band stepped in with Hubert Bath's *Honour and Glory* with Fodens coming back in 1932 to win with John Ireland's *A Downland Suite*. (Fodens victories were to continue in 1933, 1934, 1936, 1937, 1938, 1950, 1953 and 1958). Coming from one of Ireland's most fruitful periods when he abandoned some of his earlier complexity and went for more transparent textures—he had written one of his finest works, the Piano Concerto, in 1930—he found the textures of the brass band an interesting challenge. Unlike Elgar, Ireland revelled in the pastoral sonorities of gentle brass and in *A Downland Suite* produced something that was almost too subtle for its purpose. The following year Granville Bantock wrote a romantic piece called *Prometheus Unbound*. He had already written his *Oriental rhapsody* for brass band in 1930 and was to indulge in quite a spate of brass music in the years 1942-5. *Prometheus* was well written but undistinguished.

John Ireland's *Comedy Overture* of 1934 (known in its later orchestral version as *London Overture*) is a brilliant and melodious piece that leaves us to decide on the ambiguous rightness of its themes in relation to its two titles. Its rather ominous opening might well be portraying tragedy rather than comedy. The melody is heard on the bass instruments with comments from the cornets, before a cadenza starting on the euphonium and continued by a cornet leads to the allegro where the cornets have the the distinctive phrase which in the 'London' version is said to be the voice of a London bus-conductor calling 'Picc-adilly' and is handled by the violins. It is gradually taken up by the whole band with an effective use of cross-rhythms. A beautiful *tranquillo* section displays the rich tones of the brass before we are back to the original rhythmic theme and a brilliant coda. Munn & Felton's interrupted the Fodens years in 1935 when they won with their playing of Kenneth Wright's *Pride of Race*. In 1936 it was the turn of Arthur Bliss, then considered quite an avant garde composer, to show his brass capabilities with *Kenilworth*. It struck many as being daringly, even offensively, modern and has been described as 'the most extrovert music ever written for band' and comprised exotic fanfares, lavishly romantic scenes 'by the lake' and, its most popular section, a rousing march, *Kenilworth*, written in homage to Queen Elizabeth.

Herbert Howells succeeded Gustav Holst as director of music at St Paul's Girls' School in 1936 and followed in the steps of the master with his suite *Pageantry* originally written for the Belle Vue contest in 1934 and used for the National Contest in 1937. It is a strong work and worthy of revival. For the 1938 competition Fletcher's classic *Epic Symphony* was brought back. The competitions again went into abeyance for the war period 1939-44 and returned in 1945 with Denis Wright's *Overture for an Epic Occasion*.

On paper it looks as though a golden age of brass band writing was at an end for there was apparently no obvious candidate for a new piece in the 1940s. 1946 saw the return of Geehl's *Oliver Cromwell*; 1947 Hubert Bath's *Freedom*; 1948 Geehl's *On the Cornish Coast*; 1949 Ireland's *Comedy Overture*; 1950 Howells' *Pageantry*; 1951 Fletcher's *Epic Symphony*. Perhaps the organisers were too busy re-organising and doing the good work that put the contest on a new and thorough basis of regional heats and an Albert Hall finale; but it was no bad thing to revive worthy test-pieces from the past as trials for a new generation of brass band players. The movement remains fairly conservative in its musical tastes and the spiky cleverness of many modern composers would hardly please the brass-bound public. A pity, perhaps that composers like Britten or Walton were never persuaded; but there was (and is) still plenty of potential to come.

It was with the specific aim of providing attractive music, combined with pointful testing qualities, that the expert arranging talents of Frank Wright were so frequently 'put to the test' in the 1950s and 1960s. The results were consistently brilliant and satisfying—arrangements of Bantock's overture *The Frogs of Aristophanes* (1952); Bailey's *Diadem of Gold* (1953); Beaver's *Sovereign Heritage* (1954); Eric Cundell's very tuneful *Blackfriars* (1955); Lalo's *Le Roi d'Ys* overture (1959)—which had an inspired performance from the Black Dyke Mills Band that was described at the time as the finest exposition of brass and playing heard in the history of the contests; it was used again in 1971; Berlioz's *Les Francs Juges* (1961); Verdi's *The Force of Destiny* (1962); Berlioz *Le Carnaval Romain* (1966); Wagner's Prelude to *The Mastersingers* (1968). The movement owes a great debt to Frank Wright both as adjudicator and provider of first-rate brass music.

Between times the fruitful years of the 1930s were finding an echo in the 1950s and 60s as the organisers resumed the tradition of commissioning test-pieces from established academic composers which, combined with the work of the brass-band specialists like Eric Ball, was to help establish a very sound repertoire and a respectable catalogue of purpose-written brass band works. No history of brass band music would be valid without a substantial credit to Eric Ball. Born in 1903, he began his band career with the Salvation Army as conductor of their Staff Band. Since then he has conducted most of the principal bands and in 1946 led the Brighouse & Rastrick Band to victory in the National Championships. He has literally toured the world as conductor, lecturer and adjudicator. His first piece for brass-band was *Resurgam* which was the test-piece at Belle Vue in 1950 and is still regarded by many as his finest work. Also known as a prolific writer of church music (including several fine cantatas), it is not surprising to find that the inspiration for *Resurgam* is to be found in the words from the Apocrypha: 'The souls of the righteous are in the hands of God'. The motif echoing this is heard several times in the piece. The music moves into strange emotional levels, sometimes harsh and discordant, a painting of worldly chaos and violence in contrast to the peace of God. The music rises to the revelatory 'I shall rise again' and ends with the calm assurance of the opening theme. It was an ambitious piece which showed to what extent the brass band could be used for romantic imagery—a far remove from the marches and cornet pieces of earlier days. In 1956 Eric Ball provided the National test-piece *Festival Music*, an exultant display piece in three contrasting movements. In 1967 he wrote the test-piece *Journey into Freedom*. This is W.A. Chislett's description of it: 'Ball's piece is modern in outlook and style containing six well defined sections but there is no break in continuity. It opens *moderato e feroce* in a style which suggests machine-like materialism, then moves to a march of protest or revolt after which the opening mood returns, now even more unyielding and harsh in a section marked *moderato e molto feroce*. Escape is sought though the agency of human love, then there is a section of the utmost high spirits and gaiety. In the final *andante cantabile* the love music returns in sublimated and idealised form'. Which all suggests that Eric Ball is something of an idealist as well as a brass band musician.

In 1969 he wrote *High Peak* for the National Championships and has supplied his own programmatic notes: the first section 'Vision' portraying 'the ever changing light, colour and cloud as one contemplates from below a great mountain'—'Aspiration'—the climber of the mountain must plan and prepare; the music has a busy, bustling feeling. 'Ascent'—resolute in mood, 'Alpine' effects and a storm. 'Attainment'—the summit is reached and joy is expressed in the achievement. When he wrote *A Kensington Concerto* for the 1972 National event, Eric Ball dedicated it 'To Olive Rose (his wife) and that gay company of friends, now scattered, who in times past met annually in the Royal Albert Hall, London, on the occasion of the National Brass Band Championships'. Geoffrey Brand has written of the work: 'it is reflective, not in exact quotation, but by the style which many will recognise and enjoy—as Eric Ball's way. The opening melody, for one cornet, followed by the full band, serves as an introduction to a succession of moods—a lively Scherzo; a lyrical Grazioso, a majestic Moderato, a gay Giocoso, and so on. Finally, surrounded by misty muted cornets, the opening melody returns, this time on the mellow-toned horn, as if announcing that the day is done. For the student of music, it is interesting to note that *A Kensington Concerto* is in three/four time throughout. Yet how much variety of mood and feeling the composer captures'.

One sorts out the Eric Ball test-pieces for their particular distinction, but he has written so much good music for brass; exploring, romantic, interesting music that has taken brass music well away from its operatic selection days. And, of course, as well as his brilliant original compositions we are greatly indebted to him as a skilful arranger. In 1976 he wrote his *Sinfonietta for Brass*—'The Wayfarer' especially for the championships. Again it follows the typical pattern of three distinct sections all linked together without a break. The sections are sub-titled 'Adventure', 'Exile' and 'Homeward Journey'. The work opens with a quiet theme painting a picture of peace and the contented home. As the wayfarer's journey begins the music changes in mood, first arrogant and gay, then uncertain and sad, with memories of home often returning. The 'homeward journey' is announced by a march theme played in unison by trombones and B flat bass, the music then moving purposefully toward a triumphant restatement of the 'home' theme and a triumphant close.

We move back to 1957 to note the entry of the distinguished name of Ralph Vaughan Williams into the championship arena. The composer had always shown a strong interest in the brass band movement as an extension of his interest in folk and national music. But he was coming up to his 85th birthday before he turned his hand to some specific brass writing. In 1956 he had presented the prizes at the National Brass Band Championship and the same year he had written a *Prelude on Three Welsh Hymn Tunes* for the Salvation Army Band and had attended one of their concerts in Dorking. Obviously intrigued by the possibilities of brass, he followed up the invitation to write a test-piece by writing the *Variations for Brass Band* which was used for the 1957 championship on October 26. *The Times* rather condescendingly and sweepingly described it as 'unquestionably the best piece ever written for this unwieldy medium'. It was certainly a skilfully written work with a strong theme for its variations and obviously ideal for its medium for it is far less effective in the orchestral arrangement by Gordon Jacob. It is in the same vein as his 5th Symphony, and is made up of a theme and 11 variations ending in an impressive Chorale for the ensemble. The instrumentation was for E flat soprano cornet, solo B flat cornet, repiano B flat cornet and flugel horn, two B flat cornets, solo E flat horn and two E flat horns, two B flat baritone saxophones, two B flat trombones and bass trombone, one B flat euphonium, two bass tubas, drums and timpani. Twenty-one bands competed and the winners were Munn & Felton's (Footwear) Band from Kettering (later GUS). At the concert in the evening the work was played by the massed Fairey, Carlton Main, Clydebank Burgh, CWS Manchester, Morris Motors and Munn &

Felton bands conducted by Karl Rankl. Also in frequent use was his *English Folk Song Suite* (arranged for brass by Gordon Jacob) originally written for military band in 1923; and his quick march *Sea Songs* for military and brass bands written for the British Empire Exhibition at Wembley in 1924.

Edwin Vaughan Morris has the following recollections of the composer: 'Ralph Vaughan Williams had long made his prodigious contribution to music before I made his acquaintance. In fact he was in his eighty-fifth year, but the old maestro was still very alert mentally and music continued to engross him. He had, of course, throughout his life showed much practical sympathy with popular movements in music, such as the Competition Festival Movement and, especially, the Folk Dance Movement. He had also edited *The English Hymnal*. It was with these thoughts in mind that I decided to approach him with a view to his writing the music to be set as the test-piece for the 1957 National Brass Band Finals at the Royal Albert Hall. Much to my delight he agreed to write an original work for the purpose and his *Variations for Brass Band* was the outcome. He was anxious to hear the performances by the competing bands and he came along to the Royal Albert Hall for this purpose.

'Prior to his arrival at the Royal Albert Hall I had invited him to the Festival Concert in the evening, so that he could hear the first performance of his *English Folk Songs* Suite. I had also suggested he might present the Awards to the winning Bands in the Championship Section. These Bands had played his *Variations for Brass Band* at the competition stage of the proceedings earlier in the day. This he agreed to do.

'It was explained to him that the concert programme was, perforce, subject to strict timing, and more especially as a live BBC transmission was involved. Consequently, no time for speech making was available and the presentation of the awards would be a slick operation, based on the relevant and individual announcements by Frank Phillips, acting as link man.

'When the Presentation of Awards spot was reached and Vaughan Williams walked on the platform the most extraordinary and spontaneous demonstration was experienced. With no prompting, and no lead of any kind being given, the vast audience which packed the hall rose to its feet and applauded for minutes on end. It seemed as if the intensely warm and emotion-charged greeting would not come to an end. This was an amazing display of the affection and admiration these thousands of music lovers had for this great musician, even in the winter of his life.

'Understandably, he was moved considerably and he turned to me and asked for the microphone so that he could speak for a few moments. I could not gainsay him this privilege in the circumstances. Actually he spoke for eight minutes and each of these minutes played havoc with my planned running time, along with the added anxiety of the scheduled live pick up time by the BBC approaching ominously. Swift thinking and adjustment in the forward programme had to be done in consequence. What had transpired was indicative of the gratefulness and appreciation of a nation for a worthy son who had brought it honour and glory along the way. He died the following year at the age of eighty-five'.

In 1958 the National test-piece was *Variations on 'The Shining River'* by Edmund Rubbra. The composer has told us of his initial hesitation at accepting the commission as he did not have the special knowledge demanded by brass band scoring where 'everything except the bass trombone and drums is written in the treble clef'. But he was encouraged by Frank Wright who promised that if the composer went ahead with the composition he would help him to translate the sounds he had in mind into brass band terms; which he did. 'The Shining River' theme used was an adaptation of a piano piece the composer had written some years earlier. Its slow legato nature, subdued tone-colouring and rhythmic shifts between two and three beats was an immediate challenge to the brass players. The first variation is a test in legato and staccato effects, the second asks for subtle and delicate harmonic effects, the third asks for forte playing and precise dotted rhythms, the fourth is mainly in a five beat dance rhythm. The final variation is particularly demanding in its shifts of rhythm which demands absolute co-ordination in playing; a short coda brings back the opening theme. Fodens Motor Works band under Rex Mortimer were the most successful negotiators of this demanding piece.

Herbert Howell's *Pageantry* had been a successful and colourful test-piece in 1934 at Belle Vue and for the National in 1937. In 1960 he returned to the brass band foray with *Three Figures*, when Munn & Feltons were again the victors. The 'three figures' of the title are three people of particular eminence in the brass band world to whom a neat and appropriate musical tribute is paid. Firstly Sam Cope (1856-1947) and a piece called *Cope's Challenge*—of a florid nature and calling for much brilliant and showy playing; secondly John Henry Iles (1871-1951) in *Iles' Interlude*—of more sombre character; thirdly, William Rimmer (1862-1936)—a typically rousing brass exultation. It is music well orientated toward the brass idiom; well scored and demanding every ounce of skill, exploiting the various sections of the band to excellent effect. It is surprising that this exciting music has been so infrequently recorded; but the Virtuosi Brass Band recording under Maurice Handford is a first-rate addition to the LP repertoire.

Sir Arthur Bliss had provided the brass band with one of its classic pieces *Kenilworth* in 1936 and had continued a close association with the movement, a frequent and regular conductor of the concerts following the championships, and in 1963 he wrote the *Belmont Variations* which W.A. Chislett has described as 'full of attractions, especially unexpected key changes, and beautifully laid out for brass'. I discussed his interest in brass band music with him two years or so before he died in 1975 and he expressed the thoughts that must have been in the minds of many composers venturing into the brass idiom. He had found it a particularly refreshing yet demanding exercise. The brass ensemble fixes obvious limitations on tone colours which a composer used to writing for the full orchestra would find particularly daunting. So the writer is always at full stretch to try to find interesting combinations of sound; revelling in the traditional timbres, particularly effective in subdued passages, yet desperately trying to find a new idea. In some ways, said Sir Arthur, it was like trying to write for the organ where one was similarly trying to find potential new routes. He would have been delighted with the brilliant effects that Eric Ball achieved in his brass arrangements of music from one of his most colourful orchestral scores *Checkmate* used as the test-piece in the 1978 championship at the Albert Hall.

If the brass world had hopefully expected the leading British composers to supply it with masterpieces, it could always rely on the backbone of its own specialist composers to supply it with quality material—the Rimmers, Wrights and Balls who naturally thought in brass terms. Another composer well-steeped in brass thoughts, though not limited to them, was Gilbert Vinter. Starting as a boy chorister at Lincoln Cathedral he studied at the Royal Academy and was a fine bassoonist who played in the BBC Military Band, the London Philharmonic and during the war with the Central Band of the RAF. His conducting experience came with the RAF and then for many years working with the BBC Midland Orchestra. He was a diverse composer but developed a very keen interest in the brass band field and was a particularly innovative composer for brass quartet. One of his first effective compositions for brass band was *Salute to Youth* commissioned in 1962 for the qualifying events of the National Championship. He brought a new, bright and original style to brass writing, clearly apparent in this effective piece, his experience in the light music field making him appreciative of the melodic appeal needed to lighten the demands of virtuosity. His *Variations on a Ninth*, the 1964 National test-piece was a 'splendid and highly taxing set of variations on a theme which lends itself admirably to such treatment' (WAC), As the name clearly states, the 'theme' is the chord of the ninth. The work begins with a brilliant exercise in triple tonguing, starting on D with the solo cornets and then going downward in thirds, repeated in semiquavers, exploring the components of careful co-ordination between trombones and cornets; variation two is a waltz; variation three is a rather unusual set of cadenzas for various instruments; and so on—one of the most ingenious pieces written for brass.

The following year Gilbert Vinter wrote *Triumphant Rhapsody* for the Championship at the Albert Hall. Of it he wrote: 'The discordant clashes of major and minor 2nds on which this work is built should *not* be unduly emphasised (unless specially marked) but played naturally and in the more lyrical passages should be quickly "caressed" with sweet tone quality'. The main theme is founded round a phrase featuring a prominent interval of a diminished third first heard in the brief *maestoso* introduction. It comes again in the following *allegro* against a syncopated background of clashing *staccato* seconds. Throughout there are contrasting lyrical passages and climaxes. The spectacular climax in 12/8 builds from a *pianissimo*. Technically it was an exciting bit of modern music and very much a virtuoso test-piece. Vinter's masterpiece is probably *The Trumpets* for large band, chorus and bass, a cantata based on the verse from the Book of Numbers—'and the Lord said unto Moses make me two trumpets of silver', in four movements, the first, called 'Blazon', uses only the cornets; the second 'Destruction' is based on the story of the walls of Jericho being destroyed by trumpets blowing (Joshua, Chapter six); the third 'Dedication' is the central theme from the Book of Numbers, quoted above; the finale is 'Revelation', the prophesy of things to come, with the choir giving thanks to God in a tremendous climax. In the Black Dyke recording under Geoffrey Brand the band was augmented to 38 players and Gilbert Vinter was able to be there to advise. By 1969 he was very ill and his final work *Spectrum* written for the 1969 Open Championship at Belle Vue, where he should have been one of the adjudicators, was never heard by him, and he died, a tremendous loss to the brass band movement, at the end of the year. *Spectrum*, as the name suggests, was a very colourful score, like Bliss's *Colour Symphony*, depicting all the tones of the spectrum in musical terms; a highly imaginative work. His own favourite work—*James Cook—Circumnavigator*—he was never able to hear performed. His interesting experiments in brass quartet writing can be heard on an intriguing disc *Quartet for Brass* which the composer made with members of the GUS (Footwear) Band.

We have concentrated so far on the test-pieces that have been used in the National Championships and elsewhere. These are important because they are the 'symphonies' as it were of the brass band repertoire, the serious challenging works. They are works to admire but their inherent disadvantage is their technicality. Great music is rarely written with the intention of being difficult to play and lyrical qualities can very quickly be lost in the search for effect. Dare we say it—we shall not be the first to do so—that some of these worthy test-pieces are inclined to be a bit dull, a little over-serious. Now and then something emerges, eg the March from the *Kenilworth* Suite, which has lasting qualities. The brass band world has not yet found its Mozart or its Beethoven. There is no reason why it should not do so when composers are found who can write with unselfconscious exuberance and melodic inspiration for brass. Such a person could spring from the brass band ranks but it seems more likely that it will be a composer of wider interest and achievement who also finds it worth while to have a full understanding of the brass idiom.

In many ways, the nearest to this ideal has been Malcolm Arnold, who has all the qualifications. He is himself an accomplished brass player, who, after studying at the Royal College of Music, spent many years as an orchestral musician, trumpet player with both the London Philharmonic and the BBC Symphony orchestras, mainly as a principal. This obviously gave him a special sympathy for the brass, and he has lavished much of his composing talent (which includes the ability to write a good tune) on brass band compositions which are both technically interesting and richly satisfying purely as music. His first *Little Suite*, written in 1967 for the Cornwall Youth Band, was in typical vein, full of light-hearted music, amusing counterpoint, rich fat chording, frivolous galops and rondos, a delight to hear as well as to play. His joy in pure sound is demonstrated in the fine *Quintet* (for two trumpets, horn, trombone and tuba) written in 1961 for the New York Brass Quintet. In 1974 he wrote the National test-piece *Fantasy for Brass Band*, the piece for the historic occasion when the Welsh Cory Band wrested the title away from the north of England for only the second time in the history of the championship. The composer supplied his own programme-note: 'The Fantasy is a form which appeals to me very much. The term is used in the Elizabethan sense of a piece of which the form is dictated by the composer's fancy—'Fancy' being another name for the same form. I have chosen this form on this occasion, as I think there are too many brass band pieces which consist of short movements. The musical difficulties of *Fantasy for Brass Band* are enormous, though the technical difficulties are probably less than one finds in many contest pieces (and when I say technical difficulties I refer to the difficulties of playing faster than anyone else, which seems to me to matter little). It is a contest piece in the sense that it is a test of musicianship, which after all is the main thing in music'. Arnold has also proved that he can unbend in the light idiom of the *Song of Freedom*, commissioned by the National Schools Brass Band Association in 1972; and that he can write a rousing march with the best—*The Padstow Lifeboat* splendidly combines both atmosphere and tune.

In recent years there has been something of an explosion of interest in writing for the particular instrumentation and sonorities of the brass band which has been encouraged by the growing capacity of the amateur bandsman to play a complicated score and by the formation of professional playing and recording groups such as those led by James Shepherd and Philip Jones. The first impetus for this academic interest came when the Championship organisers accepted some fairly advanced scores as their test pieces such as Howells' *Three Figures* in 1960, Vinter's *Spectrum* in 1969, Robert Simpson's *Energy* and Elgar Howarth's *Fireworks* (1975). There were many who thought that these were moving too far away from the tastes of the working-class society in which the brass band movement had grown. The influence of Bartók and Schoenberg seemed unlikely to impinge on the world of operatic selections and the broadly Elgarian flavour of brass band music so far. In the main this still holds good. But once the so-called 'serious' composer had tasted the satisfaction of writing for brass, the cult was bound to grow. Following in the Howells direction, and building on the work of Rubbra and Vaughan Williams, came Martin Dalby's *Music for a Brass Band* (1962), Thea Musgrave's *Variations for Brass Band* (1965), Edward Gregson's *Brass Quintet* (1967)—since recorded by the Philip Jones Brass Ensemble and the Hallé Brass Consort, Phyllis Tate's *Illustrations* in 1970. During this period there was active commissioning of such pieces by the more adventurous conductors such as Geoffrey Brand, Ifor James and Elgar Howarth.

By the 1970s, these avant-garde activities were an established part of the brass band world, at least that part of it represented by the semi-professional and professional groups. We have mentioned Simpson's *Energy*, a work that had a great influence although in itself no more outlandish than say Nielsen or Shostakovitch. More aggressively 'modern' was Harrison Birtwistle's *Grimethorpe Aria* (1973); likewise Paul Patterson's *Chromascope* (1974), Bryan Kelly's *Divertimento* and Derek Bourgeois' *Tuba Concerto*. Listings of these and other modern works will be found in the 'who's who' that follows this section.

The brass band world always seems to have been somewhat torn by its conflicting musical needs. The majority of the public that follows the art are almost certainly not particularly highbrow in their inclinations. They come from the vast middle and working classes who enjoy a good tune and a bit of romantic programming. Because many of them are brass players themselves they appreciate test-piece ingenuity, but on the whole they probably prefer something tuneful and rhythmical. To cater for this need the brass repertoire has leaned heavily on arrangements of popular classics—and indeed some of the most successful test-pieces have been cunning arrangements of attractive pieces of music like Lalo's *Roi d'Ys*, Berlioz's *Les Francs Juges* and *Carnaval Romain* overtures beautifully arranged by a master of the craft like Frank Wright. This is music that starts with soul, strength, gaiety and craft and it translates well. Many times that stalwart reviewer of brass band recordings, W.A. Chislett, has remarked that piano music is one of the finest basic ingredients upon which to base a brass arrangement—and I am much inclined to agree with him. So is opera—a composer like Verdi takes us halfway there himself with his own liking for such sonorities.

It is impossible to survey the whole of the brass band repertoire but I would like to repeat that there is a great need for a modern composer who can be both substantial and attractive in his creations. We need more composers like Joseph Horowitz to turn to the brass idiom, as he has done in a very pleasant *Euphonium Concerto*, for more delightful sets of variations like Alan Street's based on Tchaikovsky's *Rococo* Theme, for more good material like Arthur Wood's *Dale Dances*. We should not complain, for there is much to choose from already, but with the increasing support for the brass band movement, more composers will probably come to realise that there is a very worthy outlet for their endeavours in this direction.

The brass band world is not all competition. The brass band is a part of the heritage of the people, particularly of the north, and it rightly belongs in the band-stand in the park (now sadly lacking in numbers), at the local fête and in the May Day processions. I remember as a child, but then I was brought up on the good brass county of Cheshire, the land of Fodens and the Mortimers, when our local Rose Fête procession would include as many as a dozen local and neighbouring Silver Bands (as they were so frequently called then—and still are in the Fourth Section strata). And such bands must regale us, and will, with Gilbert & Sullivan, Strauss polkas and Sousa marches, nicely mixed with the stalwart works of the Rimmers and Ord Humes—the men who knew, loved and lived brass. Their spirit will never die!

Who's who in brass band music

by Peter Gammond and W.A. Chislett

The numbers in bold (as elsewhere in the book) indicate as follows: **30** = National Championship test-piece, 1930; *30* = British Open test-piece, 1930.

ALWYN, William (b Northampton, November 7 1905). Composer and teacher. Studied at the Royal Academy of Music, London where in later years (1926-56) he became Professor of Composition. For a time he was an orchestral flautist. His first work to attract widespread attention was the Piano Concerto of 1930. He is principally known by his music for films, especially *Desert Victory, On Approval, Odd Man Out, The Way Ahead* and *The Rake's Progress*. His other compositions, which are many and varied in form, include *The Moor of Venice*, a dramatic overture for brass band. *Recordings: Fanfare for a Joyful Occasion*—Locke RHS349.

William Alwyn (Lyrita/Reg Williamson).

ARNOLD, Malcolm (b Northampton, October 21 1921). Composer. Studied trumpet, piano and composition at the Royal College of Music from 1938. Trumpet player with the London Philharmonic Orchestra from 1941 and principal in 1942. After war service became second principal of the BBC Symphony Orchestra in 1945 and rejoined the London Philharmonic as principal in 1946. Decided to become a full-time composer in 1954. Has become well-known as a writer of film music, especially for *Bridge of the River Kwai* in 1957. His orchestral works include five symphonies; concertos for horn, clarinet, oboe, flute, piano duet, guitar, harmonica; the overture *Beckus the Dandipratt* (1943); popular suites of *English* (1950) *Scottish* (1957) and *Cornish* (1966) dances; incidental music for *The Tempest* (1954), the ballet *Solitaire* (1956) based on the *English Dances;* also wrote music for Ashton's *Homage to the Queen* (1953), *Rinaldo and Armida* (1955) and Helpmann's *Elecktra* (1965). He has taken a special interest in brass music and his works in this field include a *Fantasy for Tuba, Little Suites* No 1 and No 2, a *Quintet for Brass* (1961), *Song of Freedom* (1972), the well-known march *The Padstow Lifeboat* and the 1974 National Championship test-piece *Fantasy for Brass Band*. Hon D Mus, Exeter, 1970. *Recordings: Fantasy for Brass Band* **74**—Cory SB319; *Fantasy for Tuba*—Stanshawe TT001; *Fantasy for Trombone*—Jones ZRG851; *Little Suite No 1*—Black Dyke NSPL18209 & GH632, Fairey SB301, National Youth GSGL10403; *Little Suite No 2*—Black Dyke LPT1028, London SB313, Oxford 15-56; *The Padstow Lifeboat*—Black Dyke NSPL18209, BMC CSD3650, London SB313; *Quintet for Brass*—London

SB313, Hallé GSGC14114; *Song of Freedom*—London SB313; *Symphony for Brass Instruments*—Philip Jones ZRG906.

ASHPOLE, Alfred (b Somersham, Huntingdonshire 1892.) Composer, teacher and adjudicator. Studied at the Guildhall School of Music and privately with Denis Wright and James Ord Hume. He was music master at the Downham Girls' High School from 1939 to 1947. In addition to works for orchestra and songs he wrote a number of suites for brass band of which probably the best known are *Hinchingbroke* and *Suite Ancienne*.

BALL, Eric (Walter John) (b Bristol, October 31 1903). Composer, arranger and conductor. Associated for over 50 years with the worlds of brass band and choral music, he came from a Salvation Army family and it seemed inevitable that he would be active in that sphere. After the first World War he wanted to become an organist and studied the organ at St Peter's in Staines and Holy Trinity in Dartford where the family eventually moved. At 18, after an interview with Colonel Arthur Goldsmith, he joined the Music Editorial Department of the Salvation Army and though he found it a limiting world of music he was able to study scores and started writing music himself. In 1926 he became an officer in the Salvation Army and shortly after formed the Salvationist Publishing and Supplies Band. In 1921 he had heard the Cyril Jenkins test-piece *Life Divine* and was greatly influenced by it. He conducted the International Staff Band for a short time in 1942 but shortly after left the Salvation Army and went on tours abroad entertaining the troops. Soon after he met John Henry Iles of *The British Bandsman* who asked him to write a test-piece for the Belle Vue contest—which he did, calling it *Salute to Freedom*. He became editor of *The British Bandsman* and also started his brass band conducting career. His first appointment was with the Brighouse & Rastrick Band with whom he won the National Championship in 1946. He also conducted the CWS (Manchester) Band—an outfit he particularly admired—Ransome and Marles and the City of Coventry Band and won the Belle Vue Championship three times. Became known as a lecturer and a leading adjudicator. His well-known test-pieces include *Resurgam* (1950); *The Conquerors* (1951);

Festival Music (1956); *The Undaunted* (1959); *Journey into Freedom* (1967); *High Peak* (1969) and *A Kensington Concerto* (1972). He has also been keenly interested in writing for school and youth bands and choirs and in church music including, naturally, many pieces for the Salvation Army. In 1972 he wrote *A Christchurch Cantata* for the opening of the new Town Hall in Christchurch, New Zealand; and in 1973 *For All Mankind*—a cantata for chorus and band for the Newcastle Trades Council. Music (original works for brass band): *Akhnaton; American Sketches; A Psalm for all Nations; Call of the Sea; Celebration; Contest Day; Devon Fantasy; Divertimento; English Country Scenes; Everybody's Child, Festival Music; Four Preludes; Fowey River; High Peak; Holiday Overture; Holiday Suite; Homeward; Impromptu; Indian Summer; In Switzerland; Journey into Freedom; A Kensington Concerto; Main Street; Morning Rhapsody; Oasis; Peniel; Petite Suite de Ballet; The Princess and the Poet; Resurgam; Rhapsody on American Gospel Songs; Rhapsody on Negro Spirituals; 2nd Rhapsody on Negro Spirituals; 3rd Rhapsody on Negro Spirituals; Salute to Freedom; Sinfonietta—The Wayfarer; St. Michael's Mount; Sunset Rhapsody; Swiss Festival Overture; Thanksgiving; The Ancient Temple; The Conquerors; The English Maiden; The Undaunted; The Young in Heart; Three Songs*

Eric Ball.

Eric Ball as Chief Guest Conductor conducting massed bands at the Royal Albert Hall in 1970 (London Press Photos).

Without Words; Tournament for Brass; Youth Salutes a Master. Marches: *October Festival; Rosslyn; Royal Salute; Sure and Steadfast* and *Torch of Freedom.* Solos: *Conchita* (cornet); *Legend* (trombone); *Mountain Melody* (horn); *September Fantasy* (horn). Chamber: *Friendly Giants* (quartet); *Quartet for Tubas; Quid Pro Quo* (double trio). He has published well over 30 arrangements for brass band, mainly classical pieces, (notably a suite of dances from Sir Arthur Bliss' *Checkmate* which was used as the 1978 National test-piece). His works for band and choir are *A Christchurch Cantata: For All Mankind* and *Hail to the Lord's Annointed.* In addition to his brass band music the list of his Salvation Army compositions runs to about 80 items. **Recordings:** *Akhnaton*—Carlton ABL401; *By the Cool Waters*—Carlton ABL401; *Celebration*—(excerpt) GUS TB3021; *Conchita*—Carlton ABL401; *The Conquerors 51; Cornish Festival Overture*—St Dennis TB3009; *Country Fair*—Carlton ABL401; *Devon Fantasy*—Fodens LPT1029 & PEP106; *The English Maiden*—GUS TB3021 *Festival Music* **56**, **71**—CWS STL5452,

Yorkshire GSGLI0488; *Free Fantasia*—Carlton ABL401, GUS TB3021; *High Peak* **69**—Black Dyke GSGLI0453; *Holiday Overture*—Cambridge TB3020 Carlton TB3007; *Indian Summer*—All Star PEP109, GUS TB3021; *Journey into Freedom* **67**—Black Dyke GSGLI0410 & GH632, CWS LPS16256, Parc & Dare OU2105; *A Kensington Concerto* **72**—Black Dyke SB308; *Main Street* **61**—Fairey LPT1011; *Morning Rhapsody*—Desford SB328; *October Festival —Symphonic March*—GUS TB3021, National 1978 PL25192; *The Passing Years*—Carlton ABL401; *Petite Suite de Ballet*—Black Dyke GSGLI0427; *Prelude to a Comedy*—Virtuosi VR7301; *Prelude to Pageantry*—Carlton ABL401; *A Psalm for All Nations*—St Dennis 2485 010; *Quid Pro Quo*—Black Dyke CSD3652; *Resurgam 50*—Black Dyke GSGLI0427, Carlton ABL401, CWS STFL529, GUS TWOX1039 & TB3021, Yorkshire 62973; *Rhapsody on Negro Spirituals*—Black Dyke PL25089, National 1976 LSA3285, Tullis SSLX326; *2nd Rhapsody on Negro Spirituals*—National Youth GSGL1043; *3rd Rhapsody on Negro*

Spirituals—National 1968 NSPL18260; *Rosslyn*—Carlton ABL401, Stanshawe TT001; *Salute to Freedom* **46**; *September Fantasy*—Virtuosi VR7609; *Sinfonietta for Brass—The Wayfarer* **76**—Black Dyke RL25078, National 1976 LSA3285; *A Sunset Rhapsody* **58**—CWS STFL509; *Sure and Steadfast*—Carlton ABL401; *Three Songs Without Words*—(excerpt) GUS TB3021; *Torch of Freedom*—Black Dyke LFLI5071, National 1974 SPA369, Tredegar SB320; *Tournament for Brass* **54**—Munn & Felton LPT1026, National SKL5171; *The Undaunted* **59**. As conductor: see Virtuosi Brass Band.

BANTOCK, Sir Granville (b London, August 7 1868, d London, October 16 1946). As a pioneer in the Competitive Festival movement and one who was uncompromisingly democratic in his outlook on music it is not surprising that Bantock wrote more for brass bands than most of the leading composers of his day. The best known work is *Prometheus Unbound*, inspired by Shelley's lyrical drama, which was the test-piece for the 1933 National Championship. Three years later the composer used a revised version as the prelude to a larger scale work for chorus and orchestra. Other works for brass include an *Oriental Rhapsody* (Open 1930), which is based on the same composer's symphonic poem for orchestra *Lalla Rookh* and was also incorporated in a ballet of the same name, *King Lear Overture*, suites of Russian, Irish, Scottish, English and Welsh melodies respectively and the Hebridean poem *Tir-nan-og*, named after the composer's home in Birmingham, and which was one of his last works written in 1945. He also wrote a *Festival March* on the occasion of the 21st Conference of the Independent Labour Party in Bradford in 1914. **Recordings:** *The Frogs of Aristophanes* (arr Frank Wright) **52**—CWS STFL529, Fairey LPT1025, Stanshawe SB322; *The Land of the Ever Young*—Fairey LPT1025; *Prometheus Unbound* **33**—CWS STFL547. Arrangements: *The Foggy Dew*—Black Dyke PEP118.

BARSOTTI, Roger (b London, September 17 1901). Composer and conductor. He was taught music by his father, Luigi Barsotti, one-time professor at the Milan Conservatoire, and made his first public professional appearance with the Hastings Municipal Orchestra at the age of 14, as deputy flautist. On April 25 1916, he enlisted as a band boy in the East Kent Regiment ('The Buffs') and made such rapid progress that he was promoted to band sergeant at the age of 22. After a course at the Royal Military School of Music he became bandmaster of the 2nd Battalion, The Queen's Royal Regiment on August 17 1930, remaining in this position until he retired from the army on August 12 1945. In January 1946 he was appointed Director of Music of the Metropolitan Police Band and continued in this appointment until December 31 1968. A prolific composer with more than 100 published works to his credit, including the suites *Three Women, Carnaval du Bal* and *Neapolitan Suite,* and a number of waltzes and dances in Latin-American rhythms, he is best known for such marches as *Banner of Victory, The Capitol, Colonel and Commodore, The Commissioner, The King's Colour, Metropolitan March, Motor Sport, Silver Pageantry, Celebrities* and *State Trumpeters*, and a number of post horn solos and duets, including *The New Post Horn Galop, Tattenham Corner* and *Tally Ho*. Editor of the Boosey & Hawkes series *Tunes and Toasts for All Times*—a collection of 100 favourite airs for orchestra. **Recordings:** *Bell Bird Polka*—Coventry SB332, Morris A2201, Wingates 2460 246; *Fantasia on British Airs*—Fodens SB330; *Neapolitan Suite for Brass*—Ever Ready SB334; *In the Cloisters*—Cambridge TB3020; *Neapolitan Suite for Brass*—Ever Ready SB334; *Sundown*—Coventry SB332, Morris VAR 5968.

BATH, Hubert (b Barnstaple, November 6 1883, d Harefield, Middx, April 24 1945). Composer and conductor. Studied at the Royal Academy of Music where, in 1904, he won a scholarship with a one-act opera *Spanish Student*. Became conductor of a touring opera company. For many years he was musical advisor to the London County Council, his duties including the organisation of band concerts in the various parks. Collaborated with G.H. Clutsam and Basil Hood on the light opera *Young England* (1916). Took an early interest in the brass band field and wrote test-pieces—*Freedom* in 1922, *Honour and Glory* in 1931. Wrote various operas and incidental music and became especially well-known for his film music, the most popular piece, often heard as an individual work being the *Cornish Rhapsody* which he wrote for *Love Story* in 1944. In 1929 he had written the music for the first full length British talking film, Alfred Hitchcock's *Blackmail*. Died while working on the score of *The Wicked Lady*. Two light orchestral suites, *Woodland Scenes* and *Pierette by the Stream* achieved great popularity, as did his *Summer Nights* waltz of 1919. *Recordings: Freedom* **22, 47, 73**—Brighouse SB312, St Hilda's TTV099; *Honour and Glory* **31**; *Out of the Blue*—GUS TW0161.

BEAVER, Jack (b Clapham, 1900. d September 10 1963). Educated at Royal Academy of Music. Chiefly known by the background music which he wrote for feature films and documentaries, starting with silent films and writing his first talking picture score in 1932, *Baroud* for RKO pictures. Worked with Louis Levy at Shepherds Bush on such films as *The Thirty-Nine Steps*. Resident composer with Gaumont British from 1934 and regular conductor for them from 1939. From 1936-41 was responsible for scoring many radio adaptations of films and in 1946 was musical director of the series *Picture Parade*. Composer of *Sovereign Heritage*, the test-piece for the National in 1954 and used at the Open Championship at Belle Vue in 1972. *Recordings: Gay Cavalier*—All Star PEP104; *Sovereign Heritage* (arr Frank Wright) **54, 72**—Black Dyke SB308, Fairey LPT1012.

BINGE, Ronald (b Derby, July 15 1910; d 1980). Composer. Choirboy at St Andrew's Church, Derby and started piano lessons at seven years old. Studied music with local teachers but mainly self-taught. In 1927 played the organ for silent films in the local cinema and started to compose for a small, but highly critical, local orchestra. Came to London in 1930 and played the piano in theatre orchestras, cafe trios, seaside bands, dance and gipsy bands, at the same time doing a lot of arranging and some composition. Began to arrange for Mantovani in 1934 and had his works played, broadcast and recorded by the orchestra, receiving considerable help and encouragement from the conductor. Gave up playing just before the war to concentrate on writing music, his first popular success being a piece called *Spitfire*. Served in the RAF 1941-46. Married in 1945. He was then responsible for

the re-organisation of the Mantovani orchestra and for the creation of its new sound with the famous 'echo' effect. Arranged all the music played by the orchestra including the popular *Charmaine*. Such was the success of these activities that arranging became too demanding and he became a freelance still retaining an association with Mantovani. He was helped in this by the success of *Elizabethan Serenade* (1952) originally written for Mantovani, which was now taken up everywhere from pop group, to brass band and symphony orchestra. Top of the Hit Parade in Germany, the German recording brought a new wave of popularity all over the world in the 1970s. Own broadcast series *String Song* 1955-63. Now lives in rural Sussex, mainly composing but with occasional engagements as a conductor. His recent works include a *Festival Te Deum*, a symphony, a jazz fugue and popular songs. Music for brass and military band includes: *Flash Harry* (Military band) (1950); *Old London* (military band) (1958); *Cornet Carillon* (1961)—probably one of the most popular brass band pieces ever written; *Duel for Conductors* (brass) (1968) and *Trumpet Spectacular* (military) (1972); etc. *Recordings: Cornet Carillon*—All Star PEP101, Carlton GRS1020, CWS STFL509, GUS TW0418; *Duel for Conductors; Elizabethan Serenade*—Black Dyke GH362 & NSPLI8209, Morris MFP1387; *Trombonioso*—National 1974 SPA369; *Trumpet Spectacular*—Coventry SB322; *The Watermill*—Scottish GSGLI0430, Virtuosi VR7506.

BIRTWISTLE, Harrison Paul (b Accrington July 15 1934). Composer and teacher. Studied at the Royal Manchester College of Music and later at the Royal Academy of Music in London. His compositions employ the serial technique but although the sonorities of wind instruments always seem to have had a special appeal to him he wrote nothing for brass band until 1973 when he was commissioned by the Grimethorpe Colliery Band to write a piece for them. The glowering *Grimethorpe Aria* is unusually scored for brass band in that the massed instruments are often written for *divisi*. *Recordings: Grimethorpe Aria*—Grimethorpe HEAD 14.

BLISS, Sir Arthur (b London, August 2 1891; d London, March 29 1975). Com-

Sir Arthur Bliss (Lyrita/Hans Wild).

poser. Educated at Rugby, Pembroke College, Cambridge and went to the Royal College of Music in 1913. Served in the Army 1914-18. Professor of Music at the Royal College of Music in 1921, but from 1922 concentrated mainly on composing, except for a period as BBC Music Director 1941-5. Knighted in 1950 and Master of the Queen's Music from 1953. Among musical compositions of every kind the *Colour Symphony* (1922, rev 1932) and the ballets *Checkmate* (1937), *Miracle in the Gorbals* (1943), and *Adam Zero* (1948) became particularly well-known. His best-known and most important compositions for brass band were the *Kenilworth Suite* (1936) and the *Belmont Variations* (1963) commissioned as the test-pieces for the National Championships of those years. He also wrote a number of brilliant fanfares for smaller combinations of brass instruments. ***Recordings:*** *The Belmont Variations* **63**—Brighouse GSGLI0407, GUS TWOX1053; *Antiphonal fanfares* (arr Newsome)—Black Dyke SB308;

Checkmate (Dances) (arr Eric Ball) **78**—Brighouse XTRA1160, Yorkshire TT003; *Fanfares* (various)—Locke RL25081, Jones SDD274 & SPA500; *Kenilworth* **36**—Grimethorpe SXL6820, GUS TWOX1053, Stars in Brass SCX3484, Virtuosi VR7506.

BODDINGTON, Stanley H., LRAM, ARCM (b Wollaston, Northants, 1905). Began his musical career at the age of seven as cornettist with the local Salvation Army Band. At 17 he joined the well-known Kettering Salvation Army Band as a member of the solo cornet team and quickly became known as a skilled musician. In 1933 he was appointed Musical Director of the newly formed Munn & Felton's works Band (known since 1962 as The GUS (Footwear) Band). With the expert guidance and help of Greville Cook and William Halliwell he was able to shape a band of championship standards that managed, within two years of its foundation, to win the National Championship at Crystal Palace. In 1973 a celebration with the band conducted by Harry Mortimer was held in the Granada Theatre in Kettering celebrating his 60th Year in brass bands and his 40th year as musical director. He retired in 1975 and was succeeded by Geoffrey Brand. Boddington's Salvation Army beginnings are reflected in the numerous and well-known arrangements of hymn tunes that he has made for brass band. ***Recordings:*** See under GUS (Footwear) Band.

BOURGEOIS, Derek David, MA (b Kingston-on-Thames, 1941). Educated at Cranleigh School and Magdalene College, Cambridge and at the Royal College of Music. Lecturer in Music at Bristol University from 1971, specialising in conducting, the tuba and harmony. As a composer has written a considerable number of orchestral works, chamber works, songs and anthems. With a special interest in brass music he has made some important additions to the modern repertoire in this field, including several large-scale works. His 1st *Concerto for Brass Band* was written in 1974 especially for the Grimethorpe Band and its movement titles indicate an inclination towards musical humour—*Le Tombeau d'Arthur Benjamin, Monsieur Ravel Turns in his Grave* and *The War March of the Ostriches*. The 2nd *Concerto* was written in 1976, also for Grimethorpe and includes a modern experiment in writing a brass band

Stanley Boddington, conductor of the GUS band, receiving his award from Lord Harewood after winning the 1966 National Championships. E. Vaughan Morris looks on (London Press Photos).

march. This was followed by his *Concerto for Brass Quintet and Band* which was commissioned by John Ridgeon for the Redbridge Youth band and first played by them in conjunction with the Philip Jones Brass quintet. He has also written brass quartets and a *Serenade*. All his music for brass is in the virtuoso class and indicates what high standards in brass playing are expected today. **Recordings:** *Concerto 2 for Brass*—(finale) National 1977 PL25118; *Serenade*—Yorkshire TT003.

BRAND, Geoffrey (b Gloucester, 1926). Conductor, composer and adjudicator. Born into a Salvation Army family, he started to play the cornet at the age of six and at 21 won an open scholarship to the Royal Academy of Music. He entered the Academy in 1947, following military service in a military band, and studied conducting and trumpet from 1947 to 1950. In 1950 he joined the Royal Philharmonic Orchestra under Sir Thomas Beecham and toured America with them. Later he became a member of the Royal Opera House Orchestra, Covent Garden. In 1955 he joined the BBC as Producer of Music programmes on radio and TV, leaving in 1967 to devote more time to conducting and to become editor of *The British Bandsman*. In the same year he succeeded Denis Wright as Musical

Advisor to The National Youth Brass Band of Great Britain and also became Chairman of the National School Brass Band Association. In 1967 he was awarded the silver medal of the Worshipful Company of Musicians for his services to the brass band movement. In 1967 he began an oustandingly successful association with the Black Dyke Mills Band conducting them as winners in the National Championship on three occasions and twice in the British Open, as well as giving many first performances of important new works for band. In 1975 he became Director of the Rural Music Schools Association and Musical Director of the GUS Band, resigning this last post in 1978. An adjudicator for many years, he has visited Australia, New Zealand and the West Indies; New Zealand again in 1978 and Australia in 1979. From August 1978 he became associated with the Brighouse & Rastrick Band, leading them in September to their first British Open win for 42 years, and becoming their Musical Adviser. He also conducts the National Youth Brass Band of Scotland. **Recordings:** *Tuba Tapestry*—Stanshawe TT001.

BROADBENT, Derek. Started playing the trombone at the age of nine and in the same year joined the Thornton Cleveleys Band. Was principal trombone at the age of

11. Joined the Lancashire Fusiliers and was soon sent to Kneller Hall where he studied with Jack Mackintosh and won the Cousins Memorial Certificate for playing. Was accepted as a student bandmaster but decided that his future lay elsewhere. On his release from the Army in 1962 played with the Yeadon Band but very much wanted to concentrate on arranging. Managed to get some arranging work for the resident orchestra at the Leeds Majestic Ballroom and in 1963 became leader of the band. Turned professional in 1964 and became musical director at Pontin's holiday camp in Blackpool. While still playing with the Yeadon Band was appointed musical director of the Slaithwaite Band with whom he stayed for seven years, during that time organising a dance band from within the brass band which was known as Yakkity Brass and played all Broadbent pieces. The group raised over £2,000 for the band funds and was still flourishing after Broadbent left to take over the post of Musical Director of the Brighouse & Rastrick Band in 1973. One of his most remarkable successes (though received with mixed feelings in band circles) was when the Brighouse & Rastrick Band found itself in the Top 50 pop charts with Derek Broadbent's arrangement of *The Floral Dance*, in 1977. **Recordings:** *Centaur* —march—Black Dyke SB305; *Cornets a-go-go!—Brighouse* GRS1050.

BUTTERWORTH, Arthur (b Manchester, August 4 1923). Composer and conductor. He received his principal musical education at the Royal Manchester College of Music to which he won a scholarship in 1939 but was not able to take it up until 1947 because of the war. A member of the Besses o' th' Barn Band from 1939 to 1942 he joined the Scottish (now Scottish National) Orchestra as a trumpeter in 1949, transferring to the Hallé Orchestra in 1955, where he remained until 1961. Since then he has devoted his time to composing and conducting. He is permanent conductor of the Huddersfield Philharmonic Orchestra and makes periodical guest appearances with the BBC Northern and other orchestras. His major compositions include two symphonies, *A Moorland Symphony,* which is a choral work cast in symphonic form, *The Moors,* which is a suite for large orchestra, *Sinfonietta, Suite for Strings,* an organ con-

certo and a ballet, *Creatures of the Night*. He has also written chamber music and some songs. Brass band compositions include *A Dales Suite, Three Impressions for Brass, Heroic Overture, Blenheim* and a considerable quantity of educational music. Light music includes *The Path across the Moors, The Quiet Tarn, The Green Wind, Legend, Gigues, Italian Journey, Concertante* and *Duo*. **Recordings:** *A Dales Suite*—Besses TB3012; *Royal Border Bridge, 1850*—Virtuosi VR7405.

CARR, Denis. Started to play the cornet at the age of four. Won his first medal at seven, six times North of England Junior Champion and finalist in the All-British Solo Championship at ten and 11. At the age of 12 broadcast from the Dome Theatre, Brighton and became a regular broadcaster thereafter. Tutor to the National Youth Brass Band from 1965 to 1975 and musical director of the Yorkshire Schools Band since 1967. Has also conducted various local brass bands in Denbighshire, Shropshire and Swindon. First conductor of the National Youth Brass Band of Belgium in 1975. Joined Yorkshire Imperial Metals in 1977 and conducted them in their National Championship win in 1978. Has been an adjudicator since the age of 23. A teacher for many years, a lecturer at the City of Leeds College and a BBC radio producer. **Recordings:** *Four Little Maids*—suite— Black Dyke GSGLI0453.

CARSE, Adam (b Newcastle-on-Tyne, May 19 1878; d Great Missenden, November 2 1958). Studied composition at the Royal Academy of Music under Sir Frederick Corder. He is best known by his research work in the history of musical instruments but he also taught and wrote a considerable quantity of music, mostly for the orchestra. He also wrote for other media and two works for brass band are *Three Characteristic Pieces* and *Three English Pictures*. **Recordings:** *Processional March*— Rochdale SB316.

COPE, Samuel (b 1856; d November 14 1947). Son of a west of England bandmaster. Sang in a choir and played in a fife and drum band before taking to the cornet on which he became a renowned performer. Played in various bands and was then offered the conductorship of the Queen's Park (West London) Military Band in 1888. In 1887 he founded the periodical *The British Bandsman*—a monthly magazine for Bandmasters and Members of the Military and Brass Band—which in 1888 became *The British Bandsmen and Orchestral Times* and in 1891 *The Orchestral Times and British Bandsmen* and continued in 1893 as *The British Musician*. Cope also edited the *Champion Journal*, a journal of band music founded in Hull by Richard Smith in 1857.

CUNDELL, Eric, CBE, Hon RAM, FGSM (b January 29 1893; d London, March 19 1961). Studied at Trinity College of Music where he later became a professor. In 1937 he joined the staff at Glyndebourne and in 1938 he was appointed to succeed Sir Landon Ronald as Principal of the Guildhall School of Music and Drama, where he made a name for himself by his operatic productions. He was a Fellow of both the Guildhall School of Music and Drama and the Trinity College of Music. He was a considerable composer in various forms but his works never became really well known. Frank Wright arranged his *Blackfriars* as the test piece for the National Championship of 1955. *Recordings: Blackfriars* (arr Frank Wright) **55**—Munn & Felton LPT1010, Virtuosi VR7608.

ELGAR, Sir Edward William, Bart (b Broadheath, nr Worcester, June 2 1857; d Worcester, February 23 1934). It was not until he was an old man, less than four years before his death and ten years after the death of his wife which largely robbed him of the urge to compose, that Elgar wrote a work for brass band. It was *The Severn Suite*, written as a test piece for the National Championship in 1930 and dedicated to George Bernard Shaw, who in a letter advised the composer not to use the usual Italian directions but instead to use language that bandsmen would understand, such as 'Now like hell'. Incidentally Elgar marked some passages for euphonium to be played muted. No euphonium mutes existed at the time and some were made especially for the occasion, but the results were not very satisfactory and the experiment was not repeated. *Recordings: The Severn Suite,* Op 87 **30**—Besses TB3016, Black Dyke RL25078, Brighouse GSGL10372, CWS STL5452, Ever Ready SB329, Grimethorpe SXL6820.

FARNON, Robert (b Toronto, July 24 1917). Educated musically at the Toronto Conservatory, he first came to England during the second World War as conductor of the Canadian Band of the AEF. He remained here after the war being anxious to write light orchestral music in general and that for films in particular, although he had written his first symphonies when he was 19 and a second three years later. He is universally regarded as one of the most successful composers of light music of the 20th century. Much of this has been arranged for brass and he has on occasions conducted brass bands in programmes of his own music. *Recordings: Colditz March*—National TB3004; *Concorde March*—Leyland PL25175, National TB3004; *Morning Cloud*—Black Dyke PL25117; *Une Vie de Matelot* **75**—Brighouse XTRA1160, Black Dyke SB324; *Westminster Waltz*—National TB3004.

FLETCHER, Percy (b London, December 12 1879, d London, September 10 1932). He was primarily known for his light orchestral music, of which the waltz *Bal Masqué* is probably the best known, and for the score of what was called a mosaic in music and mime—*Mecca* which was produced at His Majesty's Theatre on October with a cast which included Oscar Asche, who wrote the book, and his wife Lily Brayton. But he was also a considerable figure in the brass band world before the first World War. He wrote the first original test-piece for a major contest, *Labour and Love*, for the National Championship in 1913 and *An Epic Symphony* for the 1926 contest and which was used again for those of 1938 and 1951. It is not to be confused with Denis Wright's *Overture for an Epic Occasion* of 1945. *Recordings: An Epic Symphony* **26, 38, 51, 76**—Black Dyke RL20578, CWS FJ509 and 886155, Virtuosi VR3701; *Labour of Love* **13**—Carlton GRS1020; *March of the Manikins*—All Star NTS145; *The Spirit of Pageantry*—Black Dyke LFL15071, Coventry GRS1053, National Youth GSGL10403.

GEEHL, Henry Ernest (b London, September 28 1881, d London, January 14 1961). Composer, conductor and pianist. After musical studies under various teachers he intended a career as a pianist but soon gave this up in favour of conducting and composing. He was active as a theatre conductor from 1902 to 1908. In 1918 he joined the staff of Trinity College of music, retiring in

1960 shortly before his death. He had a special interest in brass band music and the brass band movement, and his works included several well-known test-pieces. For brass: *Festival Overture; In Tudor Days; Normandy; Oliver Cromwell* **23,** *41,* **46;** *On the Cornish Coast* **24, 48;** *Robin Hood* **36,** *41;* Scena Sinfonica *52; Sinfonietta Pastorale; A Happy Suite; James Hook; Threnody* and *Thames Valley.* Also wrote many pieces for the piano and songs which included *For You Alone* (1909), the first song that Caruso sang in English. **Recordings:** *Bolero Brillante—* All Star PEP124; *Oliver Cromwell* **23,** *41,* **46—**Brighouse PVM5 & MFP5190, Stanshawe TT001, Virtuosi VR7404; *On the Cornish Coast* **24, 28—**Brighouse GSGL-10407; *Romanza—*Ever Ready SB329, Fairey NTS167, Fodens CSD3629, Parc and Dare OU2105; *Scena Sinfonica 52—*Yorkshire TT002; *Threnody—*Fodens SB341; *Variations on 'Jenny Jones'—*Brighouse GSGL-10407. **Arrangement:** *Watching the Wheat—*All Star PEP117.

GLADNEY, John (b Belfast 1839; d 1911). One of the great pioneering conductors and trainers of the developing years of the brass band movement in the 1870s and thereafter. His musical beginnings were not with brass bands but as an orchestral clarinet player; working in various opera orchestras and with the Jullien orchestra. He had played for 30 years from 1860 in the famous Hallé orchestra. He was also proficient on the cornet, trombone, flute, bassoon, violin and piano and had been given a sound musical grounding by his father who was a military bandmaster and an adjudicator at the earliest Belle Vue band contests. John Gladney learned some of his conducting with the Belle Vue Gardens band in the 1860s and in 1871 took over an amateur Volunteer band in Burnley. Heard to criticise the famous Meltham band he was bluntly asked if he thought he could improve it and said he thought he could. He was hired by the Meltham Mills band in 1873 and led them to success at Belle Vue that same year. He won the contest with the Kingston Mills band in 1873 and then achieved a remarkable hat-trick with the Meltham Mills Band in 1876, 1877 and 1878. Playing in the band was a remarkable cornettist, Alexander Owen, who was soon to become one of Gladney's great rivals. Gladney continued

for many years to dominate the brass band scene, winning at Belle Vue in 1884 with the Honley Band, in 1885, 1886 and 1887 with the Kingston Mills Band, in 1890 with the Batley Old, in 1891, 1895, 1896, 1899, 1902 and 1904 with the Black Dyke Band before being succeeded by William Rimmer, whose great reign followed, and with other bands in 1893, 1900, 1901 and 1903. It seemed that almost any brass band success had the hand of Gladney in it somewhere at the time. Black Dyke also won the National under his guidance in 1902. He had much to do with formulating the standard line-up for the brass band as each modelled itself on his successful Meltham Mills pattern, and was also a force in the abandonment of the valve trombone in 1873 in favour of the slide instrument. He said, in 1892, that the Meltham Mills Band had never been equalled in the perfection of their playing; an experienced opinion from a man who had trained some 60 bands in his time and earned the title 'father of the brass band movement'.

GODFREY, Charles (b London, January 17 1839, d London, April 5 1919). One of a family of prominent band musicians. His father Charles (1790-1863) was bandmaster of the Coldstream Guards from 1825 until his death, edited *Jullien's Journal* (military band music) from 1847 and did much to standardise military band scoring. Of his five sons, three also became military bandmasters—Daniel (1831-1903) with the Grenadier Guards from 1856-96 and the first bandmaster to be given commissioned rank (in 1887); Adolphus Frederick (1837-82) who succeeded his father as bandmaster of the Coldstream Guards from 1863 to 1880 and was well-known as an arranger; and Charles who, like his brothers, received his education at the Royal Academy of Music. He started his professional career as a clarinet player in Jullien's orchestra. In 1859 he was appointed bandmaster of the Scots Fusilier Guards at the unusually early age of 20. In 1886 he transferred to the Royal Horse Guards as bandmaster, an appointment which he held until his retirement in 1904. He was promoted to commissioned rank in 1899. He was at various times professor of military music at both the Royal College of Music and the Guildhall School of Music and he founded the military band journal *Orpheus* in which he published many of his arrangements. He became closely associated with brass band music as well, adjudicating at the Belle Vue championship contests for many years up to and including 1914. He also made many arrangements for brass band. His son Charles George (1866-1935) also followed in the tradition and became a bandmaster and arranger.

GOFFIN, Henry Charles (b Plymouth, 1883, d Wellington, New Zealand, March 15 1973). Composer and conductor. Born of Salvationist parents, he showed early evidence of unusual musical ability and at the age of 16 he became a Corps bandmaster in the Salvation Army. Three years later he was commissioned as an officer. On migrating to New Zealand with his wife and family he transformed the Wellington Citadel Band into one of the finest brass combinations in New Zealand. He became in turn Corps Officer in Foxton, Invercargill, Auckland City, Dunedin Fortress, Auckland Congress Hall, Christchurch City and Napier. In 1934 he established a band and songster department and later he was appointed Territorial Secretary for bands, special efforts and publicity. After his wife's death in 1951 Brigadier Goffin came out of retirement to command the Kilbirnie, Oamaru and Carterton Corps. He wrote many marches of which the most popular are: *The Red Shield, New Zealand warriors, Aulesbrook march,* and *Wellington tramways.* He also wrote *The Salvation Army patrol,* the only composition in this form to be published by the Salvation Army.

GOFFIN, John Dean (b Wellington, New Zealand, 1909). Composer and conductor. Son of the preceding, he started to learn to play a brass instrument at the age of nine, began to compose when he was 15 and was appointed Bandmaster of the Wellington South Salvation Army Band when he was 19. In 1932 he enlisted as a private in the 20th Battalion of the New Zealand Army, subsequently becoming Bandmaster. Later he became Bandmaster of the 4th Brigade Band, with the rank of captain. It was while serving in the Middle East that he wrote his best known composition *Rhapsody in Brass.* He directed his own band in its first performance at the *Music for All* Club in Cairo in 1942. This was subsequently adopted as the test-piece for several contests in various parts of the Commonwealth, including the September ber contest at Belle Vue, Manchester in 1949. On returning home to New Zealand he studied for and obtained his Bachelor of Music degree at the Canterbury University after which he followed his father's example by joining the Salvation Army. In 1956 he was appointed to the International Headquarters in London as National Bandmaster and later became National Secretary for Bands, being responsible for the control and overall administration of the many Salvation Army bands in Britain. He also travelled extensively. He ultimately returned to New Zealand where he now lives. Among his many compositions are the marches *Crusaders, Anthem of the free, Tylney Hall, From strength to strength,* and *Heralds of the dawn.* Other works include *Neapolis, Symphony of thanksgiving* and *My strength, my tower.* **Recordings:** *Rhapsody in Brass* **49**—GUS SCX3502, National 1978—PL25192, Virtuosi VR7301.

GOLLAND, John, LRAM, BBCM. (b Ashton-under-Lyne, Lancs, September 13 1942). Composer, conductor and pianist. Educated at the De La Salle College in Pendleton, and at the Royal Manchester

John Golland.

College of Music where he studied composition. Has always had a strong interest in brass band music and has conducted a number of bands including Walkden, Spillers Gainsborough, Stalybridge, Fodens and JSVB. His compositions include: *Concerto for Piano and Brass Band; Fives and Threes; Peace; Relay; Diversions; In Celebration; Sounds; Epic Theme; Serenade for Trombone; Christmas Overture; Cantilena; Chanson Trevaux; Bandkraft; Lesser Thorns; Brass and Voices; A Gloucester Psalm; Blest Pair of Sirens; Ring Out Wild Bells* and *Into the Ark.* Arrangements of Reznicek's *Donna Diana* Overture; Rimsky-Korsakov's *Hymn to the Sun;* Massenet's *Meditation;* Rimsky-Korsakov's *Capriccio Espagnol;* Ravel's *Pavane* and Monteverdi's *Orfeo,* as well as many popular pieces. **Recordings:** *Christmas Offering*—GSGL10514.

GREENWOOD, John A. A protégé of William Rimmer, he began playing with a local band at the age of ten in Winsford, Cheshire and by his 20s was cornet soloist with the Gossage's Soap Works Band. He now studied piano, harmony and composition and when the New Brighton Tower company went bankrupt in 1900 became a regular tutor to many local bands and played solo cornet with such bands as Wingates Temperance. He was later to conduct such prominent bands as St Hilda's, Black Dyke and Horwich and was the winning conductor at Belle Vue in 1914, 1916, 1917, the first for some years to break the hold of Rimmer and Halliwell, and in 1925.

GREGSON, Edward GRSM, LRAM (b Sunderland, Co Durham, 1945). Composer and conductor. Began to take an interest in music at about the age of eight. Came from a not particularly musical family (one brother is a successful band conductor) but began to have piano lessons at this time and also began to play in a Salvation Army band. He found some of the music he came into contact with uninspiring and at 11 started to write his own music (mainly piano pieces), went to some Hallé concerts and was made aware of the possibilities of music by hearing a performance of Brahms' 1st Symphony. Passed some musical examinations and entered the Royal Academy of Music at the age of 18 where he studied piano and composition; receiving his musical grounding from Frederick Durrant and more advanced work with Alan Bush. His first important work was an Oboe Sonata written in 1965. Won five prizes for composition at the Academy and had many works performed there. Now divides his time between teaching—Senior Lecturer in Music at the University of London Goldsmith's College—and composition. Works in a variety of musical mediums but has always had a special interest in brass band music which he sees as an individual medium with its specialised demands rather than as an extension of orchestral music. His compositions for brass include: *Concertante for Piano and Band* 1966; *Quintet for Brass* (1967); *Voices of Youth* (1967); *Divertimento for Trombone and Piano* (1968); *March Prelude* (1968); *First Quartet* (1968); *Second Quartet* (1968); *Concert Overture 'The Pacemakers'* (1969); *Essay for Brass Band* (1970); *Prelude for an Occasion* (1970); *Partita* (1971); *The Plantagenets* (1971); *Horn Concerto* (for Ifor James) (1971); *Concerto Grosso* (1972); *Intrada* (1972); *Prelude and Capriccio for Cornet and Band (or Piano)* (1972); *Two Fanfares* (1973); *Patterns* (1974); *Three Dance Episodes for Brass Octet* (1974); *A Swedish March* (1975);

Edward Gregson (Arthur Hamer).

Variations on 'Laudate Dominum' (1976); *Tuba Concerto* (for John Fletcher) (1976); *New Horizons for Beginner Brass Ensemble* (1976); *Twenty Supplementary Tunes for Beginner Brass* (1977); *Concertante for Piano and Band* (1978). For the 1977 National Championships he wrote *Connotations* which made him the youngest composer ever to be asked to contribute a test-piece. In 1976 he took on the Conductorship of the the City of London Brass, mainly made up of student players, and changed its name to the London Collegiate Brass. *Recordings:* *Concerto Grosso*—Besses TB3003; *Connotations 77*—Black Dyke PL25143; *Essay*—Solna GRA1004; *March Prelude*—Hampshire Youth SB310, Redbridge GRS1081; *Patterns for Brass*—Tredegar SB320; *The Plantagenets*—Besses GRS1042, Black Dyke LSA3254, National 73—SKL5171; *Prelude and Capriccio*—London LFL15072; *Prelude for an Occasion*—Black Dyke GSGL10477, Brighouse SB312, Parc and Dare OU2015, Yorkshire GSGL10488; *Quintet for Brass*—Hallé GSGC14114; *Three Dance Episodes*—Versatile SB314; *Voices of Youth*—National Youth GSGL10428 & GH521.

HANMER, Ronald Charles Douglas (b Reigate, 1917). Composer and orchestrator. Studied at the Blackheath Conservatory of Music. Organist at various Granada theatres from 1935 to 1948. Became a freelance and has composed some 500 light orchestral compositions, many for background records, and including more than 40 of the special ITMA arrangements. Has written music for films, theatre and radio and made adaptations of many musical shows for amateurs. Has written numerous arrangements and compositions for brass band. *Recordings:* *The Four Corners of the world*—Hampshire SB310; *Latin Americana*—Cory SB319; *March with a Beat*—Black Dyke SB305, Redbridge GRS1018; *Waltz with a Beat*—Scottish GSGL10430.

HALLIWELL, William (b Roby Mill, nr Wigan, 1865). Began his musical career as a church organist but became interested in band music and in 1881 joined the Upholland Temperance Band as a cornettist. Within a year he was principal cornet and in 1865 became bandmaster. In 1887 he joined the Wigan Rifle Band as solo cornet. His musical activities were now wide and varied

and he played with the Wigan Orchestral and Choral societies and in several bands. In 1893 he was appointed conductor of the Rifle Club Band. After experience with many local bands he came to prominence as a contest conductor and in 1910 took over from William Rimmer as conductor of the Fodens Band and triumphantly led them in the same year to a double win at the British Open and the National contests. In the next two decades he dominated these contests, winning the Open at Belle Vue in 1911 with the Hebden Bridge Band and the National in London with the Perfection Soap Works Band. In 1912 he won at Belle Vue with the Fodens Band, in London with the St Hilda Colliery Band; in 1913 in Belle Vue with the Fodens Band, in London with the Irwell Springs Band. He was conductor of the winning bands at Belle Vue in 1915, 1918, 1921, 1923, 1927, 1928, 1932, 1933, 1934, 1935 and 1936; of the National in 1920, 1921, 1923, 1924 and 1928. He remained musical director of Fodens until 1929 when he retired and handed over to Fred Mortimer. He will always be remembered as one of the most successful trainers and directors in brass band history. Arrangements: *Symphony 4— Saltarello* (Mendelssohn)—Fairey SB311.

HARGREAVES, Walter Barrow (b Glasgow 1907). Graduated at the Royal Scottish Academy of Music where he studied french horn, trumpet and piano. He played

Walter Hargreaves.

with the Reid Symphony Orchestra from 1942 to 1946 and later with other well-known orchestras. He was lecturer on Band Instruments at Edinburgh University 1946-7 and conducted the Edinburgh City Band from 1944 to 1946 when he was appointed conductor of the Cory Band. In 1963 he went to the Brighouse & Rastrick Band. Later he became professional conductor of the Stanshawe (Bristol) Band, which was renamed the Sun Life Stanshawe Band in March 1978, following sponsorship by the Sun Life Assurance Society Limited. He is professor of cornet and french horn at the Royal Marines School of Music.

HAYSOM, Peter (pen-name of Peter CRADDY). Worked on the staff of the BBC until 1974 in the Midlands as a musical producer. During his 18 years in this capacity he composed a number of pieces that have found a permanent place in the brass band repertoire. **Recordings:** *Tenderfoot Trail*—GUS SCX3502; *Variations for Brass Band* on *'The Lark in the clear air'*—Coventry SB315.

HENZE, Hans Werner (b Gütersloh, Westphalia July 1 1926). Composer. Studied with Wolfgang Fortner at Heidelberg and Rene Leibowitz in Paris. A disciple of Schönberg but he evolved his own form of the 12-note technique. Musical Adviser for ballet at the Opera, Weisbaden for a period in the 1950s. He has always been a voluminous composer of music in most forms but did not write anything for brass band until 1977 when the Grimethorpe Colliery Band commissioned a piece from him. He had no knowledge at all of the constitution of a brass band but was given a list of the instruments and a few records and with these he produced *Ragtimes and Habaneras*, a suite of 11 brilliant miniatures. **Recordings:** *Ragtimes and Habaneras*—Grimethorpe HEAD 14.

HESPE, George William, LAAM, ARCM (b London, December 6 1900). Composer and conductor. He played cornet in the band of his school in Essex from the age of eight. At 14 he enlisted as a bandboy in the Queen's Royal Regiment. After passing out from the Royal Military School of Music he was appointed Bandmaster of the 1st Battalion, The Seaforth Highlanders on June 12 1928, an appointment which he held until his retirement from the Army in 1933. Until

his final retirement in 1964 he devoted himself to military and brass bands in the North of England, conducting, training and adjudicating, in particular he conducted the Sheffield Police Band for several years from 1933, and was Musical Director of the Ferodo Works Band. During the years of the second World War he combined with these activities that of playing tuba in the BBC Northern Orchestra and the Hallé. His best known march is *King o' the clouds*. Other marches include *Kinderscout, Lone pilot, Atlantic patrol,* and *Men of steel*. Compositions in other forms are the suite *The Three Musketeers* **53**, the trombone solo *Mélodie et Caprice, Caernarvon Castle,* a *Welsh Fantasy*, and eight suites for military band and bagpipes. **Recordings:** *Fanfare*—Men O' Brass CSD3691; *Kinderscout*—Ferodo PEP123; *Melody and Caprice (Mélodie et Caprice)*—Fodens SB333, Yorkshire SB306; *The Three Musketeers* **53**—Fairey NTS167; Markham GSGL10426.

HOLBROOKE, Joseph (b Croydon, July 6 1878, d London, August 5 1958). Composer. Studied at the Royal Academy of Music and became a pianist and conductor. Eventually he achieved recognition as a composer with several operas, including the trilogy *The Cauldron of Anwen*, several ballets and orchestral and instrumental music of all kinds. For the brass band world he wrote *Clive of India* which was used as the test-piece at Belle Vue in 1940.

HOLST, Gustave Theodore (b Cheltenham, September 21 1872, d London, May 25 1934). Imogen Holst, the composer's daughter has told us that her father preferred writing for brass rather than military bands because the sound was mellower and more flexible. Even so he only wrote one composition especially for brass, the *Moorside Suite* which was commissioned as the test-piece for the National Championship at the Crystal Palace in 1928, and still remains as a prime model of its kind, testing both the technical skill and musicianship, and admirable as a concert piece too. **Recordings:** *Fantasia on the Dargason* (from *Suite No.2*)—Cory GRS1052; *A Moorside Suite* **28**—Besses TB3012, BMC ST938, Grimethorpe SXL6820, London LFL-105072, Virtuosi VR7405, Yorkshire

GSGL10488; *Suite No.1 in E* (originally for military band)—CWS FJ507.

HOROVITZ, Joseph (b Vienna, May 26 1926). Composer and conductor. Came to England in 1938 and studied at New College, Oxford and at the Royal College of Music under Gordon Jacob; later for a year in Paris with Nadia Boulanger. Director of Music Bristol Old Vic 1950-1, Ballet Russe 1952, assistant director Intimate Opera Co 1952-63, assistant conductor at Glyndebourne 1956. Professor of Composition, RCM, from 1961. Composer of operas, ballets, orchestral and instrumental music etc. One of the few 'serious' composers to write successfully in a 'light' idiom, most of his works being in a witty and ingenious vein, many using jazz and popular music styles with obvious empathy, sympathy and understanding. His light ballets such as *Les femmes d'Alger* (1952) and *Alice in Wonderland* (1955) made his name known in the 1950s and he contributed *Metamorphoses on a bedtime theme* (1958) and *Horroratorio* (1961) to the Hoffnung concerts. His musical reconstructions include the operas *The Cooper* (1956) and *Thomas and Sally* by Arne, *Beatrix*—a ballet based on Adams' *La jolie fille de Gand,* and *Blind Beggars*—an adaptation of Offenbach's *Les Deux Aveugles.* A particularly successful use of the music hall and popular idiom is to be found in his *Music Hall suite for brass quintet* (1965), one of the many specialist works written for brass, while *Four dances for orchestra* (1952), *Jazz concerto for harpsichord* or piano (1965) and *Concerto for Euphonium* (1972) were equally successful and showed his musical vitality and wit as did *Samson* and *The Dong With a Luminous Nose* and his two one-act operas *The Dumb wife* (with Peter Shaffer) (1953) and *Gentleman's Island* (with Gordon Snell) (1958). Rapidly becoming one of the most popular choral works written for children is his amusing and tuneful *Captain Noah and his floating Zoo* (1970). The success of Horovitz's musical jokes is that they are all well constructed and based on a real understanding of the idiom he parodies. **Recordings:** *Concerto for Euphonium*—GUS TW0418; *Music Hall Suite*—Hallé GSGC14114; *Sinfonietta for Brass*—Besses GSGL10510.

HOWARTH, Elgar (b Cannock, Staffs, 1935). Came into contact with brass band music at an early age as his father was the conductor of a band in the Manchester area. Elgar Howarth joined the band when he was ten and at 14 was principal cornet. Educated at Manchester University where he obtained the degree of Bachelor of Music; and at the Royal Manchester College of Music where he met Maxwell Davies and Alexander Goehr and they formed the Manchester New Music Group. Other members included John Ogden and Harrison Birtwistle. Wrote his *Suite for Band* in 1952. Called up for National Service and was fortunate in spending his time in the Central Band of the Royal Air Force. On discharge joined the Covent Garden Orchestra and spent four years with them. Went freelance in 1963 but was invited to join the Royal Philharmonic Orchestra for a tour of America under Kempe. The invitation was irresistible so he became a member of the RPO from 1963-8 and eventually became their principal trumpet. Joined the Philip Jones Brass Ensemble in 1966 and has since played with them whenever time permitted. It was Bram Gay, the brass editor for Novello & Co, who first put him in touch with the Grimethorpe Colliery Band. He was hesitant about accepting a post with them but accepted the proffered Musical Directorship in 1972. It proved a very successful partnership and has led the band toward a much wider interest in modern music, both in competition and on record. His compositions for brass include *Mosaic* (1956), *Fireworks, Ascendit in coeli, In Memoriam: R.K,* several processional fanfares and a set of variations for brass quintet. His lighter pieces are written by a friend by the name of W. Hogarth Lear. **Recordings:** *Cornet Concerto*—Grimethorpe SB325; *Fireworks* **75**—Grimethorpe HEAD 14, Wingates GRS1045; *Mosaic*—Brighouse GRS1035, Grimethorpe SB325; *Presenting the Brass*—National 1973 SKL5171. As conductor: Grimethorpe Band—*Classics for Brass Band*—Decca SXL6820; Grimethorpe Band—*Contemporary Music*—Decca HEAD 14; Grimethorpe Band—*Pop Goes the Posthorn*—Grosvenor GRS1022; Grimethorpe Band—*Sounds of Brass, Vol. 25*—Decca SB325.

HOWELLS, Herbert (b Lydney, Gloucestershire, October 17 1892). He did not write much for brass band and, of the pieces he did write in this form, by far the

Dr Herbert Howells and Sir Adrian Boult (Lyrita/Brooman).

best known, is the suite *Pageantry* which was the test-piece in the Open Championship at Belle Vue in 1934, again in 1942 and 1970 and in the National Championship in 1937 and 1950. Second to this is another suite called *Three Figures*. **Recordings:** *Pageantry* **34, 37, 42, 50, 70**—Black Dyke GSGLI0477, Yorkshire SB302; *Three Figures* **60**—Virtuosi VR7507.

HUME, James Ord (b near Edinburgh, September 14 1864, d London November 27 1932). Composer, conductor and adjudicator. He was also something of an eccentric. He once left the gas burning in his home while he fulfilled a three months engagement in Harrogate. It is not recorded what he said when he got the gas bill, nor is it recorded what his wife said when on returning from a holiday she found that large holes had been made in the floors of the upper stories of their house to accommodate the great pipes of a church organ which he had installed in the ground floor living room while his wife was away. The son of an army bandmaster, he was keenly interested in music from a very early age. As a boy he played the cornet in the band of the 3rd Battalion, The Royal Scots and in 1881 he played solo cornet in the Royal Scots Greys. He was already composing in these early

years and spent most of his spare time in the band room teaching himself to play most of the instruments, woodwind as well as brass, of the band. Irked by the limitations imposed by service life he purchased his discharge from the army after a few years and devoted himself mainly to brass bands, writing music for them in many forms, arranging the compositions of others, conducting, coaching and adjudicating at festivals and contests. He came to be almost as well known and as highly regarded among bandsmen in Australia and New Zealand as in Britain by his visits to both countries. At the first of the National Brass Band Contests at Crystal Palace (held in the Royal Albert Hall since Crystal Palace was destroyed by fire in 1936) he was invited to write the test piece and his choice was *Gems from Sullivan's Operas*, Sullivan also being closely concerned with the contest and being also a close friend and godfather to Ord Hume's son. A little earlier he had won an open competition for a march for brass bands promoted by the *British Band and Contest Field*, the leading band journal and now called *The British Bandsman*. This march, *B.B. and C.F.* (the initials of the sponsoring journal) and the later *Lynwood*, named after his London home, are probably still the best known of his many marches. He served for a time as

Musical Director of the Edmonton Council in Middlesex, was military band editor of Boosey and Company, the publishers, and was also for a time Lieutenant (Bandmaster) in the 6th Duke of Buccleuch's Lothian and Border House Yeomanry. After his death bandsmen and admirers from all over the British Empire contributed the funds with which to provide a suitably inscribed memorial in the Edmonton Cemetery where he was buried. The unveiling ceremony was attended by many hundreds from all over Great Britain and a massed band composed of players from most of the bands in and around London paid their last tribute to him. It may be doubted if anyone knows just how much music he wrote and arranged, especially when one recalls that he wrote under several pseudonyms as well as his own name, he published *Oriental March*, for instance, under the name 'William German'. One estimate is about 2,000 pieces and it is probably not far wrong if one includes his many arrangements of operatic selections and numbers from popular musical comedies. His entirely original compositions are in many forms but it is the marches by which he is now principally remembered. One of the earliest must be *The Prairie Flower* in that it incorporates as its trio a short march written while he was serving with the Royal Scots and which was then called simply *No.1*. Some are written for both military and brass bands and some were conceived for brass alone. Among the best of his marches are *On the Road, Brilliant, Bullfighters, Colonel's Parade, The Escort, The Flying Squad, The Non-Com, Sounds of Victory, Fearless, The Front Line, Hercules, Liberty Bell* (not to be confused with Sousa's march of the same name), *Old Bill, Old Nobility, Silver Trumpets, The Victor's Return, Roll Away Bet, Laddie in Khaki, Kitchener's Army, Wye Valley, Second to None, Edina* (a processional march), *Diamond Jubilee* (written on the occasion of Queen Victoria's Diamond Jubilee for the march of Colonial troops from Victorial Park to the Mansion House in London on June 9 1897), *The Monarch, Waveney* (named after the river in Norfolk, a part of the country that the composer liked greatly), *The Elephant, Avondale, The Commandant, In Command, Rank and File, Tender and True, Bab el Mandeb, Ballarat City, Boulder City, Port Lincoln* and *Kalgoorlie* (the last five commemorating visits to the Antipodes). *Mr. Hicks of New York* and *Uncle Rastus's Skating Party* are two lively two-steps, of a number of cornet solos one of the best is *Tranquility*, of 1924, and songs include the romantic *Doone Valley* (relating to the Burns country). Although immersed in music to the very end of his life it was not his only interest by any means. He was a great collector of clocks and maintained them all in immaculate working order. It was said that his wife habitually took a couple of minutes walk down the road on the hour when practicable. His main outdoor pursuit was yachting. A one-time Commodore of the Almond (Edinburgh) Yacht Club, he owned a yacht called *Shamrock* with which he won several awards. On the literary side, in addition to countless articles for various magazines he wrote a book on brass bands and a series of instrumental tutors. **Recordings:** *The B.B. and C.F.*—Big Brass PFS4143, Brighouse GSGL10372, Carlton GRS1043, Munn & Felton PEP114, Virtuosi VR7302; *Brilliant*—Black Dyke PL25025, LFL15071 & SB308, Fairey PEP131, Men o' Brass CSD3691; *The Elephant*—Burton TB3006; *Lynwood; Roll Away Bet*—Fodens PEP129, St Dennis 2485 010; *The Tit-Larks* (cornet duet)—GUS TW0282 & OU2179. Arrangements: *Lilac Time* (Schubert/Clutsam)—Brass SKL4109; *The Lost Chord* (Sullivan)—Black Dyke GH632 & NSPL18209; *Pomp and Circumstance Marches* (Elgar)—No 1: GUS SCX3550, National 1968 NSPL18260, No 4: Black Dyke PL25089, CWS STFL547, Hammonds SB327; *Ruy Blas Overture* (Mendelssohn)—Men o' Brass TW0225.

ILES, John Henry, OBE (b Bristol, September 17 1871, d May 1951). Probably the best known name in the brass band movement. A successful business man, his first musical interest was in choral music but in 1898, while on a business visit to Manchester, he found himself with some time on his hands and consulted the hotel porter as to what he might do. The porter mentioned a brass band contest that was taking place at Belle Vue. Iles came away from it 'positively astounded', to use his own words. Back in London he began to enquire as to band activities there and in the south generally. In the course of doing so he met Samuel Cope, owner of the magazine *The*

British Bandsman and resident of the London and Home Counties Amateur Band Association. Before the end of the year Iles was the owner of *The British Bandsman* but retained Cope as editor. In the following year he began to organise a war fund through the magazine in support of the Kipling Fund of the Daily Mail to help the families of the troops fighting in South Africa. In support of the funds Iles organised a huge brass band concert in the Royal Albert Hall on January 20 1900, with 11 bands from all over the British Isles including Besses o' th' Barn and Black Dyke. The high spot in the programme was Sullivan's setting of Kipling's *The Absent Minded Beggar*. Sullivan conducted and the audience exceeded 10,000, with half as many having to be turned away. It raised between £2-3,000 which was a lot of money in 1900. Sullivan was greatly moved by the occasion and asked Iles what might be done to encourage such fine instrumentalists. Remembering the contests initiated by Enderby Jackson in the 1860s, Iles had the idea of an annual contest at the Crystal Palace, and recalled that Sullivan was a director of the company which owned it. Sullivan not only supported the idea enthusiastically but also persuaded the company to put up the famous Thousand Guineas trophy as the first prize. So the National Brass Band Championship was born. It is no exaggeration to say that John Henry Iles devoted the rest of his life to brass band music in general and the National Championship in particular.

IRELAND, John Nicholson (b Bowdon, Cheshire, August 13 1879, d Washington, Sussex, June 12 1962). His two works for brass band date from the time when he began to write in less complex terms and to simplify his music; and it may well be that these commissions stimulated his interest in the orchestra for, having at the age of 57 only written two works for orchestra, he wrote five more between 1936 and 1942. *A Downland Suite* was the test-piece for the National Championship in 1932 and *A Comedy Overture* for that of 1934. *Recordings: Comedy Overture* **34, 49, 67**—Fairey LPT1026, Grimethorpe SXL6820 GUS TWOX1053, Virtuosi VR7303; *A Downland Suite* **32, 39, 66**—Besses TB3012, GUS TWOX1053.

JACKSON, Enderby (b Hull, 1827; d Hull). Impresario. Most people know the name Enderby Jackson by the contests he organised at the Crystal Palace from 1860 to 1863. They started as two-day events and the first attracted entries from 72 bands, although some had fallen by the wayside when the great day arrived. There were six platforms, each out of earshot of the others (in theory at any rate) with three adjudicators for each, whose job it was to select two bands to go forward to the finals for which all 18 adjudicators sat in judgment. The bands chose their own test pieces and the winners at the first contest were Black Dyke, first, Saltaire, second, and Cyfarthfa, third. It is sad to read that the much fancied Stalybridge Band reached the finals but got no prize because the keys of the ophicleide got entangled with the player's waistcoat pocket. At some time during the proceedings the bands were massed and Jackson himself conducted 1,390 instrumentalists. The attendance on the two days was about 27,000 so the railway companies who had been persuaded to allow people who attended to travel free would probably do quite well out of their subsidy. By 1863 the event had lost much of its popularity and become a one-day event, possibly because of a new rule that all competing bands must be tuned to the pitch of the Crystal Palace organ. Jackson came to the Crystal Palace via a contest at Burton Constable Hall near his native Hull in 1845 when he was 18, the Great Exhibition of 1851, a great contest in Hull in 1856 followed by others in Sheffield and elsewhere, all of which competed of course with the contests at Belle Vue, Manchester which had started in 1853 and the attendance at one of which inspired John Henry Iles to institute the National Championship at Crystal Palace in 1900. After the demise of his great Crystal Palace venture Jackson continued to promote contests for a short time, his last being in Hull in 1868. Then he seemed to lose interest and, after a sojourn in Australia, settled down in Hull.

JACOB, Gordon Percival Septimus (b London, July 5 1895). In addition to writing directly for brass and military bands, he has arranged a great deal of music by others for these media, and it is not putting it too highly to say that very few composers of this or any other generation have understood as well the particular genius and limitations of all the wind combinations. His *Pride of Youth* was the test-piece for the National Championship in 1970 and other notable compositions for brass include a *Suite in B* and the joyous *Prelude to Revelry*. His *Rhapsody for Three Hands and Brass Band* was, of course, written for Phyllis Sellick and Cyril Smith. **Recordings:** *Music for a Festival*—Locke RL25081; *Pride of Youth 70; Salute to USA*—Locke RHS349; *Swedish Rhapsody*—Besses GRS1042; *Symphonic Study for Band*—Coventry TB3019; *A Victorian Rhapsody*—Men o' Brass CSD3691.

JAMES, Ifor, Hon ARAM (b Carlisle, 1931). Son of William James who was solo cornet with the then famous Carlisle St Stephens Band in the 1920s and 1930s and his wife—the soprano Ena Mitchell. Ifor also played cornet but changed to the horn and studied at the Royal Academy of Music under Aubrey Brain. He has played the horn, mainly as principal, with the Hallé, the Liverpool Philharmonic, the London Symphony, the Philharmonia, and other orchestras at different times but ultimately decided upon a solo career. Professor of the Horn at the Royal Academy of Music and teaches at Colchester College of Further Education. Played in the Philip Jones Brass Ensemble and with his own Ifor James Horn Trio. For many years musical advisor to the Carlisle St Stephens Band, and eventually returned more actively to the brass band world in 1973 when he became conductor of the Besses o' th' Barn Band. His best-known composition for brass is probably *Solitude*. **Recordings:** *Solitude*—Besses TB3012; *Windmills from Amsterdam*—Besses GRS1042. As conductor: Besses—*Capriccio Brilliant*—Pye GSGLI0510; Besses—*English Brass*—Pye TB3012; Besses—*English Brass, Vol. 2*—Pye TB3016; Besses—*Music from Vale Royal*—Pye TB3003; Besses—*Viva Vivaldi*—Grosvenor GRS1042.

JENKINS, Cyril (b Swansea, October 9 1889; d Hove, March 15 1978). Studied under the Welsh composer Harry Evans and took organ lessons from W.G. Alcock; and while in his teens travelled regularly to London to take piano lessons from Herbert Sharpe and lessons in composition from Sir Charles Stanford. In 1922 he was appointed Director of Music to the London County Council, but ill health made it desirable that he should live in Australia for some years. He wrote music in most forms, other than opera. Among the best known of his compositions for brass band are *Coriolanus; Life Divine* and *Victory*, which were test-pieces for the National Championships in 1920, 1921 and 1929 respectively; and *Saga of the North* which was the test-piece for the Open Championship at Belle Vue in 1965. **Recordings:** *Coriolanus* **20**—CWS STFL509, Hampshire Youth SB310; *Life Divine* **21, 63**—Carlton GRS1043, CWS STFL509, Massed Brass TW0240, National 1977 PL25118, St Hilda's TTV099; *Saga of the North* **65**—Fairey SPT1019.

JOHNSTONE, Maurice (b Manchester, 1900). Studied at the Royal Manchester College of Music (of which he is a Fellow) and the Royal College of Music in London. Started a career as a musical administrator as secretary to Sir Thomas Beecham 1932-5. Worked in the BBC Music Department 1935-60, as Head of North Region Music 1938-53 and Head of Music Programmes (Sound) in London 1953-60. Retired from the BBC in 1960 and devoted more time to freelance activities in writing and composition with special interests in the orchestra and its repertoire, the brass band and Gilbert and Sullivan. Wrote orchestral, instrumental and vocal works of a varied nature and has made many well-known arrangements of Wagner, Weber and other composers. His works for brass band include concert marches, overtures and a fantasia *The Tempest* **44**. **Recordings:** *Sea Dogs*—Overture—Wingates 2460 246; *Beaufighters*—March—Fairey SB304; *County Palatine*—March—Black Dyke PEP132, Yorkshire TT003.

JONES, Philip, ARCM (b Bath, 1928). Educated at the Royal College of Music. From 1948 to 1971 held various posts, mainly as principal trumpet with the Royal Opera House Orchestra, Royal Philharmonic Orchestra, Philharmonia and New Philharmonia Orchestras, London Philharmonic Orchestra and BBC Symphony Orchestra. Founder and director of the Philip Jones Brass Ensemble which has pioneered performances of ancient and present day brass chamber music in this country. **Recordings:** (Philip Jones Brass Ensemble) *Baroque Brass*—Argo ZRG898; *Classics for Brass*—Argo ZRG731; *Divertimento*—

ZRG851; *Easy Winners*—ZRG895; *Fanfare* —ZRG870; *Golden Brass*—Argo ZRG717; *Just Brass*—Argo ZRG655; *Modern Brass*— Argo ZRG906; *Pictures at an Exhibition*— Argo ZRG885; *PJBE Plays*—Argo ZRG813; *Renaissance Brass*—Argo ZRG823; *Strings and Brass*—Argo ZRG644; *Voices and Brass*—Argo ZRG576; *The World of Brass*—Decca SPA464.

JOSEPHS, Wilfred, BDS (b Newcastle-upon-Tyne, 1927). Composer & conductor, he studied music at the Guildhall School and privately in Paris with Max Deutsch. A proflific composer of orchestral music, he has written a *Concerto for Brass Band.*

KEIGHLEY, Thomas (b Stalybridge, October 15 1869). Studied at the Royal Manchester College of Music from 1895-8 and became Mus Doc, Manchester in 1901. Organist at Ashton-under-Lyne; Professor of Harmony at the Royal Manchester College of Music from 1898. He wrote many text books on music and composed numerous part-songs, anthems and piano pieces. He became particularly interested in the brass band movement as teacher and adjudicator; and created something of a record for test-pieces for the Open Championship at Belle Vue, writing *Macbeth* for 1925, *A Midsummer Night's Dream* for 1926, *The Merry Wives of Windsor* for 1927, *Lorenzo* for 1928, *The Crusaders* for 1932 and *A Northern Rhapsody* for 1935. **Recordings:** *The Crusaders* **32, 41**—Rochdale GRS1054; *Lorenzo* **28, 42, 64**—Fodens LPT1020, Munn SCX3424, Virtuosi VR7404.

KELLY, Bryan, ARCM (b Oxford January 3 1934). Composer and conductor. He was a choirboy at Worcester College, Oxford, then went to the Royal College of Music and later studied in Paris with Nadia Boulanger. First professional appointment was on the staff of the Royal Scottish Academy of Music in Glasgow from 1958 to 1960. Then in September 1962 he was appointed Professor of Theory and Composition at the Royal College of Music, an appointment which he still holds. He approves of the description applied to him by Francis Routh in *Contemporary British Music* who described his technique as that of 'a Kapellmeister, whose function is to oblige with whatever is requested; a church service, a light overture, something for a choir to sing at a festival, a childrens' opera'. His first light composition to achieve real popularity was the *Cuban Suite* which was introduced at a Light Music Festival in the Festival Hall, London. His modern church music has helped to start a new outlook which allows popular music to be used in the Church without embarrassment. His major works include a Sinfonia Concertante; the *Cookham Concerto* for chamber orchestra, a *Piano Sonata* and a *Concertino for Oboe and Strings.* His works for brass band include: *Provence Overture; Washington D.C.*—march and *Divertimento for Brass Band* which was commissioned as the test-piece for the second section in the *National Championships* in 1972. He has also written a *Sonatina for Brass Sextet.* A fairly recent work is *Edinburgh Dances*, a four movement suite commissioned in 1978 for the National Youth Brass Band of Scotland. Has written numerous light orchestral pieces and music for children which includes two operas. **Recordings:** *Divertimento for Brass* —Davis GRS1048, Versatile SB321; *Provence* —Brighouse GRS1035; *Free As Air*— London Brass ETMP7.

KENNEY, H. Arthur (Major), LRAM, ARCM. Educated at Wells Cathedral Grammar School and a chorister in the cathedral from 1925-34. Enlisted in the Somerset Light Infantry in 1934 as a band-boy. In 1945 went to the Royal Military School of Music, Kneller Hall as a student bandmaster and won the Gold Medal of the Worshipful Company of Musicians as the most outstanding student of the year. Also gained the Director of Music's prize for conducting and the Commandant's prize for the best original march composition. Appointed Bandmaster of the Oxfordshire and Buckinghamshire Light Infantry in 1949; subsequently Director of Music of the Royal Artillery (Plymouth) Band, the Alamein Band of the Royal Tank Regiment and finally gained the senior appointment of Director of Music of HM Welsh Guards. Became Musical Director of the Cory Band in October 1970. **Recordings:** *St. Julian*— Cory 2485 014. As conductor: Cory Band— *Trumpets Wild*—Polydor 2485 014; Cory Band—*Sounds of Brass, Vol.19*—Decca SB319.

LAMB, Leonard (b 1910; d 1973). Best-known as bandmaster of the Fairey Band which he conducted in three consecutive wins at Belle Vue in 1961, 1962 and 1963 and as winners of both the British Open and the National Championships in 1965. He was forced to retire from the brass band scene through severe illness soon after.

LANGFORD, Gordon, LRAM, ARCM (b Edgware, Middx, May 11 1930). Real name is Gordon Colman. Son of a precision diamond tool-maker. A sister and brother are both musical but have not taken it up professionally. He had piano lessons at five and early attempts at composition were rewarded by the public performance of one of his pieces when he was nine. Won a Middlesex Scholarship to the Royal Academy of Music and studied piano, composition and trombone from 1947 to 1950. Served in the Royal Artillery Band (Woolwich), then spent several years touring with a jazz band as vibraphone player and pianist, plus a short period as trombone player with the D'Oyly

Gordon Langford.

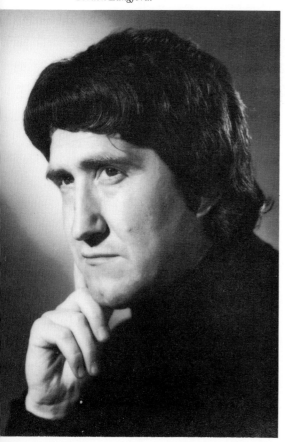

Carte Opera Company and the Lew Stone band. Was married in 1954 and has one son and one daughter. Travelled the world as a ship's musician and guest entertainer. In the 1960s and 70s has worked as session composer, arranger and conductor and has been involved in many West End theatrical productions. Has written music for films (some original scores and orchestrations for John Williams, Henry Mancini and Gerry Goldsmith). Won the Ivor Novello Award for his March from *The Colour Suite*. His first score for brass band was *Merry Mancunians.* His working life is now divided between studio work as composer, arranger, conductor and pianist and writing for brass bands and recording sessions, with regular appearances as guest conductor with various bands and BBC orchestras and as a solo pianist. His original compositions for brass band include: *Harmonious Variations on a Theme by Handel; Merry Mancunians—* march; *March of the Pacemakers; Prelude and Fugue; Salute to the Six* (for three cornets and three trombones); *The Seventies Set—* march; *Sinfonietta for Brass Band; Titan March; Carnival Day—* march; *Metropolis—* overture. His popular fantasias include: *Christmas Fantasy; Famous British Marches; Fantasy on British Sea Songs; Marching with Sousa; New World Fantasy; North Countrie Fantasy; Rhapsody on Sea Shanties; Stephen Foster Fantasy;* and *Sullivan Fantasy.* Has written many transcriptions and arrangements in frequent use by bands—*All through the night; Blow the wind Southerly; Greensleeves; La Danza* (Rossini); and *Drink to me only* (soprano cornet solo); *My love is like a red, red rose* (B flat cornet); *Take a pair of sparkling eyes* (B flat cornet); *The lark in the clear air* (E flat tenor horn); *The Ash Grove* (B flat trombone); *Trombone Concerto* (Rimsky-Korsakov); *Blaydon Races* and *Believe me if all those endearing young charms* (euphonium) and many more. ***Recordings:*** *Carnival Day Dance—* Black Dyke CSD3652, Stanshawe PL25185; *Christmas Fantasy—* Black Dyke RS1083; *European Fantasy—* National 1978 PL25192; *Fantasy on British Sea Songs—* Black Dyke PL25025, Men O' Brass CSD3691; *Harmonious Variations on a Theme of Handel—* Black Dyke PL25143; *Heritage—* London Brass ETMP7; *A London Scherzo—* London LFL15072; *Merry Mancunians—* Fodens CSD3629; *Metropolis—* Stanshawe PL25185; *North*

Countrie Fantasy—Brighouse NTS147, Ever Ready SB329; *The Pacemakers*—Black Dyke LFL15071, Coventry GRS1053; *Prelude and Fugue*—Black Dyke LSA3270, Fodens SB333; *Rhapsody on Sea Shanties*—Black Dyke PL25117; *Rhapsody for Trombone and Band*—Black Dyke LSA3270, National 1975 TB3004; *Salute to the Six*—National 1976 LSA3285; *The Seventies Set*—Desford SB328; *Sinfonietta*—Black Dyke LSA3270; *Titan March*—Leyland PL25175; *West Countrie Fantasy*—London LFL15072. Arrangements: *All through the night* (trad)— Black Dyke PL25025, Fairey INTS1331; *Après un rêve* (Fauré)—Stanshawe PL25185; *Believe me if all those endearing young charms* (trad)—Cory SB319, Fairey INTS1331; *Billy Boy* (trad)—Black Dyke LSA3270; *Blaydon Races* (trad)—Black Dyke PL25025; *Blow the wind southerly* (trad)—Fairey IN-TS1331, Fodens SB330; *The British Grenadier* (trad)—Black Dyke PL25025; *Cushy Butterfield* (trad)—Stanshawe PL25185; *Drink to me only with thine eyes* (trad)—Black Dyke PL25025; *Fairies of the Water* (Lacombe)—Fairey INTS1331, Hammond SB327; *Famous British Marches*— Fairey INTS1331, Massed TW0240; *The girl I left behind me* (trad)—Black Dyke PL25025, Burton TB3006, Fairey REC302; *Greensleeves* (trad)—Black Dyke PL25025; *The Irish Washerwoman* (trad)—Black Dyke LSA3270; *La Danza* (Rossini)— Black Dyke PL25025; *La Prophète* (Meyerbeer)—Black Dyke LFL15071; *Marche Militaire* (Schubert)—Fodens CSD3665; *Marching with Sousa*—Black Dyke PL25025 & LFL15071; *My love is like a red, red rose* (trad)—Webb Ivory GRS1075; *New World Fantasy* (Dvorák)—Men O' Brass TWOX1033, Festival 15-69; *Our Boys will shine tonight* (trad)—Fairey INTS1331; *Pavane* (Fauré)—Black Dyke LSA3270; *Phil the Fluter's Ball* (French)—Black Dyke PL25089, Yorkshire 62937; *Russalka*—Song to the Moon (Dvorák)—Black Dyke PL25117; *Sarie Marais* (trad)—Grimethorpe PL25046; *Scarborough Fair* (trad)—Stanshawe PL25185; *Siciliana & Giga* (Handel)—Black Dyke PL25117; *The Slow train* (Swann)—Leyland PL25175; *A Sullivan Fantasy*—Black Dyke LSA3270; *Under the Double Eagle* (Wagner)—Black Dyke LFLI5071; *Waltzing Matilda* (trad)—Black Dyke LSA3270; *When the Saints go Marching In* (trad)—Men O' Brass CSD3691;

Will ye no come back again (trad)—Black Dyke PL25089.

LEIDZEN, Erik Gustaf (b Stockholm, Sweden, March 25 1894). Composer, conductor and teacher. He was educated at the Swedish Royal Conservatory of Music, emigrated to the United States in 1915 and became naturalised in 1928. He was Director of the Swedish Glee Club of Brooklyn from 1930 to 1936 and in 1933 began to arrange music for the Goldman Band. For some time he was head of the theory department of the Ernest Williams School of Music and also taught at the National Music Camp and University of Michigan. His compositions include two *Swedish Rhapsodies*, several overtures and a number of quartets for cornets and trombones. His marches include *Land of the Free, Nordic, Pressing On, Steadily Onward* and *Brass Band on Parade*. His *Sinfonietta for Brass* was used as a testpiece for the 1955 Open Championship at Belle Vue. **Recordings:** *Sinfonietta for Brass Band 55*—Brighouse PVM5 & MFP5190, Cory 2485 014, Ferodo LPT1011; *Swedish Rhapsody No.2*—Solna PL25147.

LUCAS, Leighton Hon RAM, Hon ARAM (b London, January 5 1903). Largely self-taught musically. Musical Director of the Birmingham Repertory Company 1921-2 and after conducting a performance of Rutland Boughton's *Immortal Hour* in 1923 decided to make conducting his main occupation. Was with the Markova-Dolin Ballet Company in 1934, Arts Theatre Ballet Company 1940-1. After being demobilised from the Royal Air Force he formed his own orchestra in 1946 and with it gave performances of many modern and unfamiliar works. He is probably best-known as a composer by his music for many short films including *Target for Tonight*. Other works include *Symphonic Suite for Brass Band*. He is a Professor of the Royal Academy of Music. **Recordings:** *Choral and variations*—Black Dyke SB305.

MATHIAS, William James, D Mus (Wales) FRAM (b Whitland, S Wales, 1934). Composer. Educated at the University College of Wales, Aberystwyth and the Royal Academy of Music. Music Lecturer at University College of North Wales, Bangor 1959-68; Senior Lecturer in Music at University of Edinburgh 1968; Head of Department of

Music, University College of North Wales, Bangor 1970. Has written music in many forms but his first venture into the field of brass bands was when commissioned to write his *Vivat Regina* to commemorate the Silver Jubilee of HM Queen Elizabeth II. It was first played at the Royal Albert Hall on June 11 1977 by massed brass bands conducted by Walter Susskind. **Recordings:** *Vivat Regina*—suite—Black Dyke PL25143.

MORRIS, Haydn. Educated at the Royal Academy of Music. Organist and choirmaster in Llanelly and a well-known adjudicator at the National Eisteddfod and other festivals in Wales. He wrote an opera but most of his compositions were for orchestra or brass band. Of the latter, the best-known is *Springtime Suite* which was commissioned as test-piece for the 1931 Open Championship. Died December 21 1965.

MORTIMER, Alex. Son of Fred Mortimer. Played in bands under his father's direction on euphonium, including many years with the famous Fodens band. Became musical director of the CWS (Manchester) Band in 1954, retiring from the post in 1970 but remaining Musical Advisor to the band, still maintaining a very active interest and conducting on occasions until his death in 1976. Much of the band's success in the 1950s was due to his experienced leadership. **Recordings:** As conductor: see under CWS (Manchester) Band. Arrangements: *Marching with Sousa*—Fairey NTS167.

MORTIMER, Fred. (b Hebden Bridge, Yorks, 1880, d Elworth, June 20 1953). Interested in brass playing from his boyhood, Fred Mortimer studied music and the cornet under William Rimmer. At 17 he was appointed bandmaster of the Hebden Bridge Prize Band where he developed his individual style of conducting with the left hand so that he could play the cornet with his right at the same time. In 1912 he became bandmaster of the Luton Red Cross Band, enlisting in 1914 to serve in France as Bandmaster of the 36th Divisional Band. After the war he rejoined the Luton Band and was with them on the memorable occasion in 1923 when a band from the south first won the National title. In 1924, on the retirement of Thomas Hynes, he was offered and accepted the post of Bandmaster with the Fodens band. Up to this time the band had always been led by a professional conductor in con-

tests but in 1929 it was decided that Fred Mortimer would take full charge of the band for all occasions as their first permanent Musical Director. He was known as a strict disciplinarian in all matters, but he was much liked and admired by all who played with him and he was a great encourager of young players. In addition to his conducting and leading the Fodens band to its incredible run of victories in the 1930s, he was also an accomplished composer and arranger and was much in demand as an adjudicator. His eldest son, Harry, joined the band with him as principal cornet, the second son, Alex, had already preceded him as principal euphonium and the third son, Rex, also played in the band under him. All three were to make their mark as Musical Directors. Between them the Mortimers gave a total of 145 years service to the Fodens Band. In 1953 Fred collapsed just before the qualifying round of the National Championship and Harry took over the band and led them to their win that year. Fred died while the band was playing for the Coronation festivities in one of the London parks. In his honour the BBC inaugurated the Fred Mortimer Memorial Competition for the composition of a march and a suite. **Recordings:** *Mac & Mort*—All Star PEP107.

Fred Mortimer.

MORTIMER, Harry (b Hebden Bridge, Yorks, April 10 1902). Eldest son of Fred Mortimer. He was given his first cornet at the age of seven and was soon playing in the Hebden Bridge Prize Band under his father's direction. The family moved to Luton in 1912 when Fred took over the Luton Red Cross Band and Harry played in its ranks and was still with the band on that notable occasion in 1923 when it became the first southern band to win the National Championship at the Crystal Palace under the conductorship of William Halliwell. In 1924 the family moved to the north-west when Fred Mortimer became the first musical-directing Bandmaster of the Fodens Band in Sandbach, Cheshire. Again it was very much a family affair as Harry and his two brothers, Alex and Rex, were all cornermen in the band—Harry on cornet, Alex on euphonium, Rex on E flat bass. (Incidentally, these are their correct Christian names; Fred, Harry, Alex and Rex, not familiarised versions.) Harry Mortimer has perhaps been one of the most influential cornet players in the brass band movement and has done much to create the modern cornet style. Taught at one time by the famous William Rimmer, he managed to make his instrument sing (almost talk) in a way that would have been unimagined earlier; a sort of parallel to what Louis Armstrong was doing in the jazz world. At the age of 21 in 1923 he won the National cornet solo award and the following year was asked to play a cornet solo at the great festival concert. He played with the Luton Band from 1913 to 1924 (and previously in the local theatre orchestra); with Fodens from 1924 to 1956. He was principal trumpet with the Hallé and the Royal Liverpool Philharmonic orchestras from 1930 to 1941 and Professor of Trumpet at the Royal Manchester College of Music from 1936 to 1940. Further successes were to come when he followed in his father's footsteps and became a conductor. As professional conductor of the Black Dyke Mills Band he was in charge when they performed the hat-trick at the 1947, 1948 and 1949 National Championships. His total of victories in the National Championships is nine, and the same number in the Open Championship at Belle Vue. From 1942 to 1964 he was Brass and Military Bands Supervisor at the BBC and from 1935 to 1970 he was Musical Director of the Fairey Band. His recording activities

Harry Mortimer (EMI Records).

are, of course, well-known particularly with regard to his skill in handling massed bands and large festival forces; most especially with the Men O' Brass which he founded—the combined bands of Fairey, the City of Coventry and Morris Motors (with Fodens later replacing the Coventry band). He made two trips to Australia in 1953 and 1956 and took the Men O' Brass to Canada in 1961. In 1966 he was asked to form the first 'English-style' brass band in Helsinki, Finland. He is still very active, directing concerts at home and abroad, broadcasting and recording, teaching, advising and adjudicating and is still the Musical Director of the Morris Concert Band—a post he has held since 1947. He is very much the pivot of brass band activities in this country, 'Mr Brass' himself; and was awarded the OBE in 1950 for his services to music. ***Recordings:*** see under Fairey, Fodens, Morris Motors and the numerous items listed in Section B of the discography under Massed Bands, Men O' Brass, etc.

MORTIMER, Rex. Son of Fred Mortimer. Like his brothers Harry and Alex played in bands under his father's direction, notably the famous Fodens band where he played euphonium and E flat bass. Fred Mortimer died in 1953 and Rex became Musical Director of Fodens in 1956, a post that he held with great distinction, leading the band in the National Championship win of 1958 and their British Open win of 1964. He retired from the post in 1975 after 50 years service with Fodens. ***Recordings:*** see under Fodens.

MOYLE, William Edward. Lived most of his life in Newquay where he taught music and was conductor of the Newquay Town Band in the 1940s and 50s. His best-known composition is the *Cornish Cavalier* march. ***Recordings:*** *Cornish Cavalier*—Brighouse NTS147, Camborne RSR101S, Virtuosi VR7302; *Cornish Rock*—St Dennis TB3009; *Restormel*—St Dennis TB3009, *Thornton*—St Dennis 2485 010.

NEWSOME, Roy (b Elland, Yorks, July 17 1930). Conductor, composer, adjudicator and Senior Lecturer in Band Studies at the Salford College of Technology. Comes from a musical family, being the fifth generation to be closely associated with brass bands. He

Roy Newsome conducting massed bands for the first performance of his 'Concerto for Band and Piano' in 1969 (London Press Photos).

was only six when his father taught him to play the piano and at ten he joined the Elland Silver Band playing cornet. At 17 the organ attracted him strongly and he resolved to make organ-playing his career, but at 21 he returned to the brass band world and the Elland Silver Band. In 1961 he was appointed Musical Director of the Slaithwaite Band. He left five years later for freelance conducting and adjudicating but joined Black Dyke a year later and remained with them until 1978 when he was appointed professional conductor of the Sunlife Stanshawe Band of Bristol. Professional conductor of Stanshawe Band and Musical Director of Besses o' th' Barn. Holds a degree of Bachelor of Music (Durham), is a Fellow of the Royal College of Organists and an Associate of the Royal College of Music. He has written a good deal of music for brass band of which his *Concerto for Piano and Band*, first played at the Royal Albert Hall in 1968, the cornet solo *Concorde* and *Suite for Switzerland* are best known. In demand as both conductor and adjudicator, recently fulfilling engagements in both capacities in USA, Australia, Norway and Switzerland. ***Recordings:*** *Bass in the Ballroom*—GUS TWOX1039; *Concerto for Piano and Band*—Black Dyke GSGLI0463; *Concorde*—Black Dyke PL25025; *Tredegar Castle*—Tredegar SB320.

NICHOLL, Joseph Weston (b Halifax 1876, d London, April 27 1925). Composer and conductor. He received his first tuition in music from his father who was the organist at the Harrison Road (later Carlton) Chapel in Halifax. At 19, on the recommendation of the great violinist, Joseph Joachim, he went to the Staatliche Hochschule für Musik in Berlin of which Joachim was the first Director when it was founded in 1869, and where Nicholl studied organ, piano, violin and theory. He became the school's foremost organ student and often played concertos with Joachim conducting. Later he became in turn a pupil of Rheinberger in Munich and Guilmant in Paris. He came back to England in 1901, returning to his native town and becoming a recitalist on both organ and violin. His first appointment as a conductor was to the West Riding Military Band in Bradford, in 1908. By this time he had become immensely interested in the brass band movement and in 1910 he was appointed professional conductor of the Black Dyke Mills Band. That he only retained the appointment for a couple of years was because of persistent ill health. He enlisted as a private in the West Yorkshire Regiment in the 1914-18 war. He was soon promoted to Bandmaster but was later declared unfit for foreign service and invalided out of the army. Despite retirement from the professional conductorship he retained a keen interest in and close relationship with Black Dyke and its doings throughout his life. He continued to make arrangements for them and many of these are still used regularly. As an organist himself it is not surprising that not infrequently he turned to organ music for arrangements for brass. Two particularly successful ones are those of the Reubke *Organ Sonata 'Psalm No.94'* and the fugue of Bach's *'Little' Prelude and Fugue in G minor*. His finest original work for brass is the tone poem *The Viking* which was recorded, by Black Dyke of course, in 1923 (Regal G8070-1). When the composer died the St Hilda Colliery Band, then the reigning National Champions, came to Halifax from the north-east to join with Black Dyke in a massed band performance in Halifax, and a very moving tribute it was. Compositions for military band include a *Festival Overture* and a *Commemorative Ode and March,* the latter being written for the Jubilee of the opening of the People's Park in the composer's native Halifax. Works in other forms include a *Scherzo for Organ and Piano* written while he was a student in Germany, a *Concert Overture for Organ and Orchestra* which won first prize at the Dover Triennial Festival in 1904, a piano solo called *Carillon* which is a study in bell tones, and a number of part and solo songs. In his last years he devoted much of his time and sadly depleted energies towards the establishment and running of a comprehensive competitive festival in Halifax, the success of which was largely due to his enthusiasm and efforts. He died of tuberculosis in the Brompton Hospital, London and was buried in a churchyard in Ovenden, Halifax. The headstone of the grave most appropriately bears the subject of one of his favourite Bach fugues cut in music type.

ORR, Buxton (b Glasgow, 1924). Composer and conductor. Pupil of Benjamin Frankel. Professor of Composition and General Musicianship at the Guildhall School of Music. Has composed music for theatre and films, including *Suddenly Last Summer,* vocal, chamber and orchestral music and an opera *The Wager,* music for radio and TV. His important works for brass are the *Trumpet Concerto* (written for John Wilbraham) and the *Trombone Concerto* (written for Dennis Wick). **Recordings:** *Concerto for Trombone and Brass Band*—Passacaglia—Brighouse GRS1035.

OSGOOD, Hubert Albert Jack (b Horfield, 1919, d October 1979). Educated at Drayton Manor Grammar School, London. Appointed music master at Featherstone Secondary School for Boys in 1947. Was bandleader and euphonium soloist with the band of the Southall Citadel, Salvation Army before the war. Served in the Royal Artillery from 1940 to 1946. Music Instructor in Royal Artillery 1945-6. Since the end of the war has been engaged primarily in music teaching in general and brass band training in particular. Music Director of the Hangleton Band. **Recordings:** *The Buccaneer*—Brighouse NTS147; *Flying Feathers* —Redbridge GRS1018; *Round the Clock*— Fairey CSD3645, Virtuosi SONO25BS, Watney MFP1313.

OWEN, Alexander (b Swinton, Nr Manchester, 1851, d 1920). Of a somewhat obscure background and said to have been brought up in an orphanage, he got his musical training as a military bandsman and first made his mark in the brass band world in Stalybridge at the age of 16 where he showed remarkable skills as cornettist and conductor of the Stalybridge Old Band. Formed the Stalybridge Borough Band in 1871. He played as star soloist in the Meltham Mills band under John Gladney, at the same time training and conducting other bands, beginning at Boarshurst in 1877 and taking on the famous Black Dyke Mills Band from 1879 to 1888. With Meltham Mills and Gladney barred from the Belle Vue contest because of three wins in 1876-8, Owen now became the dominating figure there winning with the Black Dyke Band in 1880 and 1881, completing a hat-trick themselves begun in 1879 under J. Fawcett. He himself went on to win again in 1882 with the Clayton-le-Moor Band. The contests in those days seemed to be divided between Gladney,

Swift and Owen and Owen was the winner again in 1892 and 1894 with the Besses o' th' Barn Band, which he had taken over in 1884, and with the Mossley Band in 1897. A favourite piece of Owen's was his own difficult arrangement of *Reminiscences of Rossini* with which he won many contests. The Besses o' th' Barn Band used it 27 times in competitions and his arrangement of Berlioz's *Damnation of Faust* 21 times. He used it and won with it so often that it led to a ban on such repetitions and more contests following the footsteps of Belle Vue in commissioning special new contest pieces each year. At some contests he was known to conduct as many as ten bands and in 1900 won with the Denton Original Band in the first National Championship at the Crystal Palace; again in 1903 with Besses o' th' Barn.

PATTERSON, Paul Leslie, LRAM (b Chesterfield, 1947). Composer and teacher. Educated at the Royal Academy of Music, has taught brass instruments since 1967 and has been composer in residence for the English Sinfonia. Has written film music and has a great interest in electronic music. For brass ensembles he has written the experimental *Chromascope; Countdown; Cataclysm;* and a *Brass Quintet.* Has also written a *Horn Concerto* and a *Trumpet Concerto.* **Recordings:** *Chromascope*—Besses TB3016.

PEARCE, Arthur Oakes (b Halifax, 1872; d Halifax, January 13 1951). Conductor and Adjudicator. Perhaps the first thing to be said about him is that although he always wanted to be and was known as Arthur O. Pearce only a few intimates knew what the O stood for. He started one of the most notable of all band careers by playing the side-drum at the age of 13 in what was then known as the Ovenden Bethel New Connexion Band, Ovenden being a northern suburb of Halifax. Later he was playing the soprano cornet and then became solo cornet with the nearby Copley Mills Band. These appointments with other bands in the Halifax area, including the Brighouse & Rastrick and King Cross bands, led to his being appointed bandmaster of the Black Dyke Mills Band in January 1912, an appointment he held for 37 years during which time the band won 51 first prizes, 37 seconds and 17 thirds with prize money

totalling well over £12,000, a lot of money in those days. He came to be known as the 'Prime Minister of Brass Bands' and during his years with Black Dyke they made 50 or so records and gave over 200 broadcasts, the first being from the Wembley Exhibition in 1925. In 1948 he was presented with a gold medal by the Worshipful Company of Musicians, an honour given occasionally to a person of distinction in the world of music. He was the first brass bandsman to be so honoured. During the second World War he undertook the conductorship of the Halifax Special Constabulary Band with which he gave 178 concerts free of any charge. One of his proudest moments was conducting the King Cross Band before King George V on the day before his coronation in 1911. For many years he was one of the most trusted and respected adjudicators at contests.

POWELL, Thomas James (b Tredegar, Mons, October 12 1897, d Mellingriffith, January 8 1965). Composer and conductor. Started playing with the Tredegar Salvation Army Band at the age of eight and later joined the Tredegar Town Band. During the first World War he served in the band of the Royal Marines at Portsmouth. In 1920 he was appointed Conductor of the Melingriffith Band with which he remained until his death 45 years later. He trained many Welsh and West Country brass bands. His most ambitious composition was *Snowdon Fantasy* for brass band but he remains best-known by some of his numerous marches such as *Caernarvon Castle, Castell Coch* (the best-known of all), *The Bombardier; Cardiff Castle, Castell Caerdydd, Castell Caerffili, The Contestor, The Gay Hussar, The Spaceman and Thunderclouds;* also *The Tops*—a quintet for soprano and cornets. **Recordings:** *Appreciation*—Webb Ivory GRS1075; *Bandstand*—Fairey PEP129; *The Bombardier*—Fodens 2485 015; *Caernarvon Castle*—Exelsior MAL1139; *Cardiff Castle; Castell Caerdydd*—Excelsior MAL1139; *Castell Caerfilli*—Excelsior MAL1139; *Castell Coch*—Excelsior MAL1139, Ransome MALS1418, Virtuosi VR7302; *The Contestor*—Black Dyke GSGLI0410, Excelsior MAL1139, Greenock NTS157; *Duo for Euphoniums*—Rochdale SB316; *The Gay Hussar*—Fodens 2485 015, Excelsior MAL1139; *Salute to Wales*—Excelsior MAL1139; *The Tops*—GUS SCX3455,

Hampshire SB310, Yorkshire SB302, All Star NTS145.

PRICE, Richard Maldwyn (b Welshpool). Educated at University College of Wales, Aberystwyth. Music Master at St Anne's School, Redhill and later at Wells House School, Malvern Wells. Appointed organist and choirmaster at St Mary's Church, Welshpool in 1933. A considerable composer in many forms. His *Owain Glendwr* and *Henry V* were the test-pieces for the Open Championship at Belle Vue in 1938 and 1947. He also wrote a *Welsh Fantasy for Brass.* Died November 11 1952.

RIMMER, Drake. Nephew of the famous William Rimmer. Received his musical training in Edinburgh, Manchester and Hamburg. Had an early interest in brass band music and conducted a band at the age of six. Became editor of *Cornet*—a journal that his uncle once edited. Has written and arranged prolifically, his original pieces including the tone poems *Homage to Pharaoh; King Lear; Macbeth; Midsummer Eve; Othello; Quo Vadis; Rufford Abbey; Spirit of Progress; The Golden Hind* and *Venus and*

Drake Rimmer with the Baton of Honour at the Royal Albert Hall in 1968 (London Press Photos).

Adonis. Also: a symphonic prelude *Via Stellaris;* a symphonic rhapsody *The Flame of Freedom;* and a suite *Holiday Sketches.* **Recordings:** *Othello*—Scottish CWS MFP1137. Arrangements: *Espana* (Waldteufel)—Big Brass PFS4143; *The Pirates of Penzance* (Sullivan)—Brass SKL4109; *Scheherazade* (Rimsky-Korsakov)—Fairey LPT1021; *Plaisir d'amour* (Martini)—Fairey LPT1021.

RIMMER, William (b 1862, d February 9 1936). Composer, conductor and trainer of brass bands. His father, Thomas Rimmer, was bandmaster of the then Southport Rifle band and it was from him that the boy received his first musical instruction. He joined his father's band as drummer at the age of 15 but soon changed to cornet, and he played solo cornet when the band competed at the Belle Vue contest in 1882 under the direction of Henry Round, the well-known composer, conductor and editor. A few years later he transferred to the Besses o' th' Barn Band but after a short time ill health forced him to resign. In 1889 he was appointed bandmaster of the Southport Artillery Volunteers, and he also conducted the Skelmerdale Old Band, raising them to such heights that within a few months they began to win prizes at contests and competitions all over England. At the age of 30 he became a professional brass band trainer and directed many of the finest bands in the country, including Irwell Springs, Wingates Temperance, Black Dyke Mills, Hebden Bridge, Fodens and Besses o' th' Barn. His success with the first of these was quite remarkable. For 13 years, under his direction, they were rarely out of the major prize lists. In 1909 he was the trainer and conductor of five of the six prize-winning bands at the September Belle Vue contest. In 1910 he retired from conducting and devoted himself to composing and arranging. He arranged many operatic selections as test-pieces for the Crystal Palace Championships in 1910, 1911 and 1912 and in 1913 was appointed music editor of the Liverpool music-publishing firm of Wright & Round. After the first World War he was persuaded to assume the conductorship of the Southport Corporation Military Band, an appointment he held for two years. On March 21 1936, the BBC paid a final tribute in the shape of a broadcast programme called *Homage to Rimmer* which included many of his compositions and arrangements. Although he wrote music in many forms he is chiefly remembered by his marches, notably *Punchinello* and *The Cossack* (which was adopted by Fodens as their signature tune). Other marches include *Avenger; The British Flag; The Carnival King; The Comet; Dauntless; Dawn of Freedom; Faithful and Free; For Freedom and Honour; Kings of the Air; Jack o'the Lantern; Knight of the Road; Monarch; Ravenswood; Sergeants of the Guard; Sons of Victory; The Virtuoso* and *The Wizard.* Cornet solos that are still often played include *Hailstorm* and *Cleopatra.* **Recordings:** *The Australasian—* Black Dyke PL25165, Burton TB3006, Markham GSGL10394, Ransome MALS1418; *Black Night—*Black Dyke PS25165, Wingates MFP1099; *The Cossack—*Black Dyke PL25165, Brighouse GSGL10372, Fodens 2485 015 & CSD3665, Ransome MALS1418, Tulliss SSLX326, Virtuosi VR7302; *Cross of Honour—*Cory MFP1313; *Dawn of Freedom—*Mirrlees MALS1317; *For Freedom and Honour; Hailstorm—*Morris CSD3650; *Honest Toil—* Black Dyke CSD3652, Webb Ivory GRS1075; *Irresistible—*Black Dyke PL25165; *My Syrian Maid—*Scottish MFP1137; *The North Star—*Black Dyke PS25165; *Punchinello—*Black Dyke 25165, Brighouse GSGL10372, Fodens PEP129, Grimethorpe GSGL10392, GUS OU2179 & TWO256, Ransome MALS1418, Virtuosi VR7302; *Ravenswood—*Fairey PEP131, Ransome MALS1418; *Rule Britania Overture* (after Arne)—Cory GRS1052, Crossley GSGL10395, CWS SB309, Mirrlees GRS10-69; *La Russe—*Carlton 583 071; *Slaidburn—* Wingates MFP1099; *Victor's Return—*Scottish CWS MFP1137; *Viva Birkinshaw—* Black Dyke SB324. Arrangements: *The Bronze Horse* (Auber)—BMC CSD3650; *Domino Noir* (Auber) *12—*Cory OU2165; *The Flying Dutchman* (Wagner)—Carlton 2928 002; *Hungarian Rhapsody No.2* (Liszt) —Fairey CSD3668; *Italian Girl in Algiers* (Rossini)—Fairey SB318; *A life for the Czar* (Glinka)—Fodens 2485 015. *The Magic Flute* (Mozart)—Desford SB328; *Nabucco* (Verdi)—Brighouse GRS1023, Black Dyke GSGL10391; *Les Préludes* (Liszt)—Black Dyke GSGL10391, CWSNLPS16256, Fairey NTS167 & LPT1005, GUS OU2179 & TWO256; *Tancredi* (Rossini)—Fairey LP-TI021; *Zampa* (Hérold)—Fairey CSD3645.

RUBBRA, Edmund (b Northampton, May 23 1901). Composer. A Senior Lecturer in Music at Oxford University from 1947 to 1968 and Professor of Composition at the Guildhall School of Music and Drama from 1961. A fertile and versatile composer. His *Variations on 'The Shining River'* was the test-piece for the 1958 National Championship. **Recordings:** *Variations on 'The Shining River'* 58—Black Dyke RL25078, Fodens.

SHEPHERD, James (b Newbiggin-by-the-Sea, Northumberland, 1936). At the age of 13 played in the local colliery band, joined the Army at 18 and became principal cornet in the Staff Band of the Royal Army Medical Corps. On demobilisation he became in turn principal cornet in the Pegswood Colliery, Carlton Main Colliery (1960) and Black Dyke Bands (1964). He was nominated champion soloist of Great Britain in three successive years, 1962, 1963 and 1964 and in 1971 was awarded the Insignia of Honour, an annual award to a 'working instrumentalist who has given long years of devoted service, coupled with a singular contribution to brass bands'. Brass Instructor for the West Riding of Yorkshire Education Authority from 1964, and founded the Queensbury Music Centre in 1969. In 1972 he formed the James Shepherd Versatile Brass, a brass chamber group of selected soloists. **Recordings:** (Versatile Brass) *Sounds of Brass, Vol. 14—*Decca SB314; *Sounds of Brass, Vol. 21—*Decca SB321; *Sounds of Brass, Vol. 31—*Decca SB331.

SIEBERT, Edrich (b London, May 9 1903). Composer. His real name is Stanley Smith Masters. Started his musical career as a boy musician in the Cheshire Regiment, playing flute and piccolo at first and then saxophone, and soon became attracted by the sonorities of brass instruments. He claims to be virtually self-taught but acknowledges the great help he received during his army service, especially in learning at an early age what each instrument is capable of playing in competent hands. He was recalled to the army during the second World War, and with the regimental band he travelled more than 10,000 miles entertaining the troops in Sicily, Italy and Austria, each concert ending with a Good-Night Song written, composed and conducted by himself. While in Austria the band broadcast weekly from Graz on the Forces Network when he acted as announcer as well as playing. On returning to civilian life in 1946 he decided to become a full-time composer and arranger. He says that it was a red-letter day for him when Harry Mortimer formed his All-Star Brass Band and included in their first recording session *Three Jolly Sailormen* and *Polished Brass*, and asked him to make some special arrangements for the band. Other compositions include the marches *The Queen's Guard* and *Marching Sergeants;* the suites, *Brass Band Sketches* and *The Rising Generation;* a 'spring fantasy', *The Cuckoo and the Bumblebee;* bass solos, *The Bombastic Bombardon* and *Dear to my heart;* a cornet trio, *Three Jolly Sailormen;* a trumpet solo, *The Lazy Trumpeter;* the Latin-American number, *The Cucarumba;* and the galop, *Over the Sticks* which was adopted as the signature tune of the *Mid-day Music Hall* programme. ***Recordings:*** *Bees-a-buzzin*—Fodens SB333, GUS MFP1167; *Bombastic Bombardon*—Cory 2485 014, Fairey PEP126; *Brass Band Boogie*—GUS SCX3455; *Brass Band Bounce*—Creswell PEP128; *Carillon Waltz*—Fodens CSD3665; *Cucurumba*—Morris VAR5968; *Fiorella*—Cory MFP1313; *Gipsy Wedding Dance*—Paxton PEP110; *Hawaiian Hoe-Down*—Oxford 15-56; *Hawaiian Samba*—Creswell PEP128, Hanwell EROS8023; *The Lazy Trumpeter*—All Star PEP103, Watney EROS8129; *La Mascarada*—Watney EROS8129; *The Queen's Trumpeters*—Fairey LPT1019; *The Rover's Return*—Fodens CSD3629, Men O' Brass TWOX1033, Watney MFP1303; *Sunday Morning*—Fairey PEP120; *Swing Along*—Fodens CSD3665, Big Brass PFS4143; *Tango Taquin* (with Barratt)—Men O' Brass TWOX1033; *Three Jolly Sailormen*—All Star PEP102, Men O' Brass CSD3691; *Warriors Three*—All Star PEP123. Arrangements: *The Accursed Huntsman* (Franck) **73.**

SIMPSON, Robert (b Leamington, March 2 1921). Composer and music critic. Studied privately with Herbert Howells and took DMus at Durham in 1952. Worked with the BBC and has written various books on music. Music includes three symphonies and various orchestral and chamber works. Wrote *Energy* for the short-lived World Championship in 1971, and *Volcano* for the 1979 National Championship.

STEADMAN-ALLEN, Raymond Victor (Ray) BMus (Durham). (b Clapton, 1922).

Has devoted all his life to music for the Salvation Army (now holding the rank of Lieutenant Colonel) as composer, arranger and editor; with more than 300 instrumental and vocal compositions of many kinds to his credit. His compositions range from a *Fantasia for Band and Piano* and *The Holy War*—a tone poem for brass band to a lively trombone quartet called *Sparkling Slide.* ***Recordings:*** *Whitburn*—Carlton 583 071.

STREET, Allan. Began his musical career as a cornet player in a boys' band at the age of seven. He was principal soloist and took over the conducting at the age of 15. Gravitated toward the trumpet on which he obtained his LRAM diploma; also studied the piano, theory, harmony and composition under various teachers. Leaving the world of brass bands for some 25 years, he became a professional trumpet-player and conductor in orchestral music, dance music, the theatre and opera. He led his own octet, for which he wrote over 100 arrangements, with which he broadcast regularly for many years. Served

Allan Street.

in the RAF and after his discharge was accepted for training as a teacher specialising in schools music of all kinds in Secondary Modern and Grammar Schools. Was eventually appointed Senior Lecturer in Music at the Nottingham Teacher Training College (now the Trent Polytechnic), retiring from this post in 1977. Getting caught up in the brass band movement again some years ago, he has since conducted such bands as Ransome and Marles (now Ransome, Hoffmann & Pollard), Markham Main Colliery, Dalmellington and Whitburn Borough, Ibstock; and he is now with the Teversal Colliery Welfare Band. He has now become widely known as a composer and arranger and director of many successful contest appearances, with some hundred odd broadcasts, television shows and recordings. Founded and conducted the Derby Light Orchestra, broadcasting and appearing with some of the country's leading soloists. He was commissioned to write a series of testpieces for brass including *Rococo Variations; Embassy Suite; Song and Dances; Dean Valley;* and *Nottingham Town;* most of which have also been played in military band arrangements by Guards bands and RAF and Royal Marines bands with whom he has appeared as guest conductor. For some years he was chief arranger for Chappell & Co, and at present is Music Adviser for Brass and Military Bands for Boosey and Hawkes. His many arrangements and compositions are played regularly by brass bands. ***Recordings:*** *Embassy Suite—*(Finale) Wills CSD 3675; *Doon Valley—*Morris VAR5968; *High Heels—*Markham GSGL10394; *Just Jane—*Markham GSGL10426; *Kim—*Wingates MFP1099; *Student Days—*Fairey PEP120; *Three Sketches—*Markham GSGL10394; *Rococo Variations on a Theme by Tchaikovsky* —Black Dyke LPT1028 & RL25078, Coventry SB315, Fodens LPT1015. As conductor: *Markham Main Colliery Band—*Pye GSGL10426; *Markham Main Colliery Band—*Pye GSGL10394.

SWIFT, Edwin (b Linthwaite, Nr Huddersfield 1842, d Linthwaite, 1904. Bandmaster and conductor who was one of the domineering figures in the brass band scene and the Belle Vue contests of the 1870s and 80s. He was the son of a weaver and was taught to play the flute by a local temperance

hotel landlord. When he himself went to the mill at the age of nine he began to play the cornet in the local band. While still in his teens he became bandmaster and assistant conductor of the Linthwaite band. In 1869 the band became a unit of the 3rd West Yorkshire Rifle Volunteers and entered the Belle Vue contest. Finding his dedication to playing a strain he concentrated on conducting and in 1874 led the Linthwaite band to success in the British Open Championship, beating his great rival, John Gladney and the Meltham Mills Band. It was not until he was 32 in 1875 that he gave up his job at the mill and became a full-time arranger, composer, conductor and adjudicator. He continued to have Belle Vue success with the Littleborough Public Band (1883), the Wyke Temperance Band in 1888, 1889 and 1898 and also conducted the Lindley Band and many others. With Alex Owen and John Gladney he was a dominating figure in the development of the brass band movement in his day and was in constant demand to help various bands achieve the standards of success.

TATE, Phyllis Margaret Duncan, FRAM (b Gerrards Cross, 1912). Composer. Educated at Camden House School and the Royal Academy of Music. Has written music for most combinations from orchestra to solo works and has composed operas and cantatas. For brass band she has written *Illustrations* (1969) which was commissioned by the York Festival. Its five movements are prefaced by quotations from Shakespeare and it is full of exploratory devices.

TOMLINSON, Ernest (b Rawtenstall, Lancs, 1924). Composer. Educated at the Manchester Cathedral Choir School. At 16 won a scholarship to Manchester University and the Royal Manchester College of Music where he studied composition, organ, piano and clarinet. From 1943 to 1946 he served in the Royal Air Force and then returned to Manchester to complete his studies. After graduating in 1947 he moved to London and, for several years, worked as a publisher's arranger. From 1948 he was, for some time, the organist of the 3rd Church of Christ Scientist in London. In 1949 several of his lighter compositions were broadcast and since 1955 he has devoted himself entirely to composition. He has written music in many forms and styles but is best-known

Edwin Vaughan Morris and Raymond Horricks.

for his *Little Serenade*, which has been adopted as the signature tune for at least five radio and television programmes here and abroad, and his *Suite of English Folk Dances* (1951) from which *Dick's Maggot* was also singled out as a signature tune—for the BBC's *Invitation to Music*. He was Chairman of the Composers' Guild of Great Britain in 1964 and in 1966 was elected a Director of the Performing Rights Society Ltd. His other compositions include many pieces of light music, organ works, songs and a great deal of background music for films, TV and radio (some of it written under the name of 'Alan Perry'). *Recordings: Best Foot Forward*—Black Dyke PL25025 & LFLI5071, Watney MFP1303; *Cornet Concerto*—National 1974 SPA369; *Little Serenade*—CWS STFL576, Fairey CSD3668, National 1974 SPA369, Rochdale SB316; *The Sceptred Isle*—National 1968 NSPL18260; *Waltz for a Princess*—Black Dyke CSD3652.

VAUGHAN MORRIS, Edwin, MBE (b Holyhead, Anglesey, 1901). Educated at Holyhead County School and Owen's College. Starting as a reporter, became circulation manager, promotions manager on regional and national newspapers. A member of the Circulation Managers' Committee and the Newspaper Proprietors' Association, London and Manchester. Wrote as 'Scrutineer' in *World Press News* and as 'Vivamus' in *The Booksellers Review*. During the war years was Administration Officer and Chief Executive Officer (Midlands) and Regional Controller (Northern) in the Ministry of Labour and National Service. From 1945 to 1971 he was Producer of the National Brass Band Championships of Great Britain and Producer of the Annual National Brass Band Festival, Royal Albert Hall. Affiliations—Hon General Secretary of the National Brass Band Council of Great Britain; President of the Wessex Brass Band Association; Chairman of London & Southern Counties Regional Brass Band Committee; Chairman of the Western Counties Regional Brass Band Committee; Executive Member of Standing Conference on Amateur Music; Executive Member of National Music Council of Great Britain; Vice-President of National Association of Brass Band Conductors. Resuscitated and organised annual St Cecilia's Day Festival in London; and devised, organised and produced inaugural annual St David's Day Festival in the Albert Hall. Member of Livery of Worshipful Company of Musicians and Freeman of the City of London. Awarded the MBE in 1968.

VAUGHAN WILLIAMS, Ralph (b Down Ampney, Gloucestershire, October 12 1872, d London, August 26 1958). Composer. Although an enthusiastic admirer of brass bands and the work they did he wrote very little specifically for them. Best-known is the *English Folk Song Suite* but this is an arrangement of music originally written for military bands by Dr Gordon Jacob in 1924. His *Variations for Brass Band* was the test-piece for the National Championship in 1957 but the score included parts for two B flat baritone saxophones. The *Sea Songs March,* written for the Wembley Exhibition of 1924, was published simultaneously in brass and military band forms. The *Prelude on Three Welsh Hymn Tunes* was written for the Salvation Army, and first played privately with the first public hearing on March 12 1955 when it was broadcast by the BBC. *Recordings: English Folk Song Suite* (arr Frank Wright)—CWS STFL547, GUS TWO418; *Variations for Brass Band* *57*—Besses TB3016.

VINTER, Gilbert (b Lincoln, May 4 1909, d Tintagel October 10 1969). Composer and conductor. Boy chorister at Lincoln Cathedral. Studied at the Royal College of Music. He was a brilliant bassoon player and was in the now defunct BBC Wireless Military Band and the London Philharmonic Orchestra. For a time he was Professor of the Bassoon at the Royal Academy of Music. In 1940 he joined the Royal Air Force, first as a member of the Central Band and from April 1 1941 to October 11 1945 he was bandmaster of various RAF bands. On demobilisation in 1946 he became staff conductor with the BBC, chiefly with the Midland Orchestra. He was a prolific and diverse composer. Perhaps his finest composition is *The Trumpets* for a large band, chorus and bass soloist —a powerful and dramatic work. He had a great interest in brass band music and amongst his best works in this medium are: *Salute to Youth* (his first brass composition); *Symphony of Marches; Variations on a Ninth; Spectrum* (the composer's last and favourite work); and *James Cook, Circumnavigator* which, alas, he never lived to hear. He had the distinction of completely revolutionising the style of writing for the brass quartet, a form of music that is now probably more popular than ever it was—after a period in the doldrums. Three outstanding works in

the field are *Elegy and Rondo; Fancy's Knell* and *Alla Burlesca.* Other compositions include *The Dover Coach; English Rhapsody; Spring Carol; Little Island Rhapsody;* the suite *New Lamps for Old,* and probably the most universally popular of all his compositions, *Portuguese Part.* **Recordings:** *Challenging Brass*—Black Dyke GH632 & NSPL8209; *The Dover Coach*—Brighouse NTS147, Leyland PL25175; *Entertainments for Brass*—Elegy—Black Dyke GSGLI0453, Stalybridge GRSI055; *James Cook, Circumnavigator 74*—GUS TWO379; *John o' Gaunt 68*—Black Dyke GSGL10427; *Portuguese Party* (arr Barsotti)—Desford SB328, Hampshire SB310, Mirrlees GRS1069; *Salute to Youth*—Ever Ready SB329, CWS FJ507 & 886 155; *Simon called Peter*—CWS STL5199; *Spectrum 69*—Black Dyke GSGL10453, Grimethorpe 8147, Stanshawe SDLB62; *Symphony of Marches*—Cory SB340; *Triumphant Rhapsody 65*—Black Dyke GSGL10489, Fairey LPT1022; *The Trumpets*—Black Dyke NSPL18265; *TUC Centenary March*—Massed TWO240; *Variations on a Ninth 64*—GUS TWO379 & SCX3550, Stanshawe SDLB62; *Vizcaya*—Scottish CWS GSGL10430; *Waltzing with Sullivan* (arr)—GUS SCX3502.

WALMSLEY, Trevor, DFC Was a pupil of Harry and Alex Mortimer. His playing career was interrupted by the war when he joined the RAF and was commissioned as a pilot. Served as a flying instructor in the USA for two years before returning to England as a Mosquito pilot with the Pathfinder Squadron when he was awarded the DFC. Kept in touch with music during this period by conducting various RAF Station bands and orchestras. After the war was musical director of various bands including Irwell Springs, Wingates Temperance and the Brighouse & Rastrick. Became Director of Music of Yorkshire Imperial Metals in 1965. *Recordings:* as conductor: Yorkshire Imperial Metals—*Brass International*—Pye TB3001; Yorkshire Imperial Metals—*Highlights in Brass*—Pye GSGLI0488; Yorkshire Imperial Metals—*Sounds of Brass, Vol. 2*—Decca SB302; Yorkshire Imperial Metals—*Sounds of Brass, Vol. 6*—Decca SB306; Yorkshire Imperial Metals—*Yorkshire Brass*—GBS52937, Embassy 31012.

WIGGINS, William Bramwell, LRAM,

ARCM, LTCL (b London, 1921). Composer, conductor, trumpeter, adjudicator. Educated Harrow Weald School, Trinity College of Music and Royal Academy of Music. Assistant Professor of Trumpet at Trinity College 1943-4; Trumpet and Principal Cornet, London Symphony Orchestra 1946-57; in Canada 1957-60; Philharmonia Orchestra 1960-5; Music Master at Stowe School from 1966. Compositions include: *Music for Bands; Mardi Gras Suite; Celebration Overture; Mediterranean Holiday Suite.* Various arrangements for brass band and trumpet tutors. *Recordings: Conversation in Brass*—Versatile SB331.

WILLCOCKS, George Henry (b London, February 23 1899, d January 12 1962). Composer and conductor. On January 25 1915 joined the 4th Battalion, Royal Fusiliers as a bandsman; and transferred to the 1st Battalion. He was appointed Bandmaster of the 2nd Battalion, the South Wales Borderers, on September 11 1926 and on January 20 1937 he was transferred to the band of the Royal Artillery on Salisbury Plain. He was commissioned as Director of Music of the Irish Guards on April 9 1938 and remained with them until he retired on April 8 1949. After his retirement he transferred to, and became closely associated with, the brass band world as trainer and conductor. His compositions include the marches *Fordson Major; Guards Armoured Division; Sarafand; Fifteen-Six; Consul* and *The Palace Forecourt*. *Recordings: Pondashers*—Black Dyke PEP113; *Will o' the Wisp*—Black Dyke PEP113.

WILSON, Thomas Brendan, MA, BMus, ARCM (b Colorado, USA, 1927). Composer. Educated at Blairs College, Aberdeen and at Glasgow University. Became a University lecturer and Staff Tutor in Music in the Extra-Mural Department of Glasgow University from 1957. Became a member of the Scottish Arts Council in 1968. Composed for orchestra, chamber groups, songs, choral works, etc, and several important modern works for brass, including *Sinfonietta*, a rhythmical piece, advanced in harmony and melody, based on the interval of a fourth; *Refrains and Cadenzas*, written in the 1970s and first performed by the Black Dyke Band under Geoffrey Brand, and *Cartoon*. *Recordings: Sinfonietta*—London Collegiate LFL15072.

WOOD, Arthur (b Heckmondwike, York, January 24 1875, d London, January 18 1953). Composer and conductor. Started his musical activities as a boy playing the violin but later moved to piccolo and flute. In 1882 the family moved to Harrogate and he received flute lessons from a member of the Spa Orchestra, Arthur Brookes, later flautist with the Boston Symphony and early conductor of the Hollywood Bowl concerts. Left school at 12 and at 14 appointed organist of the St Paul's Presbyterian Church in Harrogate. By 16 he was flautist, accompanist and deputy conductor and solo pianist with the Harrogate Municipal Orchestra under J. Sidney Jones—father of the composer of *The Geisha*. A few years later he joined the Bournemouth orchestra under Sir Dan Godfrey. In 1902 his *Three Old Dances* was published and his conducting of them so impressed the younger Sidney Jones who was present that he recommended him in 1903 as musical director of Terry's Theatre in London which made him, at 28, the youngest Musical Director in London. He conducted theatre orchestras for upward of 30 years including the Gaiety, His Majesty's, Daly's and Drury Lane. Of his own compositions the best-known (and most lucrative) is *Barwick Green Maypole* (used as the signature tune of the BBC serial *The Archers)*. It is the first of four movements of a suite *My Native Heath*. Other suites include: *Three Dale Dances; Yorkshire Moors; Three Mask Dances* and *Mother Malone;* and amongst his other works are *Barnsley Fair; On the Moor; Lancashire Clog Dance; Moorland Fiddlers; Fiddle-de-dee; Shipley Glen, Fairy Dreams* and marches such as *All Clear* and *Royal Progress*. *Recordings: Barwick Green*—Brighouse NTS147; *Concertino for Tenor Horn and Band*—Parc & Dare SB336; *Concerto for Trumpet and Brass*—Desford SB328; *Three Dale Dances*—BMC CSD3650, Brighouse MFP50112, Davis GRS1048, Wingates 2460 246.

WRIGHT, Denis, Mus Doc (B London, 1895, d London, April 26 1967). Composer and conductor. Educated at St George's School, Harpenden and the Royal College of Music. After service in the first World War he took up music teaching in schools. In 1925 he won a 100 guinea prize offered by J. Henry Iles for an original brass band composition—which first made his name known

Denis Wright receives the Baton of Honour at the Daily Herald Brass Band Contest 1958 (Daily Herald).

in the brass band world. In 1930 he was appointed General Music Editor for Chappell & Co in London. On the music staff of the BBC 1936-66. From 1955 he worked freelance, his special subjects—brass bands and scoring for brass and military bands and orchestras. Produced over 1,000 scores of which some 800 have been published. He composed numerous works, both serious and light, for band and orchestra, including a *Cornet Concerto* and eight works that have been used as test-pieces for band contests. Commissioned by the BBC in 1957 and 1958 to write works for combined brass band and orchestra for their Light Music festivals. He conducted and broadcast in Britain, Australia, New Zealand, South Africa, Rhodesia and on the Continent; specialising in massed brass band work. Founder in 1951 and Musical Director of the National Youth Brass Band of Great Britain; and first Conductor of the National Youth Brass Band of Scotland in 1958. Director of Examinations for the Bandsman's College of Music, Manchester and visiting examiner of the Trinity College of Music and Guildhall School of

Music in London from 1936. Member of the executive of the National Music Committee of Great Britain and the National Brass Band Club. In 1956 he was awarded the Worshipful Company of Musicians' silver medal for outstanding work with brass bands and in 1958 was the first recipient of the Daily Herald's 'baton of honour' in recognition of over 30 years' work for bands. ***Recordings:*** *Carol Sinfonietta*—Fairey LPT1025; *Concerto for Cornet*—Coventry SB315 & SPA413, Solna GRS1031; *Glastonbury-Overture*—Black Dyke LPT1027, Crossley SPT103; *Overture for an Epic Occasion* **45**—Coventry GRS1053; *Tam o' Shanter's Ride* **56**—CWS STFL537, Scottish CWS GSGL10430, Yorkshire TT003; *Tintagel*—Coventry SB332. Arrangements: *Academic Festival Overture* (Brahms) **37, 41**—Black Dyke GSGL10489, Fairey SB311; *Lohengrin, Prelude Act 3* (Wagner)—All Star PEP103, Cammel Laird SRY1009, Hammond SB327, National Youth GSGL10403, National 1977 PL25118; *1812 Overture* (Tchaikovsky)—Big Brass PFS4143, Black Dyke CSD1565, CWS STL5199, National 1967 NSPL18200; *Shepherd's Hey* (Grainger)—Brass SKL4109; *Symphony No.5—Themes* (Beethoven) **43**; *The Two Blind Men of Toledo-Overture* (Méhul)—Rochdale GRS-1054.

WRIGHT, Frank Joseph Henry, FGSM (b Victoria, Australia, d November 16 1970). Well-known in Australia and New Zealand as well as in Britain as an adjudicator at contests and festivals and a copious arranger of music for brass. Having established a reputation in New Zealand as a cornet soloist, he came to England in 1934 and was invited to conduct the St Hilda's Band for a touring season. Between 1952 and 1971 no less than ten of the test pieces for the National Championships were arrangements made by him. His original compositions include *Preludio Marziale, Whitehall* (a ceremonial march) and *Sirius*—diversions on an original theme. Edited *Brass Today* (Besson, 1957). ***Recordings:*** *Whitehall*—Mirrlees GRS1069. Arrangements: *Blackfriars* (Cundell **55**—Munn & Felton LPT1010, Virtuosi VR7608; *Benvenuto Cellini* (Berlioz) **78**—Black Dyke GSGL10477; *Le Carnaval Romain* (Berlioz **66**—CWS LPS16256, Grimethorpe OU2159, GUS TWO379 &

TWO161; *Crown Imperial* (Walton)—National 76 LSA3285; *Diadem of Gold**(Bailey) **53, 77**—Black Dyke PL25143, Fodens LPT1016; *Le Domino Noir* (Auber)—Rochdale SB316; *La Forza del Destino* (Verdi) **62**—Crossley LPT1013, CWS STL5199; *Les Francs Juges* (Berlioz) **61**—Black Dyke LPT1010, Ransome SB303, Virtuosi VR7609; *Lohengrin—Prelude* Act 3 (Wagner)—Cammell SRY1009, Fairey CSD3645, National 1972 SKL5143; *Marche joyeuse* (Chabrier)—National 1972—SKL-5143; *The Mastersingers—Prelude* (Wagner) **68**—Brighouse 583 047, National 1968 NSPL18620, National NSPL18260, National 1974 SPA369 *Passing by* (Purcell)—All-Star NTS145; *Le Roi d'Ys* **59, 71**—Black Dyke LPT1029 & PEP111, Virtuosi VR7608, *Sovereign Heritage* (Beaver) **54, 72**—Black Dyke SB308, Fairey LPT1012, *The Thieving Magpie* (Rossini)—Stanshawe SB322; *Trumpet Tune & Air* (Purcell)—Fairey SB311; *Thunder and Lightning Polka* (Strauss)—National 1968 NSPL 18260.

*NB: Diadem of Gold is usually attributed to G. Bailey, arr Frank Wright. The G. Bailey was, in fact Guillaume Balay, conductor of the famous Garde Républicaine Band from 1911 to 1927. He wrote the work in 1912 as a test-piece for a contest held in Paris and called it Ouverture Caracteristique.

WRIGHT, Kenneth Anthony, OBE, Chev Leg d'Hon. (b East Tuddenham, Norfolk, 1899, d London, 1975). Educated City of Norwich School and Sheffield University. Became first Director of the BBC Manchester 2ZY radio station in 1922. Personal assistant to Percy Pitt 1923-30 and Sir Adrian Boult 1930-7. Assistant Music Director BBC 1937; Overseas Music Director 1940-3; Deputy Director of Music 1944-7; Acting Director of Music 1947; Artists' Manager 1948-51; Head of Music Productions BBC TV, 1951. Retired in 1959 and transferred interest to films, becoming Director of Robert Maxwell Film Companies, of Norman McCann Agencies in London and the London Master Players Orchestra. A prolific composer of music for light orchestras, brass and military bands. Music for the latter includes: *Pride of Race*—test-piece for the 1935 National Championship and 1945 Open; *Peddars Way* —test-piece Belle Vue 1970; also suite *Tobacco* (BBC Light Music Festival 1949); *Bohemia; Irish Merry; In England; Rhapsodies* for military and brass bands, songs, operatic scores, film music, etc. Adjudicator and examiner. **Recordings:** *Dancing Valley*—Fairey LPT1025.

YORKE, Peter (RCO) (b London, December 4 1902, d London, February 10 1966). Conductor, composer, arranger and pianist. Educated at Trinity College of Music and was an organist at 16. Developed an interest in dance music and worked as pianist and arranger with Percival Mackey's band in 1927 and with Jack Hylton from 1929 to 1931. In the late 1920s he recorded with an ad hoc group working for HMV as the Rhythm Band. Formed his own orchestra in 1937. Served in the RAF during the war, much involved with music in various service orchestras. After the war continued to establish a popular reputation with his own orchestra, having his own radio series and recording prolifically for Columbia. He wrote a considerable amount of light orchestral music and 'mood' music for record libraries. His compositions for brass band include *Gallions Reach*—fantasia, *The Explorers*—overture and *The Shipbuilders* suite. **Recordings:** *Automation*—Fodens 2485 015; *The Explorers*—All Star PEP124; *The Shipbuilders*—Besses GSGL10510, Black Dyke SB308.

Recording brass bands
by Raymond Horricks

Of the two parts of Cheshire I grew up in, Heaton Moor, near Stockport, was within spitting distance of the great Fairey Aviation Works Band; and Holmes Chapel, much deeper into the county, took me within a few miles of the famous Fodens Motor Works Band at Sandbach. Moreover both 'Grandpa' and my own father were enthusiasts and every year would travel with me to the 'bandings' at Belle Vue in Manchester. They were fiercely partisan. Which meant anti-Yorkshire. It was just like going to the 'Roses' cricket match at Old Trafford. For personal reasons they supported the CWS Band, but they could stand it if Fairey or Fodens won. If on the other hand a Yorkshire band won, then the tram-and-bus journey back home was one of purgatorial silence. Followed by a tea which seemed to be choking them. Not even my mother's home-made cakes could sweeten the atmosphere . . . .

Anyway, the outcome of all this is that I grew up with the sound of brass bands very much inside my head. And 'sound' has been the key to my own, later productions of brass band recordings. For they are unique in sound: overall and internally—and if one cannot capture the nuances and subtleties on disc then the whole operation has been a throwaway of everybody's time. By comparison, a good military band will sound much 'brassier' in its impact upon the human ear; more brilliant and with a host of woodwind to take over the string parts one hears in a full, balanced symphony orchestra. A good brass band can, and often does, sound brilliant; and it can attack the ear with a fanfare-like impact if the written arrangement requires it. But between times it functions with a much more mellow, rounded sound. There is a rich, delicate interplay of the different sections and any transcribed string parts have to be handled with consummate skill by the twin rows of cornets. Harmony and counterpoint are also matters of extreme subtlety within the scoring for a brass band; likewise volume control: the light and shade of internal and external dynamics. Consequently, if the producer loses *any* one of these clever markings, distinctions and characteristics between his session and the finished disc, then he cannot claim to have recorded a brass band. He might be presenting a continuous melody-line, underpinned by a vigorous rhythm. But with the brass band what lies inside and around both melody and rhythm is of equal importance.

After many years devoted to other musical forms, including a series of military band recordings *(The Grenadier Guards, Life Guards* and even the famous *Berlin Tattoo,* then held in Hitler's 1936 Olympic Stadium), my first exploit with brass bands came in 1968 with a massed bands disc under the conducting baton of Harry Mortimer. It was a studio job (in Decca's *Hang 'em High* Number Three), involved over 100 players and gave me a real chance to grapple with the intricacies of brass band playing and writing. In the end it not only turned out well, but was received well by the critics. Harry, just up from a nasty operation for varicose veins, directed the musicians with his other hand on a walking-stick. However—and typical of him— there was no lack of gusto and style in his direction, to which the selected hundred responded favourably, creating a big, exciting, alternately fiery and facile sound. Plus an excellent blend. Also the finished record (Decca PFS4143) reflected quite dramatically the wide variety of musical sources which go into a true brass band entertainment.

The programme began with J. Ord Hume's rousing *B.B. and C.F. march*, went on to include Leroy Anderson's *Bugler's Holiday*, Ketèlbey's *In a Monastery Garden*, the Eurovision pop song, *Puppet On a String*, Chabrier's *Espana*, *76 Trombones* from the Broadway show *The Music Man* and was climaxed by two items which gave me particular pleasure, Tchaikovsky's *1812 Overture* and the well-known and much-loved hymn *Abide With Me*. The Tchaikovsky piece (arranged by Denis Wright) really does come off best with an ensemble of large resources, and one can imagine—listening to our disc—how it must have sounded at the Royal Albert Hall conducted by Sir Henry Wood in his Jubilee Year. We used five tuned percussionists and three sets of tubular bells behind the air players; and later on during the remix I had Arthur Bannister, the balance engineer, overdub the city bells of Geneva against our grand finale, giving the sound tremendous added depth and atmosphere.

In contrast, *Abide With Me* was specially arranged for the session. It displays the beautiful sonority which this kind of group, well handled, can go on to achieve. They play with solemnity, dignity and—although simple—a marvellously integrated harmony, uplifted during the last verse by the addition of fanfare trumpets. So; you might say that I was 'on my way' as regards recording brass bands.

However my involvement with the movement on a regular basis began in 1971, when I met Edwin Vaughan Morris for the first time. It resulted in my becoming the producer of records of the National Brass Festival concerts at the Royal Albert Hall, which in turn led to the founding of Decca's *Sounds Of Brass* series. The latter at present stands at more than 40 volumes, has been greatly acclaimed and has reached—in one way or another—most parts of the world (I recently received 35 pence in royalties from Malaysia!). With one exception, the series has been concerned with presenting individual bands. But these have encompassed a wide range of subject matter, performers and even age-groups. They include the big-name bands like Black Dyke, Fairey, Fodens, Brighouse & Rastrick, the City of Coventry Band and so on; deserved Championship winners such as Cory and the Tredegar Junior Band; bands of Championship class who are also very successful in their own regions like Desford in Leicestershire and the Ever Ready on Tyneside; the innovative James Shepherd Versatile Brass: and a quota of the up and coming youngsters, Tredegar and the Hampshire Youth Concert Band. Plus—the one exception—an album I was most anxious to make, revolving about the music of Malcolm Arnold. (My father has now forgiven me for including some Yorkshire bands. If 'Grandpa' was still alive though; well, I have my doubts . . . .)

Throughout the building of this series Vaughan has remained a good friend and my most valued consultant; aided and abetted by some of the most respected conductors and tutors in the movement: men of such calibre as Roy Newsome and Peter Parkes, Jim Scott, Albert Chappell, Ken Dennison, the amazing Walter Hargreaves and Alex Mortimer, Trevor Walmsley and now Howard Snell. Also certain composers and arrangers. But more about our actual working methods in just a couple of paragraphs time. Before passing on to an in-depth discussion of these, I ought to mention one other involvement with a brass band which stands somewhat apart from the *Sounds of Brass* series and not just because it belongs to another record company. Rather because it was purely experimental—but an experiment that came off; musically and then as a popular item with the general public. The album in question is *Christmas With Brass*, featuring the soprano, Helen McArthur, with the Killermont Young

Singers and the Whitburn Burgh Band conducted by Allan Street.

I had produced records with Helen intermittently over a number of years. Allan Street I knew as the result of producing his *Rococo Variations On a Theme by Tchaikovsky* with the City of Coventry Band. Anyway, when the two started doing concerts together it set me thinking. In the meantime my balance engineer, Martin Smith, had been raving about the sound of a brass band playing carols in his local town-square and, suddenly, the whole idea was born to me. I had Allan do a set of Christmas-music arrangements; and I added the Killermont Young Singers, with whom I had previously worked on Robin Hall and Jimmie MacGregor sessions. We recorded the whole package in one long, fruitful Sunday at Grangemouth Town Hall, pushed it out as quickly as we could and within a few weeks it seemed as if half the D-Js in Britain were playing tracks from the LP.

The subject matter had been exactly right. Which brings me back to the discussion of working methods. You have to get good bands but also you have to put together good programmes of music. A band of championship class can go to the Finals at the Albert Hall and win with its quality performance of a set test-piece lasting say, 12 to 14 minutes, perhaps as little as ten while the audience can see as well as hear it in action. Gramophone records, on the other hand, are an experience without vision. In other words, a very *flat* medium, which one can only alleviate by the excitement, beauty, technique, etc of the performances plus the variety, and, therefore, entertainment value of the musical contents.

Programming is the vital second-stage of the recording procedure. I can have lengthy discussions with Vaughan, then with the marketing men, about which two, three of four bands we ought to try to record in the coming year. Vaughan (I will not give away his true age, but he remains a man of undiminished vigour!) will then use his vast net of contacts to begin negotiations with the bands in question. (If it gets a bit hairy, we might negotiate together.) But in the meantime the real responsibility rests upon three people (the conductor, Vaughan and myself) jointly hammering out a satisfactory programme—one which the band can do justice to by its own standards of playing. One with enough variety to keep the individual listener happy and interested through 50 minutes of LP time and one which—as the series has become extended—avoids unnecessary duplication.

Fortunately the brass band repertoire is now an extensive one; and is continually being added to by new test-pieces, arrangements of classical and popular items, and original works by such active composers as Edward Gregson and Gordon Langford. Often too I might have an idea for a certain (current) piece of material making a good transcription from its own, original instrumentation to the typical brass band line-up. This requires a separate, special commission. Generally though I like to have a programme which will entertain the overall listening public and yet contain enough technical 'meat' to satisfy the carnivorous ears of the *aficionado*. Some fans of brass bands dislike the use of transcribed pop pieces; so I try to cater for them by inserting at least one or two pieces of basic repertoire, and ones I know the band in question will play really well.

An ideal programme, from my point of view, is one that includes say, a thoroughly demanding test-piece, two or at most three transcriptions of well-known and popular classics, a rousing march to kick things off, a novelty item with in-built technical exercises, a recent pop item and, of course, some solo content. Most name bands carry a soloist of reputation and merit. If they do not, then it is well worth while importing one for the sessions—a Maurice Murphy or a Jim Shepherd or a David Moore. There is no jealousy here, any good brass player will respond to and enjoy playing with men of this quality. One I am proudest of, in fact, was the commissioning of Gareth Wood's *Concerto For Trumpet and Brass Band*, because it brought back the superlative James Watson to play in front of Desford Colliery, the band with which he had started out on his career.

Once the programme is settled, musical matters can then be left with the conductor and the band to get on with for several weeks, or preferably even months, leading up to the sessions. Most producers are grateful for this time in between. Apart from the need for the players to get themselves note-perfect, I usually have several productions overlapping: which means I have to parcel out my close-focusing attention very carefully on whichever project is the most immediate.

However . . . there is still the business of finding a suitable location for the recording sessions. Although I have produced The Fairey Band and the James Shepherd Versatile Brass within Decca's West Hampstead complex, not many brass band recordings take place in London. Even the biggest-name bands are localised; they often include members who make their livings doing shift-work; and the problems of getting them down to the capital (except at National Championships time!) are just too great. So the mountain must move towards Mohammed. As it happens, I seem to have spent half my working life living out of suitcases in identikit hotel bedrooms. Moreover, on location the producer has to forge a very special relationship with the recording team he must head: hopefully, quite gently, but occasionally and, if necessary, forcefully (should there be any problem characters around). Also though the location—while close to the band's home-base—has to be acoustically right, meaning an extra journey with one's balance-engineer beforehand to check it out. More living out of suitcases in identikit bedrooms!

Perhaps you will be lucky and run into agreeable and co-operative staff attached to the halls, schools, etc where the recording, ultimately, will take place. If they are old grumps, well then, they can go jump in the lake before I will give them a few quid in the way of gratuities. Helpfulness has its own ways of paying off. It all works out in the end. But with the best planning in the world, so the saying goes, you can never be sure of anything in recording until you have actually got it all (performance-wise) 'in the can'. When I produced *The Music of Malcolm Arnold*, for instance, everything had been planned out months ahead. *And then*—suddenly—when it was time for the sessions, we were bang in the middle of the three-day week and the Heath Government's confrontation with the National Union of Mineworkers. The government's rationing of electricity was very strict and our recordings had to take place on a Sunday, when any use of mains electricity for such things was totally forbidden. It meant we had to hire an emergency generator for the equipment—which fortunately held out. What was worrying me much more though was would the daylight last long enough? I spent the night before, not in an identikit bedroom for once, but in a rather more comfortable room of W.S. Gilbert's former residence at Harrow. Not that I did much sleeping. And the fact that Gilbert had accidentally drowned himself in the garden-pond was hardly the best bit of information the management passed on to me during dinner . . ..

We were employing large forces. The four-part *Song Of Freedom, Opus 109*, includes 250 schoolgirl singers as well as the brass and the *Quintet (For Two Trumpets, Horn, Trombone & Tuba), Opus 73*, although extremely melodic and popular is notoriously difficult to play. In the end, of course, it did work out. Jim Watson's lead trumpet throughout the day was an inspiration to everyone and we got through the quintet with a minimum of edits while Geoffrey Brand's control and encouragement of the choir was one of the most sympathetic pieces of conducting I have seen him do. Nevertheless: it was at every point a nerve-jangling day. Malcolm dropped me a note from Ireland afterwards to say he thought the disc was 'absolutely terrific' which sort of made everything seem worthwhile. But that was when nothing else could go wrong!

This touches upon another point about brass band recordings. Apart from needing to be made on location, almost invariably they have to be made over the week-end; and usually on a Sunday. The amateur status of the brass band musician means that you can only get the whole band together then—and even if you set up the equipment the day before, it still means capturing over 50 minutes of finished performance sometimes within a single day. As that day goes on, so the strain of it all, and particularly the wear and tear upon the musicians' lips, becomes enormous. Consequently the producer must be prepared to do a lot of edits to help the band over the more difficult passages and to pace them in such a way that he helps to preserve their energies. Calling a tea-break at the right moment can be both intuitive and the right psychology. Likewise announcing that you will do an edit at an appropriate point in the score: so they do not have to go right back to the beginning and hurt their lips even more.

Personally too, I always let the conductor decide the order in which he would like to record the pieces: usually bearing little or no resemblance to my own final running-order on the disc. He has been the man in front of the music for so long. He knows the particular playing problems of each score—*and how he can help preserve the lips*. More often than not he will opt to start with a march. To warm up the instruments; and also to give us a maximum volume to set our balance levels by. Then he will most likely go for the test-piece; to get that out of the way. Again, it is good psychology to let the soloists get their items out of the way during the morning. Usually after this the band is really flying, and in the afternoon, although there are signs of tiredness, it is easy enough to mop up the wines-and-spirits part of the programme.

Any successful recording resembles making love. A marvellous moment stolen back from the night. So much can go wrong; but it does not, and all at once you know you are there and it has been a wonderful experience. 'For you, I fancy, to love is to be born', Saint-Exupery wrote in his *Southern Mail*. Well, records are also like giving birth and brass band recordings are no different to any others in this respect.

However: we have not quite got this description of making one to the point of confinement yet. Following the settling of programme, location and—hopefully—the artwork and notes for the album-sleeve, the producer must then brief his chief engineer (the actual balance-engineer) on what is involved: the music, the size and nature of the instrumentation and so on. He must tell his engineer how he wants it all laid out in stereo; and what independent controls he will require at the later, editing and re-mixing stage. Also what solos there will be. The latter's job at this point is to work out and help collect (very precisely) the amount and type of equipment necessary to satisfy the producer's particular approach to the sound. Although an independent, I have only ever worked with four balance-engineers on brass band recordings. It is a question of explaining how you like to work and the kind of sound you are looking for. Given a clear picture of this, afterwards any intelligent balance-man can do quite a lot of the technical spadework on his own. And an intelligent producer will trust his balance-engineer a lot. Otherwise he will feel compelled to use someone else.

Meanwhile other details are being bolted in. Like the booking of identikit bedrooms for the recording team, travel arrangements and so on. Also calls to the conductor: just to feel reassured that 'out in the towns and shires' all is going well at the midweek-evening rehearsals. Eventually though the great day arrives and the show is on the road. A truck filled with equipment will roll north from London or south from Edinburgh and we have the big action scenes at last. Once on location I might help to unload the truck, but I (deliberately) do none of the setting up. I will help to break down a set-up after the sessions; but the actual setting-up is based upon what I have asked for, and the balance-engineer has to be given his freedom to get things right. No point in dabbling at this stage just for the sake of trying to look important. On the other hand, I do tend to hang around at the setting-up in case the balance-man has any queries arising out of his physical involvement with seating, microphone placings and so on as they will affect the music to come.

Over the years I have tended to favour a set-up which is somewhat different to a brass band's normal competition seating. We have cornets to the left of the conductor: with the soprano (a difficult instrument to get through) joining the principal and the solo cornets on the front row; then repiano, flugelhorn and the second cornets on a raised platform behind. This way we seem to get the right amount of secondary support to the solo cornets. In the middle, directly facing the conductor, we have the three horns, backed by the euphoniums and baritones and with the percussion behind that, separated for stereo. Over on the right we have the trombones seated in front of the basses. The cornets and trombones will sit directly facing their microphones. All of the others, being upright instruments, will be miked from above.

By a process of trial and error we have found the best microphones to use are Neumanns—M49s for the cornets and trombones, 84s on the horns and percussion (several on the latter, depending on the combination) and 88s on the euphoniums, baritones and basses. With these one can count on their wide dynamic range taking in both loud and soft passages, the band's internal dynamics and its rich, rounded mellow ensemble sound. The subtle interplay of the sections within the score then becomes largely a question of balance at the control-room end.

Usually one can get away with 12 channels (microphones) on a brass session. But a lot depends on how complicated the percussion is; or again what one has in the way of solos or duets or trios. One other point here. I have usually produced brass recordings 'dry' echo-wise (alcohol-wise too!); except for the natural room reverberation. And this is not merely because artificial echo-chambers are huge and cumbersome. It is as much because conductors like to have their sections seated close together. It does a lot for fellow feeling in the playing and an easier musical blend. By recording dry, therefore, one ends up with better separation and so more independent control over the sections for the later remixing back in London. This way, too, the engineer is able to please both the conductor and his producer.

Of course, all I have been writing so far applies to the recording of a single band. For the National Festival concerts at the Albert Hall everything was different again. Being a massed bands concert we had to use 24 channels (including radio microphones) and, because we had a control-room somewhere up above, the sky communication became a great problem so we used walkie-talkies as well and closed-circuit television. Oh, yes—and the BBC in the control-room next door kindly let us have some of their land-lines. Finally I persuaded Vaughan (and afterwards his successors) to reseat the trombones *in front* of the right-hand cornets, into whose microphones they had been blowing and completely drowning them out. This eased our balance problems a lot.

But the biggest headache at the Albert Hall was one purely of timing. We could set up and achieve a good balance of the hundred odd players taking part in the Festival concert at their rehearsal the day before. Only to have to take the microphones away because the actual Championships were being held on stage from the next morning and throughout the day! Moreover we had exactly *one hour* to get the mikes out and into position between the end of the Championships and the start of the Festival concert. With the foreknowledge that being 'live' the performances themselves would allow us only one bite at the cherry! Again, though, one copes. At least we did know the problems, and so we faced up to them. Also the chance to have Sir Charles Groves conduct over 100 brass players on disc is not to be turned aside lightly.

Normal brass sessions require the producer to work very closely with the conductor—almost like riding a tandem-bicycle. The conductor can deliver to the producer what the band does best, *provided* there is a natural understanding between the two men over *what that best is*. They both have to follow their scores very carefully; with the conductor knowing when to stop and when to be stopped, and the producer knowing when to stop the conductor and when to let him go on. Furthermore they need to be in absolute accord over the selection of editing points. Between them they can cajole, persuade, lean on, instruct, squeeze and push, praise and encourage. Above all though, they must operate together with a real sense of purpose so that each hard-blowing member of the band knows that his efforts are getting somewhere. It will keep the band going through the most wearing of days *and result in a superior kind of record.*

All the rest really is anecdote. Like the time we were recording the band of Yorkshire Imperial Metals and had to get the maintenance engineers to clamber up into the roof and remove a nest of very vocal young starlings. Or at the Albert Hall— and how exciting it was to record Sir William Walton's *Crown Imperial*, his 1937 coronation march, with the full weight of five bands, Dyke, Brighouse, CWS, Fairey and Fodens. Wow! Again at the Albert Hall with Walter Hargreaves leaving the bands on their own during the middle section of the *Radetsky March* to caper about the stage and encourage the audience to clap along with the rhythm. Or for that matter Mr Hargreaves on any of his recording sessions. Yes, the Mighty Atom is certainly a fair wit! These are just fleeting glimpses; moments of recall.

When we first recorded the Fairey Band under Ken Dennison (and Philip McCann, now with Dyke, played lead cornet), the band so got the wind into its sails that we collected over 90 minutes of usable performance in a single day: enough for two LPs. In contrast Dyke—for all their greatness—are the most nervous band I have ever encountered on a recording session. *They are great players*; and they can go out and devastate the opposition at contest after contest but on a recording they just keep stopping and starting to get it right. Still, that is all part of being Dyke, I suppose. It is for posterity and so they have to try to be that much better than anyone else. It leads to cracks and slips over notes they would otherwise hardly think twice about.

There are recollections of conductors too—when Alex Mortimer got CWS through the difficult *Night On A Bare Mountain* by Mussorgsky despite having to conduct the band from a wheel-chair. When Jim Scott kept repeating 'Just give me one second, Ray'. He would take two minutes, but then the resulting performance would be a total transformation. Or again: how impressed I was by Tudor Williams, the young conductor with the Tredegar Junior Band. With talents such as this now around, the brass band movement need not have too many fears for its future. And there was a little girl of nine blowing through a cornet with the Tredegar Band. I wonder what she sounds like today?

Touching on the youth bands reminds me of John Knight and his Hampshire players. What a marvellous setting it was when we recorded them inside Winchester College. On a beautiful, Constable-like summer's day. And how well they played that day. One thinks too of the many loyal supporters and helpers around. Of the librarians and presidents and band secretaries also of the Merrie Wives of Desford. Came lunchtime and they just took over—up to the elbows in chickens and salad and peaches and cream. What a spread it was that day! Again in this context, one must keep on thinking about the ordinary fan. The guy who puts his hand in his pocket and actually buys a record. He as much as anyone is the loyal servant of the movement.

What a lift too it gives to a cornet section to have someone like Jim Shepherd sit in with them. I noticed this with the Ever Ready Band. They have a very good cornet section. On the days we recorded them Jim turned it into a great one. Memories, more memories. And soon I must stop. But I cannot let go without first saying something more about the music of Malcolm Arnold. After Sir William Walton's *First Symphony* I think that Malcolm has written the most interesting and exciting music for brass instruments of any leading English composer this century. Okay, he is an ex-trumpet player himself. Nevertheless, the fact that he has pulled himself away from his symphonic output (and his lucrative film-scores) to write so many pieces directly for brass band must be an inspiration in itself to the movement. His *Little Suite No 1 For Brass Band* was the first piece I ever recorded with an individual band (Fairey) and I remain an undisguised fan of his writing. (That recording prompted my father to drop me a note and hint that, after 15 years as a very 'internationalist' music producer, I appeared to be showing some promise at last.) My final recalls, therefore, must be of Malcolm on the one hand; a towering modern composer; and on the other of the ordinary, little known, unsung players, the backbone of the movement, who crowd into the control-room whenever we have a playback: desperate to hear if they are getting it right.

No, not quite my final ones. As I have been writing all of this, I could not help thinking from time to time about just one fact. Why was it, if my father hated me liking Dizzy Gillespie and Charlie Parker, and 'Grandpa' wouldn't have forgiven me for recording Yorkshire bands; why was it that they, fervent Manchester United supporters, never lambasted me for following Manchester City? I could openly refer to United as 'the reserves' and get away with it. Although once I had to take a caning *and* beg my headmaster at college not to tell my father when I had played truant to watch one of City's important midweek games. (It does not help to have your father's former tutor as your own headmaster.) Maybe they put it all down to teenage rebellion. But I had the last laugh when United went down into the Second Division. It is like liking and recording brass bands. One can be an internationalist in one sense and still be a man of the English north: instinctive, tribal and very much involved with local ethnic roots and craftsmanship. One can go off and away, halfway round the world—and ultimately background will out.

Brass bands on record

by Peter Gammond

A final word about brass band music on record. We have solidly based this book on the recorded repertoire because this is such an important access to the repertoire for most people. (Northern exiles in the south or those who cannot always afford to follow the yearly trail to Belle Vue or the Albert Hall). Records give us all a chance to assess bands and run our own home championships. Over the LP years (which we have covered from 1960 to the present day) the brass band enthusiast had been pretty well served. The early LP days of the 1950s were perhaps a little unbalanced. The Fontana labels showed an unswerving devotion to the CWS (Manchester) Band, Columbia faithfully served Harry Mortimer, Regal-Zonophone brought the Salvation Army inside our front-doors; then gradually, as the market demand grew, the LP began to perform the really excellent service that we have come to expect of it.

The problems of the companies in this field are akin to that in other musical areas, particularly the classical. Brass band audiences' tastes are quite clearly divided between those who like the substantial music of the test-piece world and those who like jolly, tuneful music of a popular nature. The reviews of brass band records inevitably have a coda which says either 'we wish there was some music of more substance here' or 'this is heavy going and a few lighter pieces would be welcome'. Gradually it could be seen that there would be sufficient call for specialised brass music which could occupy certain labels; that the music for popular and wider consumption could come out on more general releases; and the day come when the interest in recorded brass music was sufficient to justify an occasional mixture.

One of the first outlets to give 'serious' attention to brass bands was the Paxton *Championship Brass* series of 10" LPs and 7" EPs and, although these are now hard to come by, they were well worth including in our pages for the sake of the extensive test repertoire they offered. As they went by with the mono age, other excellent series began—the Pye *Top Brass* series and the very fine Decca *Sounds of Brass* series which both took the middle road of mixing popular and serious following the tastes of the bands and conductors. The smaller Grosvenor label also added its efforts to recording worthy bands in good stereo sound and searching into interesting corners of music. Since 1973, the Virtuosi company have recorded the Virtuosi Brass Band (which draws its personnel from bands all over the country) in an exceptionally well-balanced, mainly serious series of recordings that have taken over the Paxton mantle.

Most of the principal test-pieces since the early 1900s are somewhere on record, and we have concentrated on giving guidance as to their whereabouts in the composer list in the next chapter. It is difficult to choose outstanding records with so many excellent ones about, but probably all serious students of brass band music and its special repertoire would want to have the Grimethorpe Colliery Bands *Classics for Brass* (Decca SXL6820) for its memorable pieces, and several of the Virtuosi series would be essential acquisitions for the earnest collector. The City of London collection of Malcolm Arnold's music (Decca SB313) would certainly be high on many lists; likewise the GUS record of test-pieces (Columbia TWO379); and the Black Dyke *British Music for Brass Bands* (RCA RL25078).

For a good selection of records that offer a balanced mixture of serious and popular music the *Sounds of Brass* series on Decca should satisfy most needs. For those who wish to approach brass bands in the lightest and most entertaining manner possible there are numerous possibilities but personal enjoyment suggests that the Fairey Band's *Melodious Brass* (HMV CSD3668) was one of the very best. Otherwise one could hardly go wrong with any one of the Decca *World of Brass Bands* series conducted by Harry Mortimer; or the magnificent World Record Collection *The Best of Brass*; or the individual records of the same bands on Columbia.

Beyond the pages of the specialised magazines there are few places where one can find a substantial and well-considered view of brass band recordings. Many people will be especially grateful for the knowledgeable and tasteful views that W.A. Chislett has offered for many decades in the pages of *The Gramophone*; and I should like to end this chapter by acknowledging my own debt to his enthusiasm and wisdom.

Brass bands and their recordings—
an annotated LP & EP discography
by Peter Gammond and W.A. Chislett

Our selection of bands chosen for inclusion in this section was mainly dictated by the availability of recordings, but one or two important names are included even where no LP recordings are available. In the discography, while mainly keeping to records that are currently available, we have also included a large number of deleted items—indicated by (d)—which carry repertoire of exceptional interest. On the other hand, some current records of less outstanding interest, are omitted. Specially recommended records have an asterisk beside them.

As in the 'Who's who in brass' section the numbers in bold indicate as follows—**30** = National Championship test-piece, 1930; *30* = British Open test-piece, 1930, etc. Dates in brackets (68) indicate approximate year of issue.

†Indicates availability (listed in R. Smith & Co Ltd catalogue) at time of going to press. The conductor of the band on record is indicated by c before his name.

Whilst every effort has been made to ensure that this discography is as complete and accurate as possible, errors or omissions may occur. The author would be pleased to hear from readers who can provide any additional, relevant information.

Besses o' th' Barn Band (1853)

Became an all-brass band in 1853 and is one of the oldest, if not *the* oldest brass band to have maintained a great reputation throughout its history. It was famous as a brass and reed band long before 1853. Indeed it was the winner of a contest organised to celebrate the coronation of King George VI in 1921, when it played *God Save the King* as the 'own-choice' test-piece. It is a Lancashire band and its home was picturesquely described in a book of 1895 as follows: 'Delightfully situated on the turnpike road about five miles from Manchester on the one hand and four and a half from Bury on the other stands the quaint old village of Besses o' th' Barn'. The band has toured the world twice and is proud of the accolade 'Royal' granted by King Edward VII in recognition of its tour of France in connection with the *Entente Cordiale* celebrations. At intervals over the years it has won all the most coveted awards, some of them more than once—National Champions 1903 and British Open Champions 1892, 1894, 1920, 1925, 1931, 1937 and 1959. Its present professional and resident conductors are Ifor James and Frank Bryce respectively. Bibliography: *The Origin, History and Achievements of the Besses o' th' Barn Band* (Hampson, c 1893).

Selected LP recordings

Capriccio Brilliant—Pye GSGL10510 (74). *Capriccio brilliant* (Mendelssohn, arr Brockway); *Sonata in G minor* (Handel, arr Brockway); *Jazz intermezzo* (Sievewright); *The Shipbuilders—suite* (Yorke); *Sinfonietta for Brass* (Horovitz). c Ifor James

English Brass—Pye TB3012 (77)†. *Moorside Suite* (Holst) **28**; *A Dales Suite* (Butterworth); *A Downland Suite* (Ireland) **32**; *Solitude* (James). c Ifor James

English Brass, Vol.2—Pye TB3016 (78)†. *The Severn Suite* (Elgar) **30**; *Canzon duodecimi toni* (Gabrieli, arr Dennison); *Variations for Brass Band* (Vaughan Williams) **57**; *Chromascope* (Patterson). c Ifor James

Top Brass—Pye GGL0393, GSGL10393 (67). *World Tour* (Owen); *Sandon* (Purday); *Hungarian Rhapsody No.2* (Liszt, arr W. Rimmer); *Trombola* (Bryce); *The Gypsy*

Baron—Overture (J. Strauss, arr Winter); *Cock o' the North* (Traditional, arr Bryce); *Four Gershwin Tunes* (arr Bryce). c Frank Bryce

Viva Vivaldi—Grosvenor GRS 1042 (76)†. *Viva Vivaldi* (Vivaldi, arr Bryce); *Swedish Rhapsody* (Jacob); *Windmills from Amsterdam* (James); *Hora staccato* (Dinicu, arr Bryce); *Sonata for Horn and Band* (Eccles, arr Brockway); *Rock of Ages* (Redhead, arr Steadman-Allen); *The Plantagenets* (Gregson). c Ifor James & Frank Bryce.

Also:

Music from Vale Royal—Pye TB3003.
Pride of the North—Polydor 2928 011.
Your Favourite Hymns—Polydor 2460 195.

Black Dyke Mills Band (1855)

One of the oldest bands still flourishing in the British Isles, its earliest history can be traced back to 1815 in the town of Queensbury near Bradford. At that time 'a good reed band' was formed which was known as Peter Wharton's band after its leader. A local mill-owner John Foster was a great music-lover and, to encourage other amateurs, he joined the band as an active member. Eventually Wharton's Band was disbanded and replaced by a similar group in 1833. In 1855 this also looked in danger of disintegration so it was taken over by Messrs Foster as their works band, from which time it became known as the Black Dike Mills Band—the spelling 'Dyke' became the usual one later. Its existing members were given employment at the mill, new instruments and uniforms were provided and Mr Samuel Longbottom was engaged as musical director and instructor. The band won its first prize at a contest in Hull in 1856. Further success came in 1860 when the band won first prize at the first brass band contest to be held at the Crystal Palace in London. They won the premier award two years later at Belle Vue, the first of a long string of successes there, and again in 1863 and 1871. Mr Longbottom died in 1876 and was succeeded by Mr J. Fawcett of Eccleshill under whom they won the Belle Vue contest in 1879. In 1880 the well-known cornet player, Alexander Owen, was appointed conductor and led them to the premier award in 1880 and 1881. Owen had worked in opera orchestras in London and arranged selections from various well-known operas of the time; fore-runners of typical test-pieces that were to become very popular in coming years. Owen retired in 1888 and was succeeded by John Gladney, a well-known brass band teacher who had led the then equally famous Meltham Mills Brass Band from 1871 to 1883, during which time it won nearly £4,000 in prize money.

Between 1856 and 1888 the accounts of the Black Dyke Mills Band showed that it had won £3,343 10s—£395 of this in musical instruments, a frequent form of award. For its hat-trick at Belle Vue 1879-81 each member of the band was given a gold medal worth three guineas. By 1889 its bandmaster Mr Phineas Bower won the euphonium solo prize 12 times, earning himself £135. There was also a junior section in which younger players gained experience before graduating to the senior band. From 1900, when the official National Championships started, the Black Dyke Band has continued its distinguished career as one of the countries finest brass organisations, winning the National Championships no less than 13 times—in 1902, 1928, 1947, 1948, 1949, 1951, 1959, 1961, 1967, 1972, 1975, 1976 1977 and 1979; the World Championship in 1970. In 1967 and 1970 it was the 'BBC Band of the Year', an apt title for a Band that has made well over 400 broadcasts. In recent times it has toured many European countries.

The distinguished roll of Bandmasters of Black Dyke is as follows: John Galloway 1855-1863; William Rushworth 1863-71; William Jasper 1871-75; Phineas Bower 1875-96; Harry Bower 1896-1912; Arthur O. Pearce 1912-49; Joe W. Wood 1949, Alex Mortimer 1949-54; Edmund Hoole 1954-6; Jack Emmett 1956-63; Geoffrey Whitham 1963-6; Roy Newsome 1966-78. Resident Conductors have been Denis Carr 1971, Wilfred Heaton 1971, Roy Newsome 1972-8, Michael Antrobus 1978- . Former professional conductors have included Samuel Longbottom, John Gladney, Alex Owen, William Rimmer, Joseph Weston Nicholl, J.A. Greenwood, William Halliwell, Harry Mortimer, Major G.H. Willcocks, Leighton Lucas and Colonel C.H. Jaeger. Famous cornet soloists associated with the band are John Paley, Ceres Jackson, Harold Pinches, Harold Jackson, Owen Bottomley, Willie Lang, Maurice Murphy and James Shepherd.

Selected LP recordings

The Best of the Black Dyke Mills Band—RCA PL25025 (77), cass PK25025†. *Colonel Bogey* (Alford); *Marching with Sousa* (arr Langford); *Concorde* (Newsome); *Brilliant March* (Hume); *Best Foot Forward* (Tomlinson); *Marche Joyeuse* (Chabrier); *La Danza* (Rossini, arr Langford); *Fantasy on British Sea Songs* (Langford); *All through the night* (arr Langford); *Greensleeves* (arr Langford); *Drink to me only* (arr Langford); *The British Grenadier* (arr Langford); *Blaydon Races* (arr Langford); *The girl I left behind me* (arr Langford). c Geoffrey Brand & Roy Newsome

Black Dyke Plays Langford—RCA LSA3270 (76)†. *Sinfonietta; Rhapsody for Trombone and Band; Prelude and Fugue* (Langford). *Billy Boy; Waltzing Matilda; The Irish Washerwoman; Pavane* (Fauré); *A Sullivan Fantasy* (all arr Langford) (with Don Lusher). c Roy Newsome

Brass to the Fore—RCA LSA3088 (72)†. *Joyeuse Marche* (Chabrier arr Langford); *The Daughter of the Regiment—Overture* (Donizetti); *The Tales of Hoffmann—Barcarolle* (Offenbach); *Festival Music—Romance* (Ball); *Espana* (Waldteufel); *Fantasy on British Sea Songs* (Langford); *Greensleeves* (arr Langford); *Two Tunes for Trumpet* (Purcell); *North Country Fantasy* (Langford) c Roy Newsome

*British Music for Brass Bands—RCA RL25078, cass RK25078 (77)†. *Severn Suite* (Elgar) **30**; *The Wayfarer—Sinfonietta* (Ball) **76**; *Variations on 'The Shining River'* (Rubbra) **58**; *An Epic Symphony* (Fletcher) **26**. c Major Peter Parkes & Roy Newsome

Championship Brass—HMV CLP3652, CSD3652 (68). *The Beautiful Galathea—Overture* (Suppé); *Berceuse de Jocelyn* (Godard); *Honest Toil* (W. Rimmer); *Waltz for a Princess* (Tomlinson); *Carnival Dance* (Langford); *Quid Pro Quo* (Ball); *Alpine Echoes* (Windsor); *Betty Dear* (Agoult); *Pineapple Poll—excerpts* (Sullivan, arr Mackerras). c Geoffrey Brand & Roy Newsome

Championship Brass—Paxton LPT1010 (52). *Les Francs Juges—Overture* (Berlioz, arr F. Wright) **61**; (see also Munn & Felton). c Jack Emmott

Championship Brass—Paxton LPT1027, SLPT1027 (69). *The Mastersingers—Suite* (Wagner, arr F. Wright); *Glastonbury—*

Overture (D. Wright). c Roy Newsome & Geoffrey Brand

Championship Brass—Paxton LPT1028, SLPT1028 (69). *Rococo Variations on a theme by Tchaikovsky* (Street); *Little Suite No.2, Op.93* (Arnold); *Bandology* (Osterling). c Roy Newsome & Geoffrey Brand

Championship Brass—Paxton LPT1029. *Le Roi d'Ys—Overture* (Lalo, arr F. Wright) **59, 71** (see also Fodens). c Major G.H. Willcocks

The Champions—Pye GGL0410, GSGL10410 (68)†. *The Contestor* (Powell); *Grandfather's Clock* (arr Doughty); *David of the White Rock* (arr Willcocks); *The Merry Wives of Windsor—Overture* (Nicolai); *Iolanthe—Selection* (Sullivan) *Napoli* (Belstedt); *Journey Into Freedom* (Ball) **67**. c Roy Newsome & Geoffrey Brand

The Champions—Pye GGL0391, GSGL10391 (67). *Where'er you walk* (Handel, arr Rimmer); *Hungarian Rhapsody No.2* (Liszt, arr W. Rimmer); *Carnaval de Venice* Arban); *Nabucco—Overture* (Verdi, arr W. Rimmer); *The Nightingale* (Moss); *Les Préludes* (Liszt, arr W. Rimmer). c Roy Newsome

Champions Again—Pye GSGL10427 (69)†. *Petite Suite de Ballet* (Ball); *Resurgam* (Ball)**50**; *An Epic Symphony* (Fletcher) **26**; *John o' Gaunt—Concert Overture* (Vinter) **68**. c Geoffrey Brand & Roy Newsome

Concert Sounds of Black Dyke Mills Band—RCA LSA3254 (75)†. *Die Fledermaus—Overture* (Strauss); *Marche Militaire* (Schubert, arr Ball); *La Danza* (Rossini); *The Plantagenets* (Gregson); *Rule Britannia—Overture* (Arne, arr Rimmer); *Cossack Patrol* (Rose); *Concorde* (Newsome); *Rhapsody on Negro Spirituals* (Ball). c Roy Newsome

European Brass—RCA PL25117 (78)†. *The Bartered Bride—Polka* (Smetana, arr D. Wright); *The Thieving Magpie—Overture* (Rossini, arr D. Wright); *Russalka—Song to the Moon* (Dvořák, arr Langford); *Sylvia—Entrance of the Huntress* (Delibes, arr Newsome); *The Nutcracker—Miniature Overture* (Tchaikovsky, arr D. Wright); *Siciliana & Giga* (Handel, arr Langford); *Rhapsody on Sea Shanties* (Langford); *Morning Cloud* (Farnon); *Pomp & Circumstance March No.1* (Elgar, arr Hume). c Roy Newsome & Edward Heath

Four Contest Marches, Set 3—Paxton (45) PEP132. *Death or Glory* (Hall); *Country*

Palatine (Johnstone); *March Courageous* (Hawley); *The Astronaut* (Jakeway). c Roy Newsome & Geoffrey Brand

Golden Hour of the Black Dyke Mills Band—Pye GH632, cass ZCGH632 (77)†. *Journey Into Freedom* (Ball) **67**; *Challenging Brass* (Vinter); *Little Suite No.1* (Arnold); *Londonderry Air* (arr Willcocks); *Elizabethan Serenade* (Binge); *Napoli* (Belstedt); *Pandora* (Danmare); *Where'er you walk* (Handel, arr Rimmer); *Finlandia* (Sibelius, arr Bidgood); *The Lost Chord* (Sullivan, arr Hume); etc. c Geoffrey Brand & Roy Newsome

Handel: 'Messiah' — Excerpts — Pye GSGL10475 (71). *Overtures; And the Glory of the Lord; And a Virgin shall conceive; O Thou, that tellest good tidings; Pastoral Symphony; He was despised; Lift up your heads; Why do the Nations; Hallelujah; Behold, I tell you a mystery; The trumpet shall sound.* (arr D. Wright) (with Jean Allister, Forbes Robinson & The Bradford Festival Choral Society). c Geoffrey Brand

High Peak for Brass—Pye GSGL10453 (70)†. *High Peak* (Ball) **69**; *Four Little Maids* (Carr); *Pandora* (Damare); *Elegy* (Vinter); *Spectrum* (Vinter) **69**. c Geoffrey Brand

Ivory and Brass—Pye GSGL10463 (71). *The Corsair—Overture* (Berlioz, arr Brand); *Londonderry Air* (arr Willcocks); *Concerto Symphonique—Scherzo* (Litolff, arr Wright); *Zelda—Caprice* (Code); *Concerto for Piano and Band* (Newsome) (with Keith Swallow—piano). c Geoffrey Brand & Roy Newsome

Knight Templar—HMV CLP1787, CSD1565 (64). *Knight Templar* (Allan); *Poet and Peasant—Overture* (Suppé) *Carnaval de Venice* (arr Rimmer); *Orpheus in the Underworld—Can-Can* (Offenbach); *Thunder and Lightning—Polka* (J. Strauss II); *Mikado—Selection* (Sullivan); *Chianti Song* (Winkler); *Spanish Harlequin* (Haysom); *1812 Overture* (Tchaikovsky, arr D. Wright). c Geoffrey Witham

The Lion and the Eagle—RCA PL25089 (77)†. *The Yeomen of the Guard—Overture* (Sullivan, arr Sargent); *Suite No.2—Dargason* (Holst); *Pomp and Circumstance March No.4* (Elgar, arr Hume); *Will ye no come back again* (arr Langford); *Phil the Fluter's Ball* (French, arr Langford); *Land of my Fathers* (James); *Stars and Stripes for Ever* (Sousa); *Rhapsody on Negro Spirituals* (Ball); *Stephen Foster Fantasy* (arr Hamner); *George Gershwin Medley.* c Roy Newsome

Marching to the Black Dyke Mills Band

—RCA LFL15071 (75)†. *Under the Double Eagle* (Wagner, arr Langford); *Le Prophète—Coronation March* (Meyerbeer, arr Langford); *Brilliant March* (Hume); *Onward, Christian Soldiers* (Sullivan, arr Langford); *Torch of Freedom* (Ball); *Spirit of Pageantry* (Fletcher); *Best Foot Forward* (Tomlinson); *The New Colonial* (Hall); *The Pacemakers* (Langford); *Colonel Bogey* (Alford); *Marching with Sousa* (arr Langford); *The Dambusters—March* (Coates). c Geoffrey Brand & Roy Newsome

*Music for Brass—Paxton (45) PEP111. *Le Roi d'Ys—Overture* (Lalo, arr F. Wright) **59, 71**. c Major G.H. Willcocks

Music for Brass—Paxton (45) PEP112. *Brahms on Brass* (Brahms); *Off We Go* (Spurgin); *Jeux d'Enfants—Duo & Galop* (Bizet). c Major G.H. Willcocks & Jack Emmott

Music for Brass—Paxton (45) PEP113. *Will o' the Wisp* (Willcocks); *Trumpet Tune and Air* (Purcell); *Pondashers—March* (Willcocks); *Messiah—Hallelujah Chorus* (Handel). c Major G.H. Willcocks & Jack Emmott

Music for Brass—Paxton (45) PEP118. *Peer Gynt—Anitra's Dance* (Grieg); *Harlequin's Patrol* (Lucas); *The Water Music—Bourrée, Hornpipe & Allegro* (Handel); *The Foggy Dew* (arr Bantock). c Jack Emmott

Music for Brass—Paxton (45) PEP119. *A Midsummer Night's Dream—Nocturne* (Mendelssohn); *Tarantella Cromatica* (Stokes); *Scaramouche* (Charrosin). c Jack Emmott

Sounds of Brass, Vol.5—Decca SB305 (73)†. *Centaur March* (Broadbent); *The Mountains of Mourne* (French, arr Collison); *Tritsch Tratsch Polka* (J. Strauss II, arr Pope); *Choral and Variations* (Lucas); *March with a Beat* (Hanmer); *Hansel and Gretel—Prelude* (Humperdinck, arr Ball); *Ruy Blas—Overture* (Mendelssohn, arr Staff). c Roy Newsome

Sounds of Brass, Vol.8—Decca SB308 (73)†. *A Kensington Concerto* (Ball) **72**; *Sovereign Heritage* (Beaver, arr F. Wright) **54**; *Investiture Antiphonal Fanfares* (Bliss, arr Newsome); *The Shipbuilders—Suite* (Yorke); *Cleopatra Polka* (Damaré); *Queensbury March* (Kaye) c Geoffrey Brand & Roy Newsome

Sounds of Brass, Vol.24—Decca SB324 (76)†. *Viva Birkinshaw* (W. Rimmer); *Spanish Caprice* (Baldwin); *Hat Trick*

(Newsome); *Mexican Grandstand* (Begg); *Une Vie de Matelot* (Farnon) **75**; *The Mill on the Cliff—Overture* (Reissiger); *From the Shores of the Mighty Pacific* (Clarke); *Sandon* (Purday); *New World Symphony—Finale* (Dvořák, arr Nicholl). c Roy Newsome & Major Peter Parkes

Traditionally British—RCA LSA3186 (73)†. *Blaydon Races; Drink to me only; The British Grenadiers; Jerusalem; Charlie is my darling; My love is like a red, red rose; Loch Lomond; The girl I left behind me; The minstrel boy; Gentle maiden; The Ash Grove; All through the night; Men of Harlech* (arr Langford & others). c Roy Newsome

*Triple Champions—RCA PL25143 (78), cass PK25143†. *Connotations for Brass Band* (Gregson) **77**; *Diadem of Gold* (Bailey, arr F. Wright) **53, 77**; *Vivat Regina—Suite* (Mathias); *Harmonious Variations on a Theme of Handel* (Langford). c Major Peter Parkes & Roy Newsome

Triumphant Brass—Pye GSGL10489 (73)†. *Hungarian March* (Berlioz); *Cornet Carillon* (Binge); *Suite Gothique* (Boellmann); *Academic Festival Overture* (Brahms, arr D. Wright); *Triumphant Rhapsody* (Vinter). c Roy Newsome

*The Trumpets—Pye NSPL18265 (69). *The Trumpets—Cantata* (Vinter) (with Michael Langdon—bass, Huddersfield Glee and Madrigal Society Choir). c Geoffrey Brand

With Band and Voices—Pye NPL18209, NSPL18209 (68). *Crown Imperial* (Walton, arr Wright); *Elizabethan Serenade* (Binge); *Challenging Brass* (Vinter); *Finlandia* (Sibelius, arr Bidgood); *The Padstow Lifeboat* (Arnold); *Little Suite for Brass* (Arnold); *All in the April Evening* (Roberton); *The Lost Chord* (Sullivan, arr Hume). (with the Bradford Festival Choral Society) c Roy Newsome & Geoffrey Brand

World Champion Brass—Pye GSGL-10477 (71 & 74)†. *Prelude for an Occasion* (Gregson); *Bassoon Concerto—Allegro* (Mozart, arr Henstridge); *Pageantry—Suite* (Howells) **35, 37, 50, 70**; *Pineapple Poll—excerpts* (Sullivan, arr Mackerras); *Cornet Roundabout* (Eaves); *Recitative and Romance* (Heath); *Benvenuto Cellini—Overture* (Berlioz, arr F. Wright) **78**. c Geoffrey Brand

World Famous Marches—RCA PL25165 (79)†. *The Cossack* (W. Rimmer); *Punchinello* (W. Rimmer); *The Australasian* (W. Rimmer); *The North Star* (W. Rimmer); *Irresistible* (W. Rimmer); *Black Night* (W. Rimmer); *Flying Eagle* (Blankenburg); *Gruss und Thüringen* (Blankenburg); *Auf Heimatlicher* (Blankenburg); *Erde Nec aspera terrent* (Blankenburg); *Jubelsturm* (Blankenburg); *Unter Kaisers Fahnen* (Blankenburg); *Jugendfrühling* (Blankenburg). c Michael Antrobus & Roy Newsome

also:

Black Dyke in concert—Pye GSGL10417 (74).

A Christmas Fantasy—RCA RS1083 (76).

Christmas Festival—Pye TB3013 (79).

James Cook—Circumnavigator—RCA LSA2313 (75).

Themes from Films, TV and Stage RCA PL25220, cass PK25220 (79)†.

See also under **St Hilda's Colliery Band.**

Brighouse & Rastrick Band (1881)

A band was formed in Brighouse around 1860 (possibly earlier) originally known as the Brighouse and Rastrick Temperance Brass and Reed Band, and for many years its members had to sign the pledge, buy their own uniform and contribute 6d a week. In 1881 the reeds were discarded and it became the Brighouse and Rastrick Temperance Brass Band. They were soon taking part in the increasingly popular competitions and won their first prize at the Liverpool International Exhibition in 1885. It is interesting to note that the conductor at the time, Harry Hodgson—who was with the band from approximately 1882 to 1906, was a publican who kept the Rock Tavern at Elland Upper Edge—still a thriving public house. He was succeeded by Arthur O. Pearce 1906 to 1913 (who was to conduct the Black Dyke Mills Band from 1912 to 1949); J.C. Dyson 1913 to 1918. They became well-known in the contest world, winning prizes all over the country, and, on their first visit to the Crystal Palace in 1913 won fifth place in the championship section. The conductor from 1918 to 1924 was W. Wood followed in 1924 by Fred Berry who was to lead the band to some of its finest successes. In 1928, the year they finally changed their name to the Brighouse & Rastrick Band, they won seven first prizes, six seconds and one third, receiving over £150 in cash. They won the then important contest at Hawes in 1928, then in 1929 first won the Grand Shield in Belle Vue in July, and, at last, the British

The Brighouse & Rastrick Band.

Open in September, wresting it from Fodens who had just completed a hat-trick.

Then came their own hat-trick in 1932, 1933 and 1934—they were then barred in 1935 but came back to win again in 1936. These latter successes were under the professional conductorship of the well-known William Halliwell. In 1938 the resident bandmaster was Milnes Wood who resigned in 1941 when Fred Berry returned and Harry Mortimer was engaged as professional conductor. He had to relinquish the task in 1943 and Eric Ball accepted the position in 1944. Under him they were fourth in the National in 1945 and won the great honour in 1946. Eric Ball continued to conduct them until 1953, gaining many prizes and they were now well established as one of the top bands in the country. Fred Berry resigned in 1949 and J. Harrison became bandmaster from 1949 to 1953. In 1953 Alex Mortimer took on the conductorship until 1955; W. Wood 1956-59; Trevor Walmsley 1959-63; William Hargreaves 1963-73 (un-der whom they won the National Championship, World Championship and BBC Band of the Year award 1968, and the National Championship in 1969). In 1973, now under James Scott, they won the National yet again. In 1975 Derek Broadbent became resident Musical Director and they were Granada Band of the Year. Conductors since then have included Maurice Hanford, Lieutenant Colonel George E. Evans and Geoffrey Brand who led them to their great triumph in 1977 when their recording of *The Floral Dance* reached No 2 in the Pop charts —leading to several appearances on TV.

Selected LP Recordings

Bandstand—PVK PVM5 (78). *Oliver Cromwell* (Geehl) **23, 46**; *Sinfonietta* (Leidzen) **55**; *Finale for Band* (Smith); *Trumpet Tune* (Clarke, arr Gay); *Trombone Galop* (Clark). c Walter Hargreaves

Barwick Green—Columbia TW0253 (69),

EMI NTS147 (78). *Barwick Green* (Wood); *A North Countrie Fantasy* (Langford); *The Dover Coach* (Vinter); *The Forsyte Saga— Theme* (Coates, arr Street); *Cornish Cavalier* (Moyle); *Entry of the Gladiators* (Fucik, arr Moyle); *Trojan March* (Berlioz, arr Langford); *Caprice and Variations on a Theme by Arban* (Hargreaves); *The Buccaneer* (Osgood); *French Military March* (Saint-Saens, arr Hargreaves). c Walter Hargreaves

Blooming   Brass—Pye   GGL0372, GSGL10372 (66). *The Standard of St. George* (Alford); *B.B. & C.F.* (Hume); *Punchinello* (W. Rimmer); *The Cossack* (W. Rimmer); *Radetszky March* (J. Strauss I, arr Gay); *High Command; West Riding; The Severn Suite* (Elgar) **30**; *Marche Slave* (Tchaikovsky, arr Davies). c Walter Hargreaves

Brass   Accolade—Music   for   Pleasure MFP50112 (74). *Brass Accolade* (Brien); *Ruy Blas* (Mendelssohn, arr Langford); *The Gypsy Trumpeter* (Smith); *Three Dale Dances* (Wood); *Fearnought* (Wright); *Royal Fireworks Music—Minuet* (Handel, arr Wright); *Spartacus—Theme* (Khachaturian, arr Siebert); *Carribean Cameo—Suite* (Sharpe); *The Headless Horseman—Theme* (Goodwin); *Supreme March* (Barraclough). c Harry Brennan & Major Desmond Walker

Brass from Brighouse—Pye GGL0407, GSGL10407 (68). *Russlan and Ludmilla— Overture* (Glinka, arr Hargreaves); *The Barber of Seville—Una voce poco fa* (Rossini); *On the Cornish Coast* (Geehl, arr W. Rimmer) **24, 48**; *Variations on 'Jenny Jones'* (Geehl); *Belmont Variations* (Bliss) **63**; *Horn Concerto No.1—Rondo* (Mozart); *Peace and War* (Douglas). c Walter Hargreaves

The Brighouse & Rastrick Band— Polydor   583047   (69).   *Calder*   (W. Rimmer); *La Gioconda—Dance of the Hours* (Ponchielli, arr D. Rimmer); *La Golondrina* (Serradell, arr Siebert); *Morning, Noon and Night in Vienna* (Suppé, arr Hawkins); *Le Prophète—Coronation March* (Meyerbeer, arr Rimmer); *Long, long ago* (arr Boddington); *The Mastersingers—Prelude* (Wagner, arr F. Wright). c Walter Hargreaves

The Brighouse & Rastrick Band—Transatlantic   XTRA1160   (76),   Pickwick SHM961 (79)†. *Wellington March* (Zahle); *Summertime* (Gershwin); *The Floral Dance* (Moss, arr Broadbent); *Delicado* (Azevedo); *The Girl with the Flaxen Hair* (Debussy); *The Planets—Mars* (Holst); *Round the Clock* (Osgood); *Une Vie de Matelot* (Far-

non) **75**; *Checkmate—Ceremony of the Red Bishops & Finale* (Bliss, arr Ball) **78**. c James Scott

Champion Brass—Music for Pleasure MFP5190 (71). *The Battle of Britain* (Goodwin arr Walker); *Sinfonietta* (Leidzen) **55**; *Trumpet Tune and Ayre* (Purcell, arr Taylor); *Finale for Band* (Smith, arr Cornthwaite); *Farnham Town* (Bayce, arr Walker); *Trombone Galop* (Clark, arr Howe); *Oliver Cromwell* (Geehl) **23, 46**. c Walter Hargreaves

The Champions Remember—Grosvenor GRS1023 (74)†. *The Yeomen of the Guard— Overture* (Sullivan, arr Sargent); *The Acrobat* (Greenwood); *Melodies from 'The Merry Widow'* (Lehár, arr Douglas); *Tannhauser— Grand March* (Wagner, arr W. Rimmer); *The Stars and Stripes Forever* (Sousa); *In a Monastery Garden* (Ketelbey); *Babes in Toyland—March of the Toys* (Herbert, arr Mackenzie); *Nabucco—Overture* (Verdi, arr W. Rimmer). c James Scott

The Floral Dance—Logo 1001 (77), cass KLOGO1001†. *The Lincolnshire Poacher; Lara's Theme; Tiajuana Tuba; Zambesi; Solitaire; The Floral Dance; Bachelor Girls; Try to Remember; African Waltz; Scarborough Fair; Theme from 'Shaft'; Strawberry Fair.* c Derek Broadbent

Love You a Little Bit More—Logo 1006 (78), cass KLOGO1006†. *Tenderly; Don't take your love from me; When I fall in love; So very close to me; Love you a little bit more; She was beautiful; I'm in the mood for love; Twelfth of Never; Missing you; Misty; Till there was you; How deep is the ocean.* c Derek Broadbent

The Lusher Side of Brighouse— Grosvenor   GRS1050   (77)†.   *Concert Variations* (Lusher); *Cornets a-go-go* (Broadbent); *Almost a Lullaby* (Farnon); *Harlem Nocturne* (Hagen, arr Siebert); *Battle Hymn of the Republic* (arr Broadbent); *Making Whoopee* (Donaldson, arr Lusher); *In the wee small hours of the morning* (Mann; Hilliard, arr Broadbent); *Phil the Fluter's Ball* (French, arr Broadbent); *The Trombone Men* (Lusher); *Mood Indigo* (Ellington, arr Siebert); *The Typewriter* (Anderson, arr Lusher) (with Don Lusher—trombone). c Derek Broadbent

Mosaic for Band (The World of Brass Band Classics)—Grosvenor GRS1035 (75), Decca SPA545, cass KCSP545 (79)†· *Provence* (Kelly); *Chanson de Matin* (Elgar, arr D. Wright); *Concerto for Trombone and Brass—Passacaglia* (Orr); *Suite Gothique—Toccata* (Boellmann, arr Ball); *Mosaic* (Howarth); *Solemn Melody* (Davies, arr D. Wright); *L'Arlésienne—Farandole* (Bizet, arr D. Wright) (with Harold Nash—trombone). c James Scott

Sounds of Brass, Vol.12—Decca SB312 (74)†. *Prelude for an Occasion* (Gregson); *The Accursed Huntsman* (Franck, arr Siebert) *73*; *Scherzo* (Boekel); *The Corsair—Overture* (Berlioz, arr Brand); *Freedom* (Bath) **22, 47, 73**. c James Scott
Also:
Brighouse & Rastrick—Logo MOGO4003, cass KMOGO4003 (79)†.
Music—Logo MOGO4004, cass KMOGO-4004 (79)†.

The Cambridge Band (1900)
Formed in 1900, the Cambridge Band has worked under various titles but has established itself most firmly under the present title under which it has nobly served the community from which it takes its name. It has had some distinguished directors, notably C.B. Mott. By winning the Second Section Champion Band title in the London and Southern Region Finals in 1975 the band qualified to be upgraded to Championship status. Doing well at the National Finals in London, they then won the 1979 Championship Section of the London and Southern Counties Regional Finals and qualified for contention for the title of Champion Band of Great Britain. The band has built up a good reputation as a concert band, has been featured regularly on Radio and participated in the 1979 TV series *The Best of Brass*. David Read was appointed Music Director in 1974 and had a marked effect on band standards, following his experience with the Carlton Main Frickley Colliery Band and his long service as principal cornet with the GUS (Kettering) Band. He also teaches brass playing in the Huntingdon and Peterborough area and is in demand as an adjudicator.
LP recordings
The Cambridge Band—Pye TB3020 (80). *El Matador* (Zutano); *Where e'er you walk* (Handel); *Processional March* (Carse); *Meditation in the Cloisters* (Barsotti); *Holiday Overture* (Ball); *Entry of the Gladiators* (Fucik); *Waltz Memories of Schubert* (arr Ball); *'La Traviata'—Prelude* (Verdi, arr D.

Rimmer); *A Trumpet Piece* (Scull, arr D. Wright); *Coppélia—Selection* (Delibes, arr Bidgood). c David Read

Carlton Main Frickley Colliery Band
Formed in the 1890s, the band gradually reached championship standards and won the British Open in 1922. They really came to the fore as a top band from about 1957. They were the British Open Champions in 1958 and runners-up in 1957, 1959, 1969 and 1972. Also in 1958, they were third in the National Championships and runners-up in 1959 and 1960. They were the mineworkers National Championship winners in 1962, 1963 and 1966 and Yorkshire Champions in 1970. Since then they have undertaken several European tours. The Director of the Band from 1954 to 1970 was Jack Atherton and since 1970 it has been Robert Oughton. They were the 1978 Granada Band of the Year.
Selected LP Recordings
Banding with Ball—Amberlee ABL401 (74). *Sure and Steadfast—March; The Passing Years; Resurgam 50; Country Fair; By the Cool Waters; Prelude to Pageantry; Conchita; Akhnaton; Rosslyn March; Free Fantasia* (Ball). c Robert Oughton
Brass in Contrast—Polydor 583 071 (70), 2928 002 (71). *La Russe* (W. Rimmer); *Plaisir d'amour* (Martini, arr D. Rimmer); *El Matador* (Zutano, arr D. Rimmer); *Passion Chorale* (Bach, arr Steadman-Allen); *Fanfare and Miniature Suite* (Barratt); *Di Ballo—Overture* (Sullivan, arr Owenson); *Windows of Paris* (Osborne, arr Siebert); *The Flying Dutchman—Prelude* (Wagner, arr D. Rimmer) **09**; *Whitburn* (arr Steadman-Allen); *American Patrol* (Miller, arr Owenson). c Jack Atherton
Labour and Love—Grosvenor GRS1020 (73)†. *The Arcadians—Overture* (Monckton; Talbot, arr Wood); *Fire-Star Polka* (Carter); *Hyfrydol* (Pritchard, arr Steadman-Allen); *Labour and Love* (Fletcher) **13**; *Nibelungen March* (Wagner, arr Grant); *Aurelia* (Wesley, arr Steadman-Allen); *The Fair Maid of Perth—Romance* (Bizet, arr Oughton); *To a wild rose* (MacDowell, arr Ball); *Funeral March for a Marionette* (Gounod, arr Wright); *Cornet Carillon* (Binge); *Mephistopheles Contest March* (Douglas). c Robert Oughton & Bram Gay
Life Divine—Grosvenor GRS1043 (77)†.

The B.B. & C.F. (Hume); *Land of the Mountain and the Flood* (McCunn, arr Bragg); *Shylock Polka* (Lear); *Bobby's Tune* (arr Bolton/Banks); *Sunset* (Green); *Les Millions d'Arlequins—Serenade* (Drigo); *St. Clement's* (Scholefield, arr Wright & Round); *Life Divine* (Jenkins) **21**. c Robert Oughton
Salute to Richard Rodgers—Polydor 2485 009 (71). *Music from: The Valiant Years; Carousel; the Sound of Music; Oklahoma; Circus on Parade; South Pacific; The King and I.* c Robert Oughton
The Sound of Brass and Voices—Polydor 2460 237 (75). *Invincible* (Hawkins); *Fatherland* (Hartmann); *St Theodulph* (Teschner); *John Gilpin's Ride* (Siebert); *Quo Vadis* (Rimmer); *Faust—Soldiers' Chorus* (Gounod); *Go Down Moses* (anon); *Nobody knows the trouble I've seen* (anon); *The Dambusters* (Coates]; *The Lord's Prayer* (Malotte); *Merrie England—The Yeomen of England* (German) (with the West Mercia Men's Chorus & Harvey Boucher). c Robert Oughton
Sounds of Brass, Vol.39—Decca SB339 (79), cass KBSC339. *Signature March, F.C.B.* (Badrick); *Fingal's Cave Overture* (Mendelssohn, arr Thompson); *Serenade for Trombone* (Golland); *Masquerade—Waltz* (Khachaturian, arr Johnson); *Hunting Polka* (J. Strauss, arr Bragg); *Caractacus—Processional March* (Elgar, arr Bragg); *Gay Gnu Galop* (Barsotti); *Streets of London* (McTell, arr Ashmore); *Epic Theme* (Golland). c David James
Sovereign Brass—Pye TB3007 (76). *Holiday Overture* (Ball); *Concerto for Horn* (Kenney); *Shrewsbury Fair* (Neville); *Star of Erin* (Horobin); *Venemair* (Weston); *King Lear* (D. Rimmer); *Mors et Vita—Judex* (Gounod, arr F. Wright). c Major H.A. Kenney
Top Brass—Pye TB3022 (80)†. *Mephistopheles—March* (Douglas); *Faust—Finale* (Gounod, arr Woodfield); *Love Story—Theme* (Lai, arr Bragg); *Carnaval de Venice* (W. Rimmer); *Hava Nagila* (arr Woodfield); *Procession of the Nobles* (Rimsky-Korsakov, arr Ashmore); *Troublemaker* (Davis); *Concerto for French Horn and Brass Band* (Gregson)—soloist: Michael Thompson; *Slavonic Dance No.8* (Dvorák, arr Hanmer). c David James

City of Coventry Band (1939)

The band was formed in 1939 and has always had an impressive record of successes in competitions at Championship Grade level. It was placed first on three occasions at the Edinburgh Festival from 1965-7. In 1968 and 1969 it was runner-up in the BBC Band of the Year Competition which it won in 1972. The band has been well placed at the National and British Open Championships and in various Regional Contests. In 1964 it was the first band to tour Eastern Europe, making a nine-day visit to Czechoslovakia where it recorded and gave concerts with the Czechoslovak Army Band. There is also a junior band which gives experience to young players before they join the senior ensemble. The band has made over 300 broadcasts and gives regular concerts. Its Music Director from 1973-1976 was Albert Chappell who was succeeded by Keneth Dennison.

LP recordings

The City of Coventry Band in a Celebration of its 40th Anniversary—Pye TB3019 (80). *Fest Musik der Stadt Wien* (R. Strauss); *The Watermill* (Binge); *Mexican March* (Rosas, arr Barsotti); *The Lark in the Clear Air* (arr Langford); *Gopak* (Mussorgsky, arr Siebert); *Symphonic Study for Brass—The Line of Life* (Jacob); *Blaze of Light* (Elms); *The Swan* (Saint-Saëns); *March of the Toys* (Herbert, arr Hanmer); *Concierto de Aranjuez—Adagio* (Rodrigo, arr Bolton); *Solveig's Song & Anitra's Dance* (Grieg, arr Hanmer); *Toccata Marziale* (Vaughan Williams, arr Dennison). c Kenneth Dennison
In Concert—Grosvenor GRS1053 (77). *The Spirit of Pageantry* (Fletcher); *If* (Gates, arr Ashmore); *Capriccio Espagnol—Fandango Asturiana* (Rimsky-Korsakov, arr Dennison); *Zelda* (Code); *March of the Pacemakers* (Langford); *Overture for an Epic Occasion* (D. Wright) **45**; *Believe me if all those endearing young charms* (arr Manta); *Karelia Suite—Intermezzo* (Sibelius, arr Dennison); *Fanfare and Soliloquy* (Sharpe). c Kenneth Dennison
Sounds of Brass, Vol.7—Decca SB307 (73)†. *The President* (German); *Carmen—Suite* (Bizet, arr Wright); *Romanza* (Geehl); *The Mikado—Selection* (Sullivan, arr Sargent); *Prince Igor—Overture* (Borodin, arr Barsotti); *Men of Harlech* (German, arr Wright); *Bobbie Shaftoe* (arr Maddison); *Love Song* (Beethoven, arr Bebb); *Creation's Hymn* (Beethoven, arr Bebb). c Albert Chappell
Sounds of Brass, Vol.15—Decca SB315

(74). *City of Coventry Band* (Wood); *Yeomen of the Guard—Overture* (Sullivan, arr Sargent); *Concerto for Cornet* (D. Wright); *Variations for Brass Band* (Haysom); *The Algerian Suite—French Military March* (Saint-Saëns, arr Hargreaves); *Rococo Variations on a Theme by Tchaikovsky* (Street); *Swan Lake—Excerpts* (Tchaikovsky, arr D. Wright); *Minuet* (Paderewski, arr F. Wright). c Albert Chappell

Sounds of Brass, Vol.32—Decca SB332 (78)†. *Trumpet Spectacular* (Binge); *Dubinushka* (Rimsky-Korsakov, arr Dennison); *Love's Enchantment* (Pryor, arr Dennison); *New World Symphony—extracts* (Dvorák, arr Rimmer); *Tintagel* (D. Wright); *Bell Bird Polka* (Barsotti); *Sundown* (Barsotti); *Marche Héroïque* (Saint-Saëns, arr Dennison). c Kenneth Dennison

City of Oxford Youth Band (1968)

One of three bands (Senior, Youth and Junior) belonging to the City of Oxford Silver Band Organisation. Now plays in the top section of the Oxford and District Brass Band Association. Their conductor, Terry Brotherhood, is from a dedicated brass playing family and is principal cornet in the senior band. The Youth Band were the 1975-6 National Youth Band Champions for London and Southern Regions. World Record Holders for Non-Stop Playing (28 hours, 45 minutes—see *The Guinness Book of Records*). Several of their members are in the National Youth Brass Band. They have made many European tours and a Concert Tour of America in 1976, and have appeared on radio and TV.

LP recording

City of Oxford Youth Band—Rediffusion 15-56 (77). *Hawaiian Hoe-down* (Siebert); *Alpine Echoes* (Windsor); *Melody in F* (Rubinstein, arr Ball); *Little Suite No.2* (Arnold); *Bi-Centenary USA* (Alder); *Stephen Foster Fantasy* (arr Hanmer); *Air and Rondo* (Heath); *High Spirits* (Heath); *Our American Cousins* (Catelinet). c Terry Brotherhood

The Cory Band (1884)

Originally known as the Ton Temperance Band (Ton is a small village near Pentre) the band became associated with the Cory Brothers Workmen's Band and shortened its name to the present title when the mine closed in 1971. Between 1948 and 1950 the band began to achieve true championship status and gained runner-up prizes at both the National and British Open Championships. When Major H. Arthur Kenney became its conductor in 1970 the band moved into a winning streak, beginning with the National Mineworkers Championship 1970, 1971, 1972 and 1974 and reaching a historical peak when it became in 1974 the first Welsh band (and only the second not from the north of England) to win the National Championship since it began in 1900. Playing Malcolm Arnold's *Fantasy for Brass Band* against such stern competition as the Grimethorpe, Black Dyke Mills, GUS and the defending champions Brighouse & Rastrick, they brought joy to the Rhondda by their well-earned triumph. They were also Granada Band of the Year in 1971. The band made a notable bicentennial tour of America in 1976 under the direction of Bram Gay. Since 1978 the musical director has been Denzil S. Stephens.

Selected LP recordings

American Express—Xtra XTRA1169 (77). *Liberty Bell* (Sousa); *Glory, Glory* (trad); *Music from the Elizabethan Court* (Bull/Byrd, arr Howarth); *Iolanthe—Overture* (Sullivan, arr Sargent); *The Magic Flute—Overture* (Mozart, arr Dent); *All through the night* (arr Langford); *El Cumbanchero*. c Bram Gay

Listen to the Band No.5—Music for Pleasure MFP1313 (69). *Cross of Honour* (W. Rimmer); *Men of Harlech* (German, arr Wright); *Intermezzo in C* (Coleridge-Taylor); *Besses o' th' Barn* (Carrie); *French Comedy Overture* (Keler-Bela, arr F. Wright); *Fiorella* (Siebert); *Gold and Silver Waltz* (Lehár); *Arabella* (Chester). c John Harrison

Pride of the Rhondda—EMI 'One Up' OU2165 (77). *Maple Leaf Rag* (Joplin, arr Bryce); *The Land of the Mountain and the Flood* (McCunn, arr Bragg); *Albertie* (Stephens); *Music Hall Suite—Les Girls* (Horovitz, arr Gay); *Sweet Gingerbread Man* (Legrand, arr Banks); *The Magnificent Seven* (E. Bernstein, arr Stephens); *The Guns of Navarone* (Tiomkin, arr Woodfield); *The Black Domino—Overture* (Auber, arr W. Rimmer) *12*; *Il Silenzio* (Celeste; Brezza, arr Siebert); *The Prince of Denmark's March* (Clarke, arr Gay); *The Virginian Theme* (Faith); *Miller Magic* (arr Stephens). c Bram Gay & Denzil S. Stephens

*Salute to the New World—Grosvenor GRS1052 (77)†. *Rule Britannia Overture* (W. Rimmer); *Chorale and Rock-Out* (Huggens); *An Epic Symphony—Elegy* (Fletcher); *Dashing away with the smoothing iron* (arr D. Wright); *Manhattan Beach* (Sousa); *Jeannie* (Foster, arr Howarth); *Marche des Bouffons* (Picon); *New World Symphony—Largo* (Dvořák, arr D. Wright); *Fantasia on the Dargason* (Holst). c Bram Gay

Sounds of Brass, Vol.19—Decca SB319 (75)†. *Fantasy for Brass Band* (Arnold) **74**; *A Cotswold Lullaby* (Watters); *Carambina* (Hughes); *Allegro Preciso* (Mozart, arr Siebert); *Waltz with a Beat* (Hanmer); *Latin-Americana* (arr Hanmer); *Hootenanny* (arr Watters); *Slavonic Dance No.3* (Dvořák, arr Hanmer); *Believe me if all those endearing young charms* (arr Langford); *The Marriage of Figaro—Overture* (Mozart, arr Hazelgrove). c Major H. Arthur Kenney

Sounds of Brass, Vol.40—Decca SB340, cass KBSC340 (79)†. *Aces High* (Stephens); *Myfanwy (Arabella)* (arr Stephens); *Rule Britannia* (Hartmann, arr Stephens); *Symphony of Marches* (Vinter); *March, Opus 99* (Prokofiev, arr Stephens); *Y Deryn Pur (Pure Bird)* (arr Stephens); *The Blue and the Gray—a Civil War Suite* (Grundman); *Miller Moods: Tuxedo Junction* (Hawkins; Johnson; Dash; Feyne, arr Stephens); *Londonderry Air* (arr Stephens); *Pennsylvania 6-5000* (Gray; Sigman, arr Stephens); *Anvil Chorus* (Verdi, arr Gray & Stephens). c Denzil S. Stephens

Trumpets Wild—Polydor 2485 014 (71). *The Spaceman* (Powell); *Escapada* (Phillips, arr D. Wright); *Menuet* (Boccherini, arr Hawkins); *Calon Lan* (arr Kenney); *Bombastic Bombardon* (Siebert); *Land of Song Fantasia* (Parrott); *St. Julian* (Kenney); *Spanish Serenade* (Zutano, arr D. Rimmer); *Trumpets Wild* (Walter); *Sinfonietta for Brass Band* (Leidzen) **55**. c Major H. Arthur Kenney

Creswell Colliery Band (1899)

The band was formed in the Nottinghamshire village of Creswell, near the Derbyshire border, in January 1899 by a group of miners from the colliery. They raised their status to championship class and appeared many times at Belle Vue and the Albert Hall, winning the British Open Championship in 1925. They regularly broadcast and made their first gramophone record in 1930

Selected LP recordings

Brass and Voices—Paxton LPR203. *Creswell Crags* (Moss); *The Student Prince—Drinking Song* (Romberg, arr Rapport); *Forgotten Dreams* (Anderson, arr Woodhouse); *Rollin' the Stone Away* (arr Alexander & Falconer); *Il Trovatore—Prison scene* (Verdi, arr W. Rimmer); *South Pacific—There is nothing like a dame* (Rodgers, arr Stickles); *The Desert Song—Riff Song* (Romberg, arr Rapport); *Crystal Waltz* (Portengen, arr Siebert); *Eriskay Love Lilt* (Kennedy-Fraser, arr Roberton); *Trumpet Blues and Cantabile* (Reader); *Irgendwo* (arr Falconer); *Oh, Mary don't you weep* (arr Rhea); *Deep Harmony* (Parker, arr Greenwood). (with the Bestwood Male Voice Choir). c Ernest Woodhouse

Brass in Rhythm—Paxton (45) PEP128 (65). *Dixieland Stomp* (Lawrenson); *Brass Band Bounce* (Siebert); *Butterfly Boogie* (Falconer); *Hawaiian Samba* (Siebert). c Ernest Woodhouse

CWS (Manchester) Band (1900)

The band was started by a group of employees of the CWS Tobacco Factory (founded 1863) in Manchester in 1900; and it grew alongside the CWS expansion of the 1900s. In 1946 the band was completely reorganised and took on its present name; since when, with steady support from the CWS directors, it has risen to championship level and become well-known for its concerts throughout the British Isles. Much of its success in the 1950s was due to the inspiration of Alex Mortimer who was appointed musical director in 1954 and retired from active conductorship in 1970 to become the band's Musical Advisor, still maintaining a great interest in its affairs and still conducting on special occasions. In 1972, Derek Garside, principal cornet for 25 years, was appointed Musical Director. The band has a long history of radio and television appearances and has made over 15 LP recordings. Its competition successes include two National Championships in 1962 and 1963— and many times runner-up, four British Open Championships in 1948, 1952, 1960 and 1966; and North West Area Champions more than a dozen times.

Selected LP recordings

Brass Bounty—Fontana TFL5121, STFL547 (61). *The Barber of Seville—Overture* (Rossini); *All in the April evening* (arr Roberton); *Imperial Echoes* (Safroni); *Facilita* (Hartmann); *English Folk Song Suite* (Vaughan Williams, arr F. Wright); *Dambusters March* (Coates); *Prometheus Unbound* (Bantock) **33**; *Pomp and Circumstance March No.4* (Elgar, arr Hume); *Serenade No.1* (Heykens); *Nightfall in Camp* (Pope). c Alex Mortimer

Champion Brass—Fontana FJ507 (63) (68). *Marching Trumpets* (Seymour); *Tintagel—Two Arthurian Sketches* (D. Wright); *Cavalier* (Sutton); *Suite No.1 in E flat* (Holst); *The Flyer* (Ridewood); *Bells Across the Meadow* (Ketelbey); *Pandora* (Damare); *Hungarian Rhapsody No.2* (Liszt, arr W. Rimmer). c Alex Mortimer

CWS Band—Fontana LPS16256 (69). *Journey Into Freedom* (Ball) **67**; *Le Carnaval Romain—Overture* (Berlioz, arr F. Wright) **66**; *High Spirits* (Heath); *Les Préludes* (Liszt, arr W. Rimmer); *The Three Trumpeters* (Agostini). c Alex Mortimer

CWS Band—Fontana STL5480 (69). *Finlandia* (Sibelius, arr Bidgood); *Themes from Symphony No.5* (Beethoven, arr F. Wright); *Panis Angelicus* (Franck); *The Barber of Seville—Una voce poco fa* (Rossini); *William Tell—Ballet Music* (Rossini). c Alex Mortimer

CWS Band—Fontana TFL5066 (59); STFL509 (60). *Coriolanus* (Jenkins) **20**; *The Magic Flute—Overture* (Mozart, arr D. Rimmer); *Life Divine* (Jenkins) **21**; *A Sunset Rhapsody* (Ball); etc. c Alex Mortimer

CWS Band—Fontana TFL5158, STFL576 (61). *Fantasia in F minor* (Mozart, arr Sargent); *Oliver Cromwell* (Geehl) **23**; *The Mill on the Cliff* (Reissiger); *Little Serenade* (Tomlinson); *Spanish Gypsy Dance* (Marquina, arr Dawson); *Miss Melanie; La Belle Americaine* (Hartmann); *The Valiant Years—Theme* (Rodgers); *Two Grotesques—Balletomaine & Marche des Buffons* (Picon). c Alex Mortimer

Fanfare and Soliloquy—Fontana TL5452, STL5452 (68). *Summit March* (Seymour); *Fanfare and Soliloquy* (Sharpe); *Festival Music* (Ball) **56**; *Radetzky March* (J. Strauss I, arr Ryan); *The Severn Suite* (Elgar) **30**. c Alex Mortimer

Highlights of Gilbert and Sullivan—Fontana FJL508 (63) (68), cass CFP4004. *Pineapple Poll* (Sullivan/Mackerras, arr Gregory); *The Mikado—Selection* (Sullivan, arr Sargent); *Iolanthe—Selection* (Sullivan, arr Dawson); *Patience—Selection* (Sullivan, arr D. Wright); *H.M.S. Pinafore—Overture* (Sullivan, arr D. Rimmer); *The Yeomen of the Guard—Selection* (Sullivan, arr D. Wright). c Alex Mortimer

Music for Brass—Paxton (45) PEP125 (57). *Over the Sticks; A Woolly Tale; The*

Falcons; March of the Herald. c Alex Mortimer

Music for Brass—Paxton (45) PEP130 (57). *Dancing Clown* (Crossman); *Honeymoon Express* (Hanley; Field); *The Enchanted Garden* (Rayner); *Shaggy Dog* (Jones). c Alex Mortimer

National Champions—Fontana TL5199, STL5199 (63). *1812 Overture* (Tchaikovsky, arr D. Wright); *Spring (Elegaic Melody, Op.34/2)* (Grieg, arr Ryan); *Simon Called Peter* (Vinter); *Introduction and Allegro* (Senaillé, arr D. Wright); *La Forza Del Destino—Overture* (Verdi, arr F. Wright) **62**. c Alex Mortimer

Rhapsody in Brass—Fontana TFL5108, STFL537 (60). *Niebelungen March* (Wagner, arr Grant); *Two Grotesques—Balletomaine & Marche des Bouffoons; Tom O'Shanter's Ride* (D. Wright); *Trumpet Voluntary* (Clarke, arr Gay); *Rhapsody in Brass* (Goffin); *Cossack Patrol* (Rose); *Bugler's Holiday* (Anderson); *The Legionnaires; Jerusalem* (Parry, arr Langford). c Alex Mortimer

Salute to Youth—Fontana 680988, 886155 (62). *Zampa—Overture* (Hérold, arr W. Rimmer); *Horn Concerto No.4 in E flat—Rondo* (Mozart, arr D. Wright); *Salute to Youth* (Vinter); *Ballet Russe—Themes* (Luigini, arr Helyer); *Angels guard Thee* (Godard, arr Ball); *An Epic Symphony* (Fletcher) **26**. c Alex Mortimer

Sounds of Brass, Vol.9—Decca SB309 (74)†. *Thundercrest* (Osterling); *Serenade* (Haydn); *Plaisir d'amour* (Martini, arr Rimmer); *Night on the Bare Mountain* (Mussorgsky, arr Hurst); *Crown Imperial* (Walton, arr Wright); *Nights of Gladness* (Ancliffe); *Preludes Nos.7 & 20* (Chopin, arr Sargent); *The Nightingale* (Moss); *Rule Britannia Overture* (Arne, arr W. Rimmer). c Alex Mortimer & Derek M. Garside

This is Brass—Fontana TFL5096, STFL529 (60). *Light Cavalry—Overture* (Suppé); *Cleapatra* (Damare); *Czech Polka* (Strauss); *Resurgam* (Ball) **50**; *Slavonic Rhapsody No.2* (Friedemann, arr D. Wright); *Robin Adair* (Hartmann); *The Frogs—Overture* (Bantock, arr F. Wright) **52**; *Cornet Carillon* (Binge). c Alex Mortimer

Desford Colliery Welfare Band (1898)

The Desford Band was founded in 1898 by George Underwood and his son James as the Ibstock United Band. A photo of 1902 shows a nucleus of 17 players and by 1909 they had their first band-room on a site behind the Ram Inn in Ibstock. They engaged Albert Lawton as their first professional Musical Director in 1912 and acquired their first full set of Boosey & Hawkes instruments in 1913. Most of the band (including Tommy Underwood, son of James, still alive aged 83 in 1980) served in the war, and returned to make the Desford Band one of the most successful in the Midlands by 1919. With Albert Lawton at the helm they won many local contests and when he died in 1928, Tommy Underwood then became its Musical Director. It had gained a high reputation by 1937 and included a young cornet player, James Scott, in its ranks. The second World War deprived the band of many of its members and it never really recovered until 1956 when new instruments were supplied by the Coal industries Social Welfare Organisation and the band was logically adopted by the colliery, as most of its members were miners, and became the Desford Colliery Welfare Band. From 1956-63 the Musical Director was J. Measures, from 1963-6 William Brotherhood who built up the new band and trained young players. From 1967-9 Bernard Springett took over and led the band to championship status, and was succeeded by Ernest Woodhouse in

1969 when it made its first LP recordings and started to broadcast. In 1976 Albert Chappell became Musical Director and saw them become National Coal Board Midland Champions and Midland Area Champions in 1976 and 1977 and National Coal Board Champions in 1977. The newest musical director from July 1978 is Howard Snell. The band is actively supported and sponsored by Dowty Mining Equipment Ltd.

Selected LP recordings

Sounds of Brass, Vol.28—Decca SB328 (77)†. *The Seventies Set* (Langford); *Concerto for Trumpet and Brass Band* (Wood); *Portuguese Party* (Vinter, arr Barsotti); *Morning Rhapsody* (Ball); *Aida—Grand March* (Verdi, arr D. Wright); *The Magic Flute—Overture* (Mozart, arr D. Rimmer); *If* (Gates, arr Ashmore); *Slavonic Rhapsody No.1* (Friedemann). c Albert Chappell

Sounds of Brass, Vol.35 (Something Old, Something New)—Decca SB335 (79)†: *Fanfare for the Common Man* (Copland, arr Snell); *Zampa—Overture* (Hérold, arr Hartmann); *A Requiem Chorus* (Verdi, arr Douglas); *Feelings* (Albert, arr Ashmore); *Don Quixote—Suite* (Telemann, arr Snell); *Exhibition Can-Can* (Snell); *Who pays the ferryman* (Markopoulos, arr Peberdy); *Zelda—Caprice* (Code); *Finlandia, Op.26* (Sibelius, arr Bidgood). c Howard Snell

An early photograph of the Desford Colliery Welfare Band in 1902.

Also:
Desford Conquest—Pye GSGL10501
Viva Desford—Pye TB3002.

Dobcross Band (1875)

The Dobcross Band comes from the very heart of the traditional brass band country. Dobcross is a large village in Yorkshire but only just over the Lancashire border and its postal address is Oldham, hence the band's badge of a rose with alternate white and red petals. With several other villages bearing such intriguing names as Delph, Diggle and Denshaw among others it forms part of the administrative district of Saddleworth. Although a receipt for £5 made out to 'The late Dobcross Amateur Band' and dated 1875 reveals that there must have been an earlier band, 1875 is regarded as the date of birth of the present band and its centenary was commemorated in 1975 by a highly entertaining history written by Henry Livings, well known as a playwright and for his BBC *Northern Drift* programmes, who has long been intimately associated with the band.

It seems to have had a chequered career like many other old established bands. At the beginning of the 1970s it was very near to folding up but in 1972 a young man called Peter Watson was engaged as the Musical Director. He had much musical knowledge and great enthusiasm, but very little brass band experience. With no outside help from any other professional conductor he succeeded in raising the band to a standard which entitles it to compete in the championship class at the 1980 National Championship.

There are many tales about the doings at Dobcross. A favourite is that of a well-known member of the band called Eddie Taylor who is said to have weighed 17 stones. Once he slipped a disc and was confined to bed. A fellow member of the band called to see how he was getting on and, on being conducted upstairs he found Taylor propped up in bed with pillows. His wife was holding the music up whilst he was practising on his double B flat bass.

Ever Ready (GB) Band (1926)

Formed in 1926 as the Craghead Colliery Band in County Durham it operated under this name until 1968 when the colliery was closed. Fortunately the band was able to continue under the patronage of the Ever Ready Co, and has remained in existence under this new banner. A top quality band, one of the finest in the north, it has had an impressive record as Northern Regional Champions from 1968-70 and 1972-8. Also, since 1963, it has been amongst the finalists in the National Championships on no less than 14 occasions. It makes frequent concert appearances and has a junior section of 30 players. Their Musical Director for a remarkable 27 years was E.W. Cunningham, succeeded in 1978 by R.J. Childs, long associated with the Tredegar Band. The band toured the continent in 1970.

Selected LP recordings

Sounds of Brass, Vol.29—Decca SB329 (77)†. *High Command* (Sampson); *Crimond* (arr Hargreaves); *Theme and Variations, Op.102* (Hummel); *Salute to Youth* (Vinter); *North Countrie Fantasy* (Langford); *Romanza* (Geehl); *The Severn Suite* (Elgar) **30**. c E.W. Cunningham

Sounds of Brass, Vol.34—Decca SB334 (79)†. *Robin Hood Suite—March of the Bowmen* (Curzon); *Cavalleria Rusticana—Selection* (Mascagni); *Xerxes—Largo* (Handel, arr Ball); *Thunder and Lightning Polka* (Strauss); *Neapolitan Suite for Brass* (Barsotti); *Russian Dance* (Ostarbohle, arr Heaton); *Concerto for Two Trumpets* (Vivaldi, arr Bryce); *Symphony No.5—Finale* (Tchaikovsky, arr Ball). c R.J. Childs

Stars of the North—Dansan DS017 (79). *Fest Musik der Stadt Wien* (R. Strauss, arr Banks); *Cushie Butterfield* (arr Langford); *The Lark in the Clear Air* (arr James; Banks); *Simon Called Peter* (Vinter); *Reflections for Brass* (James, arr Banks); *Hunting the Hare* (arr James; Banks); *Blaze of Light* (Elms, arr Banks); *Cock o' the North* (James, arr Banks); *Cavatina* (Myers, arr Bolton; Banks); *Homage March* (Grieg, arr Banks); *Sleepy Serenade* (Watters); *Star Wars* (Williams, arr Farr). c Eric Banks

Also:

Plays Patrick Moore—Pye TB3017 (79)†.

Excelsior Ropes Works Band (Mellingriffith Band)

The Mellingriffith Band traces its history to the early years of the century, gradually gaining status until its first known entry in the senior championship class in 1932. Since then it has been one of the leading Welsh bands, winning all the major prizes in the main Welsh contests and many successes in England and area representatives in the

National Championships on numerous occasions. Its progress and achievement was greatly due to the remarkably sustained leadership of Thomas James Powell (qv) who was appointed its Conductor in 1920 and was their Musical Director until his sudden death in January 1965. In 1967 the closure of the Mellingriffith Works left them without a sponsor and a somewhat bleak outlook, but they were officially adopted by Excelsior Ropes Ltd of Cardiff, and have continued under their sponsorship.

LP recording

Salute to Wales—Marble Arch MAL1139. *Caernarvon Castle* (Powell); *Castell Caerfilli* (Powell); *Famous Fragments from the Marches of W. Rimmer* (arr Hawkins); *Western Knights* (Bosanko); *Castell Coch* (Powell); *Faust—Soldiers' Chorus* (Gounod); *Castell Caerdydd* (Powell); *Devil's Kitchen* (Hughes); *The Contestor* (Powell); *Silver Trumpets* (Viviani, arr Hume); *The Gay Hussar* (Powell); *Salute to Wales* (Powell). c David Thomas

Fairey (Engineering Works) Band (1937)

The band was formed at the Fairey Aviation Works, Heaton Chapel, Stockport in 1937. Well organised from the start and in established brass band country with a good supply of musicians, it had reached championship status as early as 1938 and the Fairey Aviation Band, as it was then usually known, soon took its place amongst the great bands in brass band history. By 1972 it had completed a dozen successes as the British Open Champions at Belle Vue. This remarkable success story included a hat-trick of wins from 1961 to 1963. In the National Championships they became the Champion Band for the first time in 1945 with further wins in 1952, 1954, 1956 and 1965. They were the International Champions in 1948 and 1949 and held a record in 1945, 1956 and 1965 in being holders of the double title—British Open and National Champions in the same year. They were Granada Band of the Year in 1976. As well as reaching the high technical standard needed for these achievements the band has been especially successful in combining this with the sort of light and polished style that has made them one of the most popular bands with a wide general public, ever in demand for concert appearances and in tours of Germany,

Holland, Belgium, Canada and other countries. Its radio broadcasts approach the 500 mark and it has been seen many times on TV. This all stems from its constant rehearsal and self-improvement and a professional regard of its public standards. Their present musical director is Kenneth Dennison and their musical advisor Harry Mortimer.

Selected LP recordings

Brass in Action—RCA INTS1158 (70). *Entry of the Gladiators* (Fucik); *The Gondoliers—Take a pair of sparkling eyes* (Sullivan); *Faust—Soldiers' Chorus* (Gounod); *Spring* (Grieg); *Fame and Glory* (Matt; Grant); *La Danza* (Rossini); *When the Saints Go Marching In* (trad); *Angels guard thee* (Godard); *Hungarian Dance No.5* (Brahms); *To a wild rose* (MacDowell); *Knightsbridge March* (Coates); *Marching with Sousa* (arr A. Mortimer. c Kenneth Dennison

Brilliant   Brass—HMV   CLP3645, CSD3545 (68). *Zampa—Overture* (Hérold, arr Rimmer); *Norwegian Dance No.2* (Grieg, arr Ryan); *Bellissima* (Rayner); *Beguine for Brass* (Howe); *The Three Tromboners* (McFarlane);   *The   Medallion* (Moreton); *Lohengrin—Prelude Act 3* (Wagner, arr F. Wright); *Fanfare and Soliloquy* (Sharpe); *Mini-Variations on a Welsh Theme* (Thomas); *Round the Clock* (Osgood); *Slavonic Rhapsody* (Friedemann). c Harry Mortimer & Leonard Lamb

Championship Brass—Paxton LPT1005 (62). *Les Préludes* (Liszt, arr W. Rimmer); *Wuthering Heights* (Rayner). c Harry Mortimer & Austin Rayner

Championship Brass—Paxton LPT1011 (62). *Main Street* (Ball) **61**. (See also under Ferodo Works Band). c Leonard Lamb

Championship Brass—Paxton LPT1012 (62). *Eroica—Selection from 3rd Symphony* (Beethoven, arr W. Rimmer); *Sovereign Heritage* (Beaver, arr F. Wright) **54**. c Harry Mortimer

Championship Brass—Paxton LPT1015 (65). *From the New World Symphony* (Dvořák arr D. Rimmer). (see also under Fodens). c Harry Mortimer

Championship Brass—Paxton LPT1016 (65). *Melodies from Massenet* (arr Rayner). (see also under Fodens). c Harry Mortimer

Championship Brass—Paxton LPT1019 (66). *Saga of the North* (Jenkins) **65**; *The Queen's Trumpeters* (Siebert); *Morning, Noon and Night in Vienna* (Suppé); *Encarnita* (Picon). c Leonard Lamb & Harry Mortimer

Championship Brass—Paxton LPT1020 (66). *The Frogs of Aristophanes* **52** (Bantock, arr F. Wright). (See also under Fodens). c Harry Mortimer

Championship Brass—Paxton LPT1021 (67). *Scheherazade* (Rimsky-Korsakov, arr D. Rimmer); *Tancredi—Overture* (Rossini, arr W. Rimmer); *Plaisir d'amour* (Martini, arr D. Rimmer). c Harry Mortimer

Championship Brass—Paxton LPT1022 (67). *Triumphant Rhapsody* (Vinter) **65**; *La Boutique Fantasque* (Rossini, arr Respighi). c Leonard Lamb & Harry Mortimer

Championship Brass—Paxton LPT1025 (68). *Carol Sinfonietta* (D. Wright); *The Land of the Ever Young* (Bantock); *Dancing Valley* (K. Wright). c Leonard Lamb

Championship Brass—Paxton LPT1026 (69). *Comedy Overture* (Ireland) **34** (see also under Munn & Felton). c Leonard Lamb

Four Contest Marches, Set 1—Paxton (45) PEP129. *Mephistopheles* (Douglas); *Bandstand* (Powell) (see also Fodens Motor Works Band). c Harry Mortimer

Four Contest Marches, Set 2—Paxton (45) PEP131. *Glendene* (Carr); *Ravenswood*

(W. Rimmer); *Brilliant* (Hume); *Avondale* (Verner). c Harry Mortimer

*Melodious Brass—HMV CSD3668 (69). *Polonaise in A* (Chopin, arr Martyn); *A Keltic Lament* (Foulds); *John Peel* (arr F. Mortimer); *Parade of the Tin Soldiers* (Jessel, arr Bidgood); *The Boulevardier* (Curzon, arr F. Wright); *Little Lisa* (Warr); *Waltzing Trumpets* (Stephens); *Serenata* (Hughes); *Jenny Wren* (Davis); *Little Serenade* (Tomlinson); *Hungarian Rhapsody No.2* (Liszt, arr W. Rimmer). c Harry Mortimer & Leonard Lamb

Music for Brass—Paxton (45) PEP115. *The Bartered Bride—Polka* (Smetana); *Busy Day* (Rayner); *Ich Liebe Dich* (Grieg); *Donauwellen* (Ivanovici). c Harry Mortimer

Music for Brass—Paxton (45) PEP116. *Jesu, hope of man abiding* (Bach); *Trumpet Tune in 17th Century Style* (Stewart); *The Kerry Dance* (Molloy); *From Greenland's icy mountains & New every morning is the love.* c Harry Mortimer

Music for Brass—Paxton (45) PEP120. *Eboracum* (Rayner); *Sunday Morning* (Siebert); *Student Days* (Street); *Slumber Song* (Schumann, arr Rayner). c Harry Mortimer

The Fairey Band.

Music for Brass—Paxton (45) PEP126. *The Bartered Bride—Dance of the Comedians* (Smetana); *The Bombastic Bombardon* (Siebert); *Music for the Royal Fireworks* (Handel, arr Wood). c Harry Mortimer

Polished Brass—RCA INTS1331 (72). *William Tell—Overture* (Rossini); *All through the night* (arr Langford); *Fairies of the Waters* (Lacombe, arr Langford); *Blow the wind Southerly* (arr Langford); *Trumpet Voluntary* (Clarke, arr Gay); *Famous British Marches* (arr Langford); *Our boys will shine tonight* (arr Langford); *Believe me if all those endearing young charms* (arr Langford); *Cossack Patrol* (Ball; Rose); *Thunder and Lightning Polka* (Strauss, arr Wright); *Cavalleria Rusticana—Intermezzo* (Mascagni); *Light Cavalry—Overture* (Suppé). c Kenneth Dennison

Sounds of Brass, Vol.1—Decca SB301 (72)†. *Aida—Grand March* (Verdi, arr Wright); *Enigma Variations—Nimrod* (Elgar, arr Wright); *Horn Concerto No.3—Rondo* (Mozart, arr Siebert); *Cornet Carillon* (Binge); *The Gypsy Baron—Overture* (Strauss, arr Winter); *Die Fledermaus—Overture* (Strauss, arr Winter); *Alpine Echoes* (Windsor); *Little Suite for Brass, Op.80* (Arnold). c Kenneth Dennison

Sounds of Brass, Vol.4—Decca SB304 (73)†. *Radetzky March* (Strauss I, arr Ryan); *Peer Gynt—Morning* (Grieg, arr Cook); *Buffoon* (Confrey); *Festival Overture* (Shostakovitch, arr Cornthwaite); *The Headless Horseman* (Goodwin); *Beaufighters March* (Johnstone); *La Traviata—Prelude Act 3* (Verdi, arr D. Rimmer); *Fatherland* (Hartmann, arr Owenson); *The Hunt* (Alford). c Kenneth Dennison

Sounds of Brass, Vol.11 (Concert Classics) —Decca SB311 (74)†. *Trumpet Tune & Air* (Purcell, arr F. Wright); *Rondo alla Turca* (Mozart, arr Owen); *Water Music* (Handel/ Harty, arr Holt); *Slavonic Dance No.8* (Dvořák, arr D. Wright); *Academic Festival Overture* (Brahms, arr D. Wright); *Symphony No.4—Saltarello* (Mendelssohn, arr Halliwell). c Kenneth Dennison

Sounds of Brass, Vol.18 (More Concert Classics)—Decca SB318 (75)†. *The Flight of the Bumble-Bee* (Rimsky-Korsakov, arr Dennison); *Christmas Night Overture* (Rimsky-Korsakov, arr Wright); *L'Italiana in Algeri—Overture* (Rossini, arr Rimmer); *Nabucco—Chorus of Hebrew Slaves* (Verdi, arr Ball); *A Children's Overture* (Quilter, arr Wright);

Pian' e' forte (Gabrieli, arr Dennison); *A Moorside Suite* (Holst) **28**. c Kenneth Dennison

Sounds of Brass, Vol.23 (A Concert Entertainment)—Decca SB323 (76), cass KSBC323†. *Cavalleria Rusticana—Intermezzo* (Mascagni); *The Three Bears* (Coates, arr A. Mortimer); *Carnival of Venice* (Steiger); *Russlan and Ludmilla—Overture* (Glinka); *Orpheus in the Underworld—Overture* (Offenbach); *Jesus Christ, Superstar —I don't know how to love Him* (Lloyd-Webber); *Escapada* (Phillips); *Scarboro' Fair* (arr Bolton). c Kenneth Dennison

Sounds of Brass, Vol.42—Decca SB342 (80). *Hungarian March* (Berlioz, arr Catelinet) *Chanson Indoue* (Rimsky-Korsakov, arr D. Wright); *Cossack Ride & Slavonic Dance* (Baron, arr Woodfield); *Le Carnaval Romain* (Berlioz, arr F. Wright); *Arnhem—March* (Kelly); *Salamanca* (Baker; Stone, arr Wilby); *Du bist die Ruh (You are my life)* (Schubert; Hargreaves); *Serenade* (Bourgeois); *Concert Variations* (Lusher); *Epic Symphony—Heroic March* (Fletcher). c Walter B. Hargreaves

A Souvenir of Memories—EMI NTS167 (79)†. *Marching with Sousa* (Sousa, arr A. Mortimer); *String Quartet, Op.3, No.5—Serenade* (Haydn, arr F. Wright); *Oh, my beloved father* (Puccini, arr Dennison); *Donnauwellen* (Ivanovici, arr Moss); *The Three Musketeers* (Hespe) **53**; *Radetzky March* (Johann Strauss I, arr Hargreaves); *Romanza* (Geehl); *Andante Cantabile* (Tchaikovsky, arr F. Wright); *Les Préludes* (Liszt, arr W. Rimmer). c Walter Hargreaves Also:

Champion Brass—BBC REC302.

Fodens Motor Works Band (1902)

There is a popular legend that the Fodens Band was formed to celebrate the Relief of Mafeking in 1900 but this is not accurate although some of the band's pre-history goes back to those days. In the small Cheshire village of Elworth a celebration and procession was arranged for this occasion. The nearby town of Sandbach had been caught napping in this respect and they therefore asked the Elworth committee to bring their procession to Sandbach, to which the Elworthians agreed provided that the Sandbach Volunteer Brass Band would lead the procession. This was amicably arranged with the added attraction of a diversion via Wheelock where the Wheelock Temperance band would also join the column. All went well until the return to Elworth when it was found that everyone had dispersed. A local publican had offered free beer to both bands while the speeches were going on. The Wheelock Temperance Band had deemed this an insult and went home; the Sandbach Volunteers took up the offer and were rendered incapable of further music-making. The Elworth committee were so annoyed that they decided there and then that Elworth would have its own band and within a month the band was formed and had bought a set of second-hand instruments from a band in Knutsford. The Elworth Brass Band (subsequently known as the Elworth Silver Band) therefore came into being in 1900 and, as none of its members could play a note, went into serious rehearsal.

Its first official engagement was for the memorial service for Queen Victoria in 1901 and it soon became in demand for social functions. The next important engagement should have been at the celebrations attending the Coronation of King Edward VII in 1902 but there was some dissension over whether a fee should be paid, the bandsmen demanding £4 a head. The local committee decided that this was exorbitant and hired the London and North Western Carriage

Fodens Motor Works Band and trophies, 1924.

Works Band from Crewe at an inclusive fee of £8, while the Elworth Band played at Sandbach and Smallwood. Following this domestic crisis the Elworth Band was dissolved and its instruments sold. At this point Edwin Foden (1841-1911), the young head of what was to become Fodens Ltd, makers then of agricultural machinery and portable steam engines, decided that 1902 was the time for his growing business to run its own band. So the Elworth players and their conductor were reformed, given a new set of Besson instruments and became the Fodens Band. They immediately plunged into the round of local contests and after the original Bandmaster Samuel Charlesworth retired and Alfred Jackson had been appointed in 1907 it began to win many local prizes. Early in its career the band had retained the celebrated composer and conductor, William Rimmer, as its professional coach but when he demanded an influx of new and better players the management refused and Mr Rimmer departed. Mr Jackson realised that Rimmer had been right in his demands and prevailed upon the management to reconsider their opinion. Mr Rimmer returned and the band was reconstructed with an influx of some of the finest players that could be lured to Fodens. Even some members of the Foden family were removed from the ranks as being of insufficient musical ability. This musical dedication paid off and by 1909 with Edward

Wormald as Bandmaster the band had won the British Open at Belle Vue and gained second place in the National Championships at the Crystal Palace. Having completed this task William Rimmer retired and William Halliwell took over to lead the band in 1910 to the double triumph as winners of both the British Open and National Championships. Edwin Foden's faith in the band had been justified and when he died in 1911, the cortège was led by his players.

From now on Fodens was to be one of the country's leading bands and in 1912 a decision was taken that minor contests would have to be limited and the band would concentrate on maintaining its championship status. In 1912 they won the British Open for the third time. Thomas Hynes became Bandmaster in 1913. This continuing pressure began to tell and in 1915 half the band went on strike. They were dismissed and the band had to rebuild after the war, not getting back to its former level until around 1924. It was in this memorable year

that Fred Mortimer was appointed as bandmaster and the band went into a period of glory that has never been matched. They won the Open in 1926, 1927 and 1928 bringing their total to eight victories and made the Belle Vue Challenge Cup their own. In 1929 William Halliwell retired and Fred Mortimer became Musical Director with his son, Harry, taking over as Bandmaster. In 1930 they won the National Championship again and then completed the famous triple win of 1932, 1933 and 1934, which barred them from entering in 1935, but they came back to repeat the achievement in 1936, 1937 and 1938. In 1938 it played by Royal Command at Windsor Castle. After the war in 1945 when the National Championships went to the Albert Hall, Fodens again came back to strength and won the event for the ninth time in 1950 when the adjudicator, Herbert Howells, who had written the test-piece *Pageantry*, could hardly find words of sufficient praise for their performance. He concluded that it was nothing less than 'technical perfection'. Fred Mortimer died in 1953 and Harry Mortimer took over to lead the band to its tenth

Fodens Motor Works Band.

National victory in 1953. Harry held the fort until his brother, Rex, took over as Musical Director and he became Musical Advisor. In 1974 Harry Mortimer retired, Rex the following year and John Golland took over. He resigned in 1975 and the new musical director was James Scott. A full history of the band (to which we are much indebted) is to be found in *By Royal Command; the Story of Fodens Motor Works Band* by F.D. Burgess, published for their 75th anniversary in 1977. They had been National Champions on 11 occasions; and British Open Champions on nine by this time.

Selected LP Recordings

Brass Supreme—Polydor 2485 015. *The Gay Hussar* (Powell); *The Cavalier* (Sutton); *Marche Symphonique* (Hughes); *A Life for the Czar—selection* (Glinka, arr W. Rimmer); *The Bombardier* (Powell); *Die Fledermaus—Du und Du* (Strauss, arr D. Rimmer); *Little Lisa* (Warr, arr Boddington); *Jamie's Patrol* (Dacre); *Automation* (Yorke); *The Cossack* (W. Rimmer). c Rex Mortimer

Championship Brass—Paxton LPT1015 (65). *Variations on 'The Shining River'* (Rubbra, arr F. Wright) **58**; *Cwm Rhondda* (Hughes, arr Rayner). (See also Fairey Band). c Rex Mortimer

Championship Brass—Paxton LPT1016 (65). *Diadem of Gold* (Balay, arr F. Wright) **53**. (See also Fairey Band). c Harry Mortimer

Championship Brass—Paxton LPT1029 (66). *Lorenzo* (Keighley) **28, 42, 64**. (See also Fairey Band) c Rex Mortimer

Championship Brass—Paxton LPT1029 (67). *Devon Fantasy* (Ball). (See also Black Dyke Mills Band). c Harry Mortimer

A Christmas Offering—Pye GSGL10514 (74). *Christmas Prelude* (arr Barratt); *All on a Christmas morning* (Amers); *Christmas Offering* (Golland); *Hark the herald Angels sing* (Mendelssohn, arr Willcocks); *Carol of the Bells* (Bearcroft; Mawey); *Sans Day Carol* (arr Jordan); *Jingle Bells* (arr Charles); *Away in a manger* (arr Willcocks); *Hail to the Lord's Annointed* (arr Ball); *Ring out, wild bells* (Fletcher, arr Golland); *Drummer Boy* (arr Street); (with the Northwich & District Festival Choir). c Rex Mortimer

Four Contest Marches, Set 1—Paxton (45) PEP129. *Punchinello* (W. Rimmer); *Roll Away, Bet* (Hume) (See also The Fairey Band). c Rex Mortimer

The Fodens Sound—Pye GSGL10511 (74). *The Enchantress* (White); *Arabella* (Chester); *Rhythmic Skaters* (Waldteufel, arr Wood); *Pixie's Parade* (Saville); *Ida and Dott* (Losey); *Swedish Rhapsody* (Alfven, arr Faith); *A Festival Prelude* (Hughes); *La Chatelaine* (arr F. Mortimer); *Where'er you walk* (Handel, arr D. Rimmer); *The Magic Flute—Overture* (Mozart, arr D. Rimmer). c Rex Mortimer

Marches and Waltzes—HMV CSD3665 (69). *Colonel Bogey* (Alford); *Imperial Echoes* (Safroni); *The Cossack* (W. Rimmer); *Swing Along* (Siebert); *Marche Militaire* (Schubert, arr Langford); *Marching with Sousa* (arr A. Mortimer); *Nights of Gladness* (Ancliffe); *Red Letter Day* (Heath); *Waltzing with Gung'l* (arr Seymour); *Carillon Waltz* (Siebert); *Skater's Waltz* (Waldteufel). c Rex Mortimer

Music for Brass—Paxton (45) PEP106. *Devon Fantasy—Suite* (Ball); *Merry Macdoon* (Foulds); *Franz Schubert—Overture* (Suppé). c Harry Mortimer

Music for Brass—Paxton (45) PEP114. *Early one morning* (trad); *Brass Band Blues* (Gould) (see also Munn & Felton Works Band). c Harry Mortimer

Sounds of Brass, Vol.30—Decca SB330 (78)†. *Nibelungen March* (Wagner, arr Grant); *Blow the wind southerly* (arr Langford); *Silver threads among the gold* (Danks, arr Boddington); *Things to Come—excerpts* (Bliss, arr Beresford); *Fantasia on British Airs* (Barsotti); *The Talisman Suite—Prelude* (Hughes); *La Sonnambula* (Bellini, arr Adolphe); *Slavonic March* (Tchaikovsky, arr Davies). c James Scott

Sounds of Brass, Vol.33—Decca SB333 (78). *Prelude and Fugue* (Langford); *The Sea* (Thalassa) (D. Wright); *Melody and Caprice* (Hespe); *Bees-a-buzzin'* (Siebert); *Semper Fidelis* (Sousa); *Die Fledermaus—Overture* (Strauss, arr Winter); *Patterns in Brass—Intermezzo* (Hughes); *Casse-Noisette Suite—March & Trepak* (Tchaikovsky, arr D. Rimmer); *La Reine de Saba—Overture* (Gounod). c James Scott

Sounds of Brass, Vol.41—Decca SB341† (80) cass KBSC341. *Rhapsodic Symphony—Intrada & Scherzo* (Hughes); *Shylock* (Alwyn); *Eugene Onegin—Waltz* (Tchaikovsky); *Pride of Youth—Overture* (Jacob); *Oberon—Overture* (Weber); *Threnody (A Tribute to Fred Mortimer)* (Geehl); *Jenny Jones; Sylvia—Prelude Dance of the Huntress & Procession of Bacchus* (Delibes). c Derek Garside

Also:
Festival band Series, Vol.4—Saga 8148 (70).
Sounding Brass—HMV CLP3629 (67).

Greenock and District Silver Band

A well-known band from the West Coast of Scotland, playing in the Championship section of the Scottish Amateur Brass Band Association. Its policy is to promote music within the local community and it has represented Greenock in many public performances given in the area. The musical director of the band since 1971 has been Mr A.G.T. Clucas.

LP recording

Sailing from the Clyde—EMI NTS157 (78). *The Contestor* (Powell); *Scotland the Brave* (arr Keenan); *The Green Oak Tree* (arr Keenan); *Song of the Clyde* (Gourlay); *Stranger on the Shore* (Bilk); *Sailing* (Sutherland); *Betty Dear* (Agoult, arr Siebert); *Jesus Christ Superstar* (Lloyd Webber); *Men of Harlech* (arr Langford); *Hawaii Five-O* (Stevens); *Scots wha'ha'e* (arr Keenan); *My love is like a red, red rose* (arr Langford); *Frolic for Trombones* (Heath); *Bramwyn* (Carr). (with the Choir of St Michael's Academy, Kilwinning). c A.G.T. Clucas

Grimethorpe Colliery Band (1917)

Grimethorpe village, now submerged in the bustling activities of a thriving colliery, is right in the heart of the South Yorkshire coalfield some seven and a half miles from Barnsley. The pit band was founded in 1917—its full title (still officially in use) the Grimethorpe Colliery Institute Band. The band, of course, is very much an institution itself and its high standards are maintained through the enthusiastic interest of the Committee of the Colliery Institute at both Grimethorpe and Ferrymoor Collieries, backed by the support of the General Manager and staff of the South Barnsley Area. The standards were considerably raised in the 1960s when the Coal Industry Social Welfare Association completely equipped the band with new instruments with the satisfying result that they became the first prize winners for three years in succession at Blackpool and won the British Open title at Belle Vue in 1967 and 1969

when they played Gilbert Vinter's *Spectrum*. They were Mineworkers' National Champions in 1967, 1968, 1969, 1973, 1974, 1975 and 1976. In 1970 they won the National Championship at the Albert Hall. They have remained in the top flight of band competition and have a great reputation as a concert band. Many of their successes were under George Thompson, their conductor for many years, and the band has produced some first-rate soloists such as David Moore who won the Senior Championship as euphonium soloist on several occasions. Elgar Howarth became musical director in 1972 in which year, and in 1973, they won the title of Granada Band of the Year.

Selected LP recordings

*Band of the Year—RCA PL25046 (77), cass PK25046†. *The NYBBS March* (Thomson); *The lark in the clear air* (arr Langford); *Sarie Marais* (arr Langford); *The Sleeping Beauty—Waltz* (Tchaikovsky, arr Newsome); *Cleopatra* (Damare); *Suite No.1 in E flat—March* (Holst); *Overture on Famous English Airs* (Tomlinson); *Cavalleria Rusticana—Intermezzo* (Mascagni, arr Wright); *Trumpet Voluntary* (Clarke, arr Wright); *Variations on a Theme by Lully* (Cavie). c Bryden Thomson.

Brass Versus the Classics—Decca BYK714 (73). *A Night on the Bare Mountain* (Mussorgsky, arr Ashmore); *Tantalusqualen—Overture* (Suppé); *Lieutenant Kije—Troika* (Prokofiev, arr Ashmore); *Egmont Overture* (Beethoven); *La Fille de Régiment—Overture* (Donizetti); *The Planets—Jupiter* (Holst). c Derek Ashmore

*Classics for Brass Band—Decca SXL6820, cass KSXC6820 (77)†. *A Moorside Suite* (Holst) **28**; *The Severn Suite* (Elgar) **30**; *Comedy Overture* (Ireland) **34**; *Kenilworth* (Bliss) **36**. c Elgar Howarth

Escape from the Dark—EMI EMC3148 (77). *Music for the Film 'Escape from the Dark'* (Goodwin). c Ron Goodwin

Festival Band Series, Vol.3—Saga 8147. *Oliver—March* (Thompson); *Springtime* (Heath); *Square Dance* (Parker); *Three Lazy Gents* (Barraclough); *Simoraine* (Barraclough); *Danse Hongroise* (Delibes, arr Siebert); *Spectrum* (Vinter) **69**; *Don Pasquale—Overture* (Donizetti, arr Thompson). c George Thompson

*Grimethorpe Special (Contemporary Music)—Decca HEAD14 (77)†. *Fireworks* (Howarth); *Grimethorpe Aria* (Birtwistle);

Garden Rain (Takemitsu); *Ragtimes and Habaneras* (Henze) (with the Besses o' th' barn Band). c Elgar Howarth

Highlights in Brass—Polydor 583086 (70), 2928 008 (72). *San Marino* (Hawkins); *Showers of Gold* (Clarke); *Ocean Bounce* (Walmsley; Thornton); *Rienzi—Overture* (Wagner, arr Jones); *British Mouthpiece* (Doughty); *Light Cavalry—Overture* (Suppé, arr Greenwood); *Song of India* (Rimsky-Korsakov, arr Thompson); *1812 Overture* (Tchaikovsky, arr D. Wright). c George Thompson

Hymns of Praise—Pye PKL5509 (73). *23 Hymns* c Dennis Wilby

Hymns You Love—Marble Arch MALS1388 (71). *18 Hymns* c George Thompson

Music from Films and Shows—Decca BYK712 (73). *Music from: Godspell; Those Magnificent Men in Their Flying Machines; The Challengers; Where Eagles Dare; The Dambusters; Big Country; 683 Squadron; Goldfinger; Turnbull's Finest Half Hour; Pathfinders; The Magnificent Seven; Love Story.* c Derek Ashmore

Pop goes the Posthorn—Grosvenor GRS1022 (74)†. *Pel Mel* (Lear); *Pavane* (Bull, arr Howarth); *The King's Hunting Jigg* (Bull, arr Howarth); *Sinfonietta—Finale* (Horovitz); *Pop goes the Posthorn* (Lear); *A Londonderry Air* (arr Howarth); *Moonlight Serenade* (Miller, arr Howarth); *Lohengrin—Prelude Act 3* (Wagner, arr W. Rimmer); *Cops and Robbers* (Lear); *Galliard* (Farnaby, arr Howarth); *Mal Sims* (Farnaby, arr Howarth); *Yo-ho-ho-an' Sebastian Bach* (Bach, arr Howarth); *Divertimento—March* (Kelly); *Trumpeter's Holiday* (Paige, arr Wilboy); *Embraceable you* (Gershwin, arr Howarth); *Russian Sailors' Dance* (Glière, arr Dodds). c Elgar Howarth

Salute to Gershwin—Polydor 2485 008 (71). *Strike up the band* (arr Thompson); *Oh, lady be good* (arr Wiggins); *Fascinating rhythm* (arr Beckingham); *Liza* (arr Wiggins); *Bidin' my time* (arr Jordan); *Embraceable you* (arr Jordan); *The man I love* (arr Wiggins); *Rhapsody in Blue* (arr Thompson); *S'wonderful* (arr Wiggins); *Somebody loves me* (arr Jordan); *I got rhythm* (arr Thompson); *Gershwin for Brass* (arr Duro). c George Thompson

*Sounds of Brass, Vol.25—Decca SB325 (76), cass KSBC325†. *Red Sky at Night* (Lear); *Hogarth's Hoe Down* (Lear); *I dream of Jeannie with the light brown hair* (Foster); *Barney's Tune* (Lear); *Cornet Concerto* (Howarth); *Chinese Take-Away* (Lear); *Parade* (Howarth); *Paris Le Soir* (Lear); *Mosaic* (Howarth); *Stars and Stripes Forever* (Sousa). c Elgar Howarth

Top Brass—Pye GGL0392, GSGL10392 (67). *Queen of Sheba—March* (Gounod); *Starlight* (D. Rimmer); *The Three Grenadiers* (Ashpole); *Fingal's Cave—Overture* (Mendelssohn, arr Thompson); *Mill on the Cliff—Overture* (Reissigar); *La Belle Americaine* (Hartmann); *I-Tiddley-I-Tie* (Roper); *Silver threads among the gold* (Allison); *Punchinello* (W. Rimmer). c George Thompson

GUS (Footwear) Band, (Munn & Felton—1933-62)

The band was formed in 1933 as Munn & Felton's Works Band, made up entirely of employees of the firm based in Kettering in the County of Northampton. Its original, and outstandingly long-serving, Musical Director was Stanley Boddington (b 1905) who under the guidance of Greville Cook and William Halliwell, soon shaped a band of the highest standards which won the National Championship in 1935, within two years of its formation. The conductor on that occasion was William Halliwell. They won the British Open in 1954 and the National Championship in 1955, 1957, and 1960 and, under their new name, when the firm became Gus Footwear Ltd, in 1962, in 1964 and 1966. The Midland Area Championship came their way on numerous occasions and in 1966 they won the National Quartet Championship in 1966 and 1967. They have toured Holland, Denmark and Switzerland and became one of the most prolific recording bands. The band is kept in the championship class by exacting twice weekly rehearsals on the top floor of the factory warehouse. The band is said to travel an average of 10,000 miles a year to play in concerts and competitions.

Selected LP recordings

1) As Munn & Felton's Band:

Bandstand No.4—Columbia 33SX1266, SCX3335 (60). *The Swashbuckler* (Moreton); *Poet and Peasant—Overture* (Suppé); *Silver Threads* (Danks, arr); *Fairy on the Clock; Florentiner March* (Fucik); *Military Polonaise* (Chopin, arr Sargent); *Marinarella* (Fucik); *Belive me if all those endearing young charms* (arr Langford); *Horbury; Circus Capers.*

c Stanley H. Boddington & Harry Mortimer
Bandstand No.5—Columbia 33SX1391, SCX3424 (62). *Wellington* (Zeele); *Poème* (Fibich); *Snow Flakes* (Charrosin); *The Long Day Closes* (Sullivan); *The Thieving Magpie—Overture* (Rossini, arr F. Wright); *Under the Double Eagle* (J.F. Wagner); *Lorenzo* (Keighley) **28**; *Facilita* (Hartmann arr H. Mortimer); *Morgenblätter* (Strauss); *Fandango* (Perkins). c Stanley H. Boddington & Harry Mortimer
Championship Brass—Paxton LPT1010 (62). *Blackfriars* (Cundell, arr F. Wright) **55**. (See also under Black Dyke). c Harry Mortimer
Championship Brass—Paxton LPT1026 (69). *Tournament for Brass* (Ball) **54**. (See also under Fairey Band). c Stanley H. Boddington
Munn & Felton's Works Band—Columbia 33S1089 (57). *Royal Standard* (Chesterton); *Napoleon Galop* (Martyn); *Bees-a-buzzin'* (Siebert); *Christmas Lullaby (Cornet Carillon)* (Binge); *Rimington* (Duckworth, arr Boddington); *Washington Post* (Sousa); *Liberty Bell* (Sousa); *Early one morning* (arr Seymour); *Brass Band Blues* (Gould); *Crimond* (Grant, arr Boddington); *Washington Greys* (Grafulla). c Stanley H. Boddington & Harry Mortimer
Music for Brass—Paxton (45) PEP114. *BB & CF* (Hume); *The Joys of Sport* (See also Fodens). c S.H. Boddington
2) As GUS (Footwear) Band or GUS (Kettering) Band:
Bandstand No.6—Columbia 33SX1466, SCX3455 (62). *Rendine March* (Martyn); *Posthorn Polka* (Strauss, arr Seymour); *Variations on a Theme* (Weber, arr Boddington); *Little Lisa* (Warr); *Robert the Devil—Ballet Music* (Meyerbeer); *Masaniello—Overture* (Auber); *Onward Christian Soldiers* (Sullivan); *Brass Band Boogie* (Siebert); *The Tops* (Powell); *Copacabana* (Stephens). c Stanley H. Boddington & Harry Mortimer
Bandstand No.7—Columbia 33SX1582, SCX3502 (64). *The Medallion* (Moreton); *Waltzing with Sullivan* (arr Vinter); *Plymouth Hoe* (Ansell, arr Wright); *The Swing o' the Kilt* (Ewing, arr Mackenzie); *Dear Lord and Father of Mankind* (Parry, arr Boddington); *Tenderfoot Trail* (Haysom); *London Bridge* (Coates, arr Wright); *Date with a Square* (Sefton); *Rhapsody in Brass* (Goffin) **49**; *Fiddle-di-di* (Stephens); *Seventy-six Trombones* (Willson, arr Duthoit). c

Stanley H. Boddington & Harry Mortimer
Bandstand No.8—Columbia 33SX1621, SCX1621 (64). *Queen Anne's Ride; Moment Musical* (Schubert); *Mac and Mort* (Mortimer); *Skye Boat Song* (Kennedy-Fraser); *Spanish Harlequin* (Haysom); *Lustspiel—Overture* (Keler-Bela); *Knightsbridge* (Coates arr Denham); *Carnival Variations; Shepherd's Hey* (Grainger, arr Wright); *Capriccio Italien* (Mendelssohn); *Portuguese Party* (Vinter, arr Barsotti); *Through all the changing scenes of life* (arr Boddington). c Stanley H. Boddington & Harry Mortimer
Bandstand No.9—Columbia 33SX1720, SCX3550 (65). *Number One March* (Willett-Robertson, arr Boddington); *Bolero* (Ravel, arr Boddington); *Variations on a Ninth* (Vinter) **64**; *Hymn Tune—Moscow* (arr Boddington); *Ballerina* (Bootz, arr Mackenzie); *The President* (German); *Hymn Tune—Harewood* (arr Boddington); *Die Felsenmühle—Overture* (Reissiger, arr Rimmer); *The lark in the clear air* (arr Haysom); *Solemn Melody* (Walford-Davies, arr Hume); *Pomp and Circumstance March No.1* (Elgar, arr Hume). c Stanley H. Boddington & Harry Mortimer
Bandology—EMI 'One Up' OU2179 (77). *Bandology* (Osterling, arr Wright); *Mary Poppins—Selection* (Sherman, arr Wright); *Slavonic Rhapsody No.2* (Friedemann, arr Wright); *Tit-Larks* (Hume); *Amparito Roca* (Texidor, arr Winter); *Congratulations* (Martin; Coulter, arr Siebert); *Who would true valour see* (arr Boddington); *Punchinello* (W. Rimmer); *The Arcadians—Overture* (Monckton, Talbot, arr Wood); *Les Préludes* (Liszt, arr W. Rimmer); *Coronation Street* (Spear, arr Langford); *Beautiful Colorado* (De Luca, arr Boddington); *No Hiding Place* (Johnson, arr Siebert); *Praise my soul, the King of Heaven* (arr Boddington). c Stanley H. Boddington
Best of Brass—EMI 'Starline' SRS5033 (70). *Zampa—Overture* (Hérold, arr Hartmann); *Anchors Aweigh* (Zimmermann, arr Newton); *Morgenblätter* (Strauss); *Spanish Gypsy Dance* (Marquina, arr Dawson); *Post Horn Polka* (Strauss, arr Seymour); *Pomp and Circumstance March No.1* (Elgar, arr Hume); *Knightsbridge* (Coates, arr Denham); *Poet and Peasant—Overture* (Suppé); *March of the Cobblers* (Barratt; Siebert); *Waltzing with Sullivan* (arr Vinter); *Comedians Galop* (Kabalevsky); *Abide with me* (Lyte, Monk, arr Boddington). c Stanley H. Boddington &

Harry Mortimer
The Best of the GUS Band—EMI 'One Up' OU2102 (76). *Imperial Echoes* (Safroni); *Gold and Silver* (Lehár); *Sabre Dance* (Khachaturian, arr Siebert); *A Little Suite—March* (Duncan, arr Siebert); *The Lost Chord* (Sullivan, arr Hume); *Ballycastle Bay* (Barratt; Siebert); *Ballerina* (Bootz, arr Mackenzie); *Out of the Blue* (Bath); *The Thieving Magpie—Overture* (Rossini, arr F. Wright); *National Emblem* (Bagley, arr Siebert); *España* (Chabrier, arr D. Rimmer); *All in the April evening* (Tynan, arr Roberton); *Shepherd's Hey* (Grainger, arr F. Wright); *Swedish Rhapsody* (Alfven, arr Faith & Pope); *Dear Lord and Father of Mankind* (Parry, arr Boddington). c Stanley H. Boddington & Harry Mortimer

Brass in Perspective—Columbia TWO195 (68). *Sabre Dance* (Khachaturian, arr Ball); *Belle of the Ball* (Anderson, arr Tomlinson); *National Emblem* (Bagley, arr Siebert); *Puppet on a String* (Martin, Coulter, arr Siebert); *O God, our help in ages past* (Watts, arr Boddington); *Colonel Bogey on Parade* (Alford); *The Black Domino—Overture* (Auber, arr W. Rimmer); *Calling All Workers* (Coates); *Cossack Patrol* (Rose, arr Ball); *Scherzo* (Boekel); *Oh, listen to the band* (Monckton, arr Duthoit); *Abide with me* (Lyte, arr Boddington). c Stanley H. Boddington

Cornet Carillon—Columbia TWO418 (73). *Post Horn Galop* (Koenig, arr Herbert); *Cornet Carillon* (Binge); *Euphonium Concerto* (Horovitz); *When the Saints go marching in* (arr Langford); *Rock of Ages* (Redhead, arr Boddington); *Entry of the Gladiators* (Fucik, arr Siebert); *Spartacus—Adagio* (Khachaturian, arr Siebert); *English Folk Song Suite* (Vaughan Williams, arr F. Wright); *Perils of Pendragon* (Isaac); *Chit-Chat Polka* (Strauss, arr Pope); *I heard the voice of Jesus say* (Hutcheson, arr Boddington). c Stanley H. Bodington & Joseph Horovitz

Going Home—Columbia TWOX1039 (75). *Aida-Grand March* (Verdi, arr Wright); *Going Home (from the New World Symphony)* (Dvořák, arr Boddington); *Galloping Home* (King, arr Woodfield); *Bass in the Ballroom* (Newsome); *Hark! Hark! my soul* (Faber; Smart, arr Boddington); *Scheherazade—Festivities at Baghdad—The Sea* (Rimsky-Korsakov, arr Hume); *Totem Pole* (Osterling, arr Banks); *Bless this House* (Brahe); *The Piper in the Meadow* (arr Barratt; Siebert); *Greensleeves* (arr Woodfield); *How sweet the*

name of Jesus sounds (Newton; Reinagle, arr Boddington); *Resurgam* (Ball) **50**. c Stanley H. Boddington

Gold and Silver—Columbia TWO256 (69). *Punchinello* (W. Rimmer); *Coronation Street* (Spear, arr Langford); *Amparito Roca* (Texidor, arr Winter); *March of the Cobblers* (Barratt; Siebert); *Les Préludes* (Liszt, arr W. Rimmer); *Fight the good fight* (arr Boddington); *No Hiding Place* (Johnson, arr Siebert); *The Arcadians—Overture* (Monckton, arr Wood); *A Little Suite—March* (Duncan, arr Siebert); *The Last Rhapsody—Theme* (Wreford); *Gold and Silver* (Lehár); *Praise my soul* (arr Boddington). c Stanley H. Boddington

★Great British Music for Brass—Columbia TWOX1053 (76). *Comedy Overture* (Ireland) **34, 49, 67**; *The Belmont Variations* (Bliss) **63**; *A Downland Suite* (Ireland) **32, 39, 66**; *Kenilworth* (Bliss) **36**. c Stanley H. Boddington

Kings of Brass—Columbia TWO161 (67), EMI 'One Up' OU2159 (77). *Out of the Blue* (Bath); *Spanish Gypsy Dance* (Marquina); *Le Carnaval Romain—Overture* (Berlioz, arr F. Wright) **66**; *Espana* (Chabrier, arr F. Wright); *Sons of the Brave* (Bidgood); *Angelus* (arr Boddington); *R.A.F. March Past* (Walford-Davies); *Estudiantina* (Waldteufel); *Samum* (Robrecht, arr Dawson); *Bells Across the Meadow* (Ketelbey); *American Patrol* (Meacham); *The New Colonial—March* (Hall). c Stanley H. Boddington

Land of Hope and Glory—Columbia SCX6406 (70). *Faust—Soldiers' Chorus* (Bizet); *The Student Prince—Marching Song & Drinking Song* (Romberg); *Tannhauser—Pilgrims' Chorus* (Wagner); *The Lost Chord* (Sullivan); *Finlandia* (Sibelius arr Bidgood); *Jerusalem* (Parry); *Battle Hymn of the Republic* (anon); *Cavalry of the Steppes* (Knipper); *David of the White Rock* (Trad); *Il Trovatore—Anvil Chorus* (Verdi); *Abide with me* (Liddle, arr Boddington); *Land of Hope and Glory* (Elgar). (With the Morriston Orpheus Choir). c Stanley H. Boddington

Listen to the Band, No.3—Music for Pleasure MFP1176 (57) (66). *Royal Standard* (Chesterton); *Napoleon Galop* (Martyn); *Bees-a-buzzin'* (Siebert); *Christmas Lullaby (Cornet Carillon)* (Binge); *Solemn Melody* (Davies, arr Ball) *The Thunderer* (Sousa, arr Mortimer); *Washington Post* (Sousa); *Liberty Bell* (Sousa); *Early one morning* (arr

Seymour); *Brass Band Blues* (Gould); *Leaps and Bounds* (Spencer; Brianne); *Galopade* (Palmer; Ball); *Washington Grays* (Grafulla). c Stanley H. Boddington & Harry Mortimer
Quartets for Brass—Columbia SX6312, SCX6312 (69)†. *Elegy and Rondo* (Vinter); *Fancy's Knell* (Vinter); *Alla Burlesca* (Vinter); *March* (Lully, arr Vinter); *Song* (Purcell, arr Vinter); *Tambourin* (Rameau, arr Vinter); *Air* (Handel, arr Vinter); *Badinerie* (Bach, arr Vinter); *Dance* (Corelli, arr Vinter); *Lullaby* (Couperin, arr Vinter); *Jig* (Loeillet, arr Vinter). c Gilbert Vinter.
Salute to Brass—Columbia TWO282 (70). *The Stars and Stripes Forever* (Sousa); *Tit-Larks* (Hume); *Mary Poppins—Selection* (Sherman, arr Wright); *Slavonic Rhapsody No.2* (Friedemann, arr Wright); *Swedish Rhapsody* (Alfven, arr Pope); *Lead us, Heavenly Father, lead us* (Filitz, arr Boddington); *Bandology* (Osterling, arr Wright); *Beautiful Colorado* (De Luca, arr Boddington); *Tango Taquin* (Barratt; Siebert); *Diadem of Gold—Overture* (Balay, arr F. Wright) **53**; *Congratulations* (Martin; Coulter, arr Sibert); *Who would true valour see* (arr Boddington). c Stanley H. Boddington
A Tribute to Eric Ball, OBE, ARCM—Pye TB3021 (80). *October Festival; Free Fantasia; Resurgam; Celebration—Festival Prelude; The English Maiden; Three Songs Without Words—Spring Humoresque; Symphonic Suite for Brass Band, Festival Music* (all by Ball). c Keith M. Wilkinson
The World Champions Play Marches and Waltzes—Columbia TWO364 (72). *King Cotton* (Sousa); *Moonlight on the Alster* (Fetras); *The Great Little Army* (Alford); *Casino Dances* (Gung'l); *The Valiant Years* (Rodgers, arr Duthoit); *Ancliffe in the Ballroom* (Ancliffe); *Liberty Bell* (Sousa); *Grenadier Waltz* (Waldteufel); *March Lorraine* (Ganne); *Wine, Women and Song* (Strauss, arr Winter); *The Dambusters* (Coates). c Stanley H. Boddington
*The World Champions Play Test-Pieces for Brass—Columbia TWO379(72). *Energy—Symphonic Study* (Simpson) **W71**; *James Cook—Circumnavigator* (Vinter) **74**; *Variations on a Ninth* (Vinter) **64**; *Le Carnaval Romain—Overture* (Berlioz, arr F. Wright) **66**. c Stanley H. Boddington
Also:
Championship Bandstand (recordings 1959-72)—EMI ONCR514 (79)†.

Incl *James Cook—Circumnavigator* (Vinter) **74**, etc.

Hammond's Sauce Works Band (1946)

The band was formed in 1946 under the direction of Mr H.B. Hawley who was its musical director until 1952. A keenly competitive band, it soon reached the highest standards and achieved championship status in 1957. Amongst its successes are the BBC Band of the Year award in 1969, Northern Eastern Counties Regional Champion and finalist in many competitions including the British Open. They have qualified on several occasions for the National Championships. In 1966, Geoffrey Witham, who had previously played with and conducted the Black Dyke Mills Band, became their Musical Director. The band is frequently seen on Yorkshire TV's *Stars on Sunday* and has made many broadcasts. They tour England and Scotland and, in 1976 made a tour of Australia. The band is very actively supported by the Hammond's Sauce Group whose Chairman, H.R. Hawley, was a playing member of the band until 1968.

Selected LP recordings
Sounds of Brass, Vol.27—Decca SB327 (77)†. *Light Cavalry—Overture* (Suppé); *Les Préludes* (Liszt, arr W. Rimmer); *Lohengrin—Prelude to Act 3* (Wagner, arr D. Wright); *Eine kleine Nachtmusik* (Mozart, arr Ball); *Pomp and Circumstance March No.4* (Elgar, arr Hume); *Fairies of the Water* (Jacombe, arr Langford); *The Swan* (Saint-Saens, arr Mott); *On the Quarter-Deck* (Alford); *Suite in D-Air* (Bach, arr D. Wright). c Geoffrey Whitham
Yorkshire Brass—Pye GSGL10498 (73). *Comedians Galop* (Kabalevsky); *Carnival of Venice* (Hartmann; Remmington); *Zorba's Dance* (Theodorakis); *The Acrobat* (Greenwood); *Miller Magic* (Miller, arr Stephens); *The Miniature* (Laycock); *Beguine for Brass* (Howe); *Chanson Indoue* (Rimsky-Korsakov); *Il Turco in Italia—Overture* (Rossini). c Geoffrey Whitham
Also:
Hootenanny—EMI 'One Up' OU2146 (76)†.
Quality Plus—Pye GSGL10439.
Quality Plus; Cleopatra; Nimrod; Fra Diavolo (Auber); *The Gladiator; Non piu andrai; Abide with me.*
Super Quality Plus—Pye GSGL10455.

The North Star; Duo for Euphonium; Romeo and Juliet; Swiss Festival Overture; Carnival of Venice; Finlandia.
Spectacular Brass†.
Spectacular Brass—Polyphonic PRL001 (80)†.

Hampshire Youth Brass Band (1965)

Founded in 1965 by John Knight, who is in charge of brass band Music for the Hampshire Education Authority, it became the Champion Youth Band of Great Britain in 1968. Continued success in these areas led to the bands promotion to championship grade and a continuing high level of attainment in spite of changing membership. The band has made tours of Austria, France, Germany, Holland and Sweden and has appeared on radio and TV.

Selected LP recordings

Sounds of Brass, Vol.10—Decca SB310 (74). *The Impresario—Overture* (Cimarosa, arr Wright); *Carnival of Venice* (Arban, arr Knight); *Chorale for Brass* (Lovelock); *Coriolanus* (Jenkins) **20**; *The Dambusters March* (Coates); *Shepherd's Hey* (Grainger, arr Brookes); *The Tops* (Powell); *Portuguese Party* (Vinter, arr Barsotti); *The Four Corners of the World* (Hanmer). c John Knight

Sounds of Brass, Vol.17—Decca SB317 (75). *Exodus—Theme Music* (Gold, arr Knight); *Sinfonietta—Allegro maestoso* (Wilson); *Cavalleria Rusticana—Easter Hymn* (Mascagni, arr Ball); *Duel for Conductors* (Binge); *Essay for Brass Band—Epigram* (Gregson); *Songs my mother taught me* (Dvořák, arr Knight); *Jesu, priceless treasure* (Bach, arr Knight); *Cossack Patrol* (Rose); *All in the April evening* (Roberton); *The Creation—The Heavens are telling* (Haydn, arr Greenwood). c John Knight

The Hanwell Band (1891)

Formed in 1891 the band had few resources in its early days and it was many years before it reached top competitive standards. It has competed in the National Championship on many occasions being placed fourth in 1946 and runner-up in 1950. There have been successes in the Nottingham Open, Hammersmith Open, National Coal Board and Reading Open Championships. In 1966 they won the BBC Challenging Brass Competition. It is entirely an amateur and self-supporting band made up of people from all walks of life. The appointment of Eric

Bravington as musical director in 1959 was of considerable benefit to the band.

LP recording

The Golden Sound of the Hanwell Band—Saga EROS8023 (68). *Cottonopolis* (Anderson); *Gold and Silver* (Lehár); *Dashing away with the smoothing iron* (arr Stewart); *Hawaiian samba* (Siebert); *Seventy-six Trombones* (Willson); *Trumpet Voluntary* (Clarke, arr Wright); *Jealousy* (Gade); *The Blue Danube* (Strauss, arr anon); *Thunder and Lightning Polka* (Strauss, arr Wright); *Stardust* (Carmichael); *Washington Grays* (Grafulla, arr Bidgood). c Eric Bravington

London Collegiate Brass (City of London Brass) (1972)

Formed in 1972 (and then known as the City of London Brass) to cater for students wishing to play brass music—especially contemporary brass music. From the beginning this non-competitive group, mainly made up of teachers and students from the London music colleges, has maintained the highest standards. They made a successful tour of Norway in 1974 and have become known through broadcasts, concerts and recordings. Notably they have given performances of a number of new works by British composers. Their conductor since 1976 has been Edward Gregson. The band differs from the normal brass band in using French horns (usually six) instead of the usual alto-saxhorns which gives a new dimension to their sound. They also use trumpets when needed. There is also a London Collegiate Brass Octet, formed in 1976 from players within the band.

Selected LP recordings

★City of London Brass—RCA LFL15072 (75). *A Moorside Suite* (Holst) **28**; *Sinfonietta* (Wilson); *A London Scherzo* (Langford); *A West Country Fantasy* (Langford); *Prelude and Capriccio* (Gregson); *Blow the wind southerly* (arr Langford). c Geoffrey Brand
★The Music of Malcolm Arnold—Decca SB313 (74)†. *The Padstow Lifeboat; Little Suite No.2; Quintet, Op.73; Song of Freedom* (with the Harrow Girls Choir). c Geoffrey Brand

Mirrlees Works Band (1949)

In spite of its comparative youth, in brass band reckoning, the Mirrlees band has achieved a high reputation and has won nearly 50 prizes in various competitions since its foundation in 1949. After some years in the lower sections it achieved championship status in 1965 and has since remained in prominence not only for its competition work but also as a well-rehearsed concert band.

Selected LP recordings

Mirrlees Makes Music—Pye MALS1317 (70). *Dawn of Freedom* (W. Rimmer); *Choral Prelude—St. Clements* (Scholefield, arr Johnstone); *Polovtsian Dances* (Borodin, arr Huckridge); *L'Italiana in Algeri—Overture* (Rossini, arr Greenwood); *St. Louis Blues* (Handy, arr Corry); *Thais—Meditation* (Massenet, arr Owenson); *Venus and Adonis* (D. Rimmer). c Jack Atherton

Snapshots—Grosvenor GRS1069 (79)†. *Bandology* (Osterling); *Rule Britannia—Overture* (Rimmer); *The Nightingale* (Moss); *Napoleon Galop* (Martyn); *Whitehall—March* (D. Wright); *Portuguese Party* (Vinter, arr Barsotti); *Jesus Christ Superstar—I don't know how to love Him* (Lloyd Webber, arr Dennison); *Swedish Rhapsody* (Alfven); *Blaydon Races* (arr Langford); *Plymouth Hoe* (Ansell). c Kenneth Dennison & Eric S. Pinkerton

Morris Motors Concert Band (1924)
(BMC (Morris) Concert Band)

Since its formation in 1924 the Morris Motors Band has been accepted as one of the country's leading bands. They have been champions of the south many times, but their activities are mainly directed toward broadcasting, recording and concerts. As the BMC Band they toured Holland, Switzerland and Scandinavia. They are a regular part of the 'Men O' Brass' ensemble and conducted by their Musical Director Harry Mortimer who took over the Morris Band in 1947 and has held the appointment ever since. All the players are employees of the car factory at Cowley on the outskirts of Oxford.

Selected LP recordings

1) As BMC Concert Band:
Burnished Brass—HMV CLP3650, CSD3650 (68). *Overture on Famous English Airs* (Tomlinson); *Three Dale Dances* (Wood); *Hailstorm* (W. Rimmer); *Red Musketeer* (Hughes); *The Bronze Horse—Overture* (Auber, arr W. Rimmer); *Horn Concerto No.3—Rondo* (Mozart, arr D. Wright); *Fanfare Polka* (Haysom); *High Spirits* (Heath); *Paperchase* (Stephens); *The*

Padstow Lifeboat (Arnold). c Harry Mortimer

2) As Morris Motors (BMC) Band:
These Happy Sounds—HMV CSD3639 (66). *Gilbert and Sullivan Selection* (arr Mortimer); *The Yeomen of England* (German, arr Carr); *Blaydon Races* (arr Langford); *Cushie Butterfield* (arr Morton); *In Cellar Cool* (Muchler; Fischer, arr Mansfield & Morton); *Myself when young* (Lehmann, arr Barsotti); *Friend o' mine* (Sanderson, arr Hume); *Shortnin' bread* (Wolfe, arr Morton); *The Trumpeter* (Dix, arr Hume). (With Owen Brannigan, The Low Fell Ladies' Choir & The Felling Male Voice Choir). c Harry Mortimer

3) As Morris Concert Band:
Brass Tracks—Meridian A22001 (78)†. *On Parade* (Elms); *The Runaway Rocking Horse* (White); *Bell Bird Polka* (Barsotti); *Echo de Bastion* (Kling); *Cairngorm Patrol* (Sutherland); *Away Lifeboat* (Kidd); *The Trombone Men* (Lusher); *Sky Watch* (Davies); *Second Thoughts* (Watters); *Wonder March* (Allen); *A Little Suite—March* (Duncan); *Prince Igor—Overture* (Borodin, arr Barsotti). c Harry Mortimer

Harry Mortimer Conducts the Famous Morris Concert Band—Music for Pleasure MFP1387 (70). *Carmen—Prelude* (Bizet, arr Martyn); *Tales of Hoffman—Barcarolle* (Offenbach, arr Mortimer); *Marche Lorraine* (Ganne); *Springtime* (Heath); *Swedish Rhapsody* (Alfven, arr Heyler); *Sullivan Medley* (arr Seymour); *Colonel Bogey* (Alford); *Alleluia* (Mozart, arr Mortimer); *Marching Sergeants* (Siebert); *Elizabethan Serenade* (Binge); *The Grand Duchess—Galop* (Offenbach, arr Seymour); *Trumpet Voluntary* (Clarke, arr Gay). c Harry Mortimer

Marching Contrasts—Polyphonic PRL-002 (80)†. *Marche Militaire—La Ronde* (Gounod, arr Sharpe); *Oh, listen to the band* (Monckton, arr Hanmer); *Bally-Castle Bay* (Barratt, Siebert); *Mancunians Way* (Barry); *The Queen's Trumpeters* (Siebert); *The St. John March* (Kennedy); *Semper Sousa* (arr Seymour); *By Royal Command* (Watters); *Bugle Call Blues* (New); *The Rover's Return* (Siebert); *The Duke of York's Patrol* (Spurgin); *Corner Flag* (Howe); *The European* (Richard); *Seventy-Six Trombones* (Willson). c Harry Mortimer

The Morris Concert Band—Canon 'Charivari' VAR5968 (76). *Burnished Brass*

(Cacavas); *Bright Eyes* (Finlayson); *The White Company* (Richardson); *Eye-Level* (Trombey, arr Richardson); *Cavalry of the Steppes* (Knipper, arr Woodfield); *Instrumentalist* (Skornika); *Wembley Way* (Elms); *If I can help somebody* (Androzzo, arr F. Wright); *Doon Valley* (Street); *Cucurumba* (Siebert); *Sundown* (Barsotti). c Harry Mortimer

Out and About in Merry England—Music for Pleasure MFP5021 (75). *Out with the Hunt* (arr Mortimer); *Scarborough Fair* (Simon & Garfunkel, arr Woodfield); *The Shepherd's Song* (Canteloube, arr Gould); *English Country Garden* (Jordan, arr Siebert); *To a wild rose* (MacDowell, arr Martyn); *Barwick Green* (Wood); *The Adventures of Black Beauty—Galloping home* (King, arr Woodfield); *Greensleeves* (arr Woodfield); *Shepherd's Hey* (Grainger, arr D. Wright); *Londonderry Air* (arr Coleman); *Merrie England—The English rose* (German); *The Horse Guards, Whitehall* (H. Wood, arr Cornthwaite). c Harry Mortimer
See also under Massed Brass, Men O' Brass, etc.

Parc and Dare Band (1894)

The band was formed in 1894 and like many colliery bands had to go through the difficult time when many collieries closed and the long established financial backing was lost. From those dark days the band has had to remain self-supporting relying on concert engagements and competition successes to maintain its existence. A forward-looking policy of training young musicians has helped to keep the standards high and the Parc and Dare Band has managed to keep in the top ranks of the bands today. In 1970, 1971 and 1972 it won the major title at the Royal National Eisteddfod and was Champion Band of Wales in 1976, 1977 and 1978. In contests it has won 102 first prizes, 51 second prizes and 38 third. The band first broadcast in 1938 and has now been heard on the radio over 200 times, and many times on TV. Much of the band's impetus has come from its Musical Director Ieuan Morgan who was originally principal euphonium with the band. He is Brass Instrumental Tutor with the mid-Glamorgan Educational Authority. The high standards in the band has led to three members joining the National Youth Orchestra of Wales.

Selected LP recordings
Rhondda Rhapsody—EMI OU2105 (75).

Rhondda Rhapsody (Jones, arr Ball); *The Headless Horseman* (Goodwin, arr Brand); *Journey Into Freedom* (Ball) **67**; *Trumpets Wild* (Walters, arr Brush); *Cwm Rhondda* (Hughes, arr Rayner); *Heroic March* (Price); *Romanza* (Geehl); *Prelude for an Occasion* (Gregson); *David of the White Rock* (arr Bebb); *Men of Harlech—March* (German, arr D. Wright). c Ieuan Morgan

Sounds of Brass, Vol.36—Decca SB336, cass KBSC336 (79)†. *Concertino for tenor horn and band* (G. Wood); *Suite for Brass* (Segers); *Cornet Roundabout* (Eaves); *Tuba Tapestry* (M. Brand); *McArthur March* (Price); *Hob Y derri dando* (Price); *I wish you love* c Ieuan Morgan

The Rochdale Band (1952)

(Rochdale-Wilsons Band, 1979)
A gap in Rochdale's eminently musical life was filled in 1952 when the Rochdale Band was formed. Starting as a youth band under the direction of Frank Mallinson, and with continued support from its President and Patron, Alderman Cyril Smith, the band quickly improved its standards to become the championship band that it is today. They made their first tour of Europe in 1960 and have since frequently toured the Continent and become well-known on radio and TV. In the competition field the band was a sectional Champion of the North-West Region in 1963, 1968 and 1969; a National finalist in 1961, 1962, 1963, 1965, 1966, 1968 and 1969. In 1972 it was in the World and National finals; in 1970 and 1971 at Belle Vue. In 1977 they were the winners of the Edinburgh Festival contest. The Musical Director from 1970 to 1978 was Norman Ashcroft who was for many years principal cornet with the Fairey Band. David M. Loukes, GGSM, took over for a time; then in 1979 the band became Rochdale-Wilsons and James Scott its musical director.

Selected LP Recordings
The Crusaders—Grosvenor GRS1054 (77)†. *Bramwyn* (Carr); *Robin Adair* (arr Hartmann); *The Crusaders* (Keighley); *The Swing of the Scale* (McFarlane); *Deep Harmony* (arr Golland); *Gypsy Rondo* (Haydn, arr O. Howarth); *I hear you calling me* (Marshall); *The Two Blind Men of Toledo-Overture* (Méhul, arr D. Wright). c Norman Ashcroft

Sounds of Brass, Vol.16—Decca SB316 (75). *Processional March* (Carse); *Little*

The Rochdale Band conducted by Norman Ashcroft on BBC TV's Champion Brass.

Serenade (Tomlinson); *Duo for Euphoniums* (Powell); *The Dream of Gerontius—Prelude* (Elgar, arr Ball); *The Love of Three Oranges—March* (Prokofiev, arr Richardson); *Valse España* (Chabrier, arr D. Rimmer); *Hungarian Dances Nos.1 & 6* (Brahms, arr Rimmer); *Jenny Wren* (Davis); *Le Domino Noir—Overture* (Auber, arr F. Wright). c Norman Ashcroft

St Hilda's Colliery Band

This band was unusual if not unique among the brass bands of Britain. It hailed from South Shields and its meteoric career got under way when in 1912 it won the National Championship for the first time with its playing of William Rimmer's arrangement of Rossini's *William Tell Overture*. The championship was suspended from 1914 to 1919 but when resumed St Hilda's came back as the winners in 1920, 1921, 1924 and 1926. Its conductor was the redoubtable James Oliver. Other conductors and band trainers then challenged the eligibility of the band to compete in amateur events. For quite a long time (the colliery had actually closed in 1925) it had been obvious that the bandsmen were earning their living by playing. In addition to the usual park concerts they had extended

summer seasons at several seaside resorts and in the winter the band played for the Bertram Mills Circus at London's Olympia. The decision was in the hands of John Henry Isles and he rightly decreed that the band was really constituted of professionals. This was accepted and true and acknowledged professionals they became. But many players shunned the idea of professionalism and left to join other bands. They were replaced, of course, by efficient players and for a time the band carried on more or less as before and still under the active management of James Southern, secretary and trombone player, but a decline in success accompanied the change of status, not the least important factor in which was that they could no longer be billed as National or Open Champions. A year or two before the war the Slaithwaite Band bought St Hilda's repertory, the band having 'just previously gone out of existence'. Shortly after the end of the second World War the name 'St Hilda's' was sold to a group of men who seem to have been more interested in money than music and the name faded out early in the 1950s.

Selected LP recording

*Original Vintage Brass—Two Ten (M)

TTV099†. *Queensbury—March* (Kaye); *Life Divine* (Parts 1 & 2) (Jenkins) **21, 63**; *Carnival of Venice* (Arban) (soloist: Jack Mackintosh); *Drinking* (Bilton) (soloist: Alex Mortimer); *Symphony No.1: Freedom* (Bath) **22, 47, 73**; *Epic Symphony—Heroic March* (Fletcher); *Zelda* (Code) (soloist: Harry Mortimer); *Kenilworth* (Bliss) **36**; *The Acrobat* (Greenwood) (soloist: Jack Pinches); *The Severn Suite* (Elgar) **30**. (with Fodens Motor Works Band c Fred Mortimer; Black Dyke Mills Band c Arthur O. Pearce; & Military Band). c Cyril Jenkins & James Oliver

Salvation Army International Staff Band (1891)

Brass band music has been a part of the Salvation Army mode of operation since its foundation in 1878 as the Christian Mission, but it was not part of its initial considered policy. At an historical gathering in Salisbury in 1878 four instrumentalists turned up—two cornets, a valve trombone and euphonium not so much with the intent of providing musical entertainment as to divert the possible hostilities of the crowd. They were Charles Fry (1837-82) and his three sons. Charles thus earned the right to be considered the first Salvation Army bandmaster, though his eldest son, Fred, had the honour of being the first bandsman, having previously played at a Mission event. There was some controversy later as to which was the first full-scale organised band; the claims of the town of Northwich in Cheshire, being superseded by a matter of months by the Consett Corps of Salisbury in March 1880. From this time on bands became a regular part of Salvation Army activities. The first London band was formed in Whitechapel in the same year and by 1882 there were bands in action at Regent Hall, Clapton Congress Hall and Chalk Farm—the latter becoming one of the best-known and its dingy Baptist Chapel centre a place of pilgrimage for many connoisseurs of Salvationist brass band music. In 1887 a national unit was formed that became known as the Household Troops Band and this became well-known through tours of America and Canada and was a great source of inspiration to the musical movement in the Army.

In 1889 the Junior Staff Band was formed made up of employees at the Army's International Centre in Queen Victoria Street.

There was also an unofficial headquarters band led by Captain George Storey. From these the International Headquarters Staff Band was officially formed in 1891. It took considerable time to organise on a permanent and satisfactory basis and it was not properly constituted until 1893. The earliest Leaders (as they were termed) or organisers of the band were playing members and included Major Thomas Marshall, Commissioner William Simpson, Colonel Edwin Le Butt and Colonel Henry Haines. Their first non-playing full-time conductor was Colonel Charles Swinfen appointed in 1931. Even more influential initially was their Bandmaster, starting with Jabez Lyne and Caleb Burgess, but five years after the foundation of the band, with Captain George Mitchell who was to be the dominating figure for the next 25 years. When he retired in 1920 the band, partly as an aftermath of war, almost ceased to exist. It was fully revived in 1923 under Major George Fuller who had been a member of the band from 1891 and deputy to Mitchell for 23 years. He was a renowned band trainer. After 51 years association with the band he died and was succeeded in 1942 by Major Eric Ball, already well-known as a composer though never a playing member of the band, who gave the unit considerable musical polish. He was succeeded by Colonel Bramwell Coles 1943-4, Lieut-Colonel William Stewart in 1944 and Lieut-Colonel Bernard Adams in 1947 under whom it has since been a thriving unit in every way, adding many recordings to its list of activities. In 1953 Ralph Vaughan Williams heard the band and, greatly impressed, wrote his *Prelude on Three Welsh Hymn Tunes* especially for it.

The International Staff Band is far from being the only important permanent organisation. There was a Home Office Band organised almost at the same time; a Trade Headquarters Band formed in 1895; a second one in 1928; a Men's Social Work Headquarters Band formed in 1924; a Salvation Army Assurance Society Band in 1928; and, of course, countless regional and local bands. Their full history and the story of their activities can be found in a volume *Play the Music, Play* written by Colonel Brindley Boon in 1966 and reprinted in 1978 for the Salvation Army Centenary; published by Salvationist Publishing and Supplies Ltd.

Selected LP recordings

International Staff Band:

Brass Band Festival—Sacred SAC5077.
Brass Band Festival—Regal Zonophone SLR4005 (64).
Brass Impact—HMV SXLP50016 (73).
Brass International—Sacred SAC5068.
Christmas Festival in Brass—HMV SXLP50014 (74).
Festival Salute—HMV SXLP50017 (76).
75th Anniversary—Regal Zonophone SLRZ4015 (66).

Scottish CWS Band (1918)

Formed in 1918, considered the finest Scottish band of all time. They have been runners-up in the National Championships four times, won the Edinburgh Festival Contest three times, the Scottish Championship on 16 occasions. Fulfils many concert engagements in Scotland and frequently heard on the radio. Its musical directors through the years include J.A. Greenwood, George Hawkins, Fred Mortimer, Alex Mortimer, W.C. Crozier. The present bandmaster is Robert Oughton, well-known as a cornet-player. The band is under the patronage of the Directors of the Scottish Co-operative Society Ltd.

Selected LP recordings

Listen to the Band, No.2—Music for Pleasure MFP1137 (67). *Victors' Return* (W. Rimmer); *My Syrian Maid* (W. Rimmer); *The Flying Scot* (Grant); *St. Cuthbert* (Dykes, arr Beckingham); *Othello* (D. Rimmer); *William Tell—Overture* (Rossini, arr Hawkins); *Baa, baa, black sheep* (Campbell); *In this hour of softened splendour* (Pinsuti); *The Bold Gendarmes* (Offenbach, arr Siebert); *Le Prophète—Coronation March* (Meyerbeer). c Robert Oughton, Gregor Grant, F.J. Beckingham & Drake Rimmer
The Scottish CWS Band—Pye GSGL10430 (69). *The Hampden Roar* (Hartley); *Waltz with a Beat* (Hanmer); *Bulgarian Bugle Boy* (Agoult); *Tam o' Shanter's Ride* (D. Wright) **56**; *The Jewels of the Madonna—Intermezzo* (Wolf-Ferrari); *Andante Scherzo* (Heath); *The Watermill* (Binge); *Vizcaya* (Vinter). c Geoffrey Brand & Robert Oughton

Sun Life Stanshawe Band
(Stanshawe (Bristol) Band) (1968)

The band was formed in 1968 and started with a good nucleus of skilled and experienced instrumentalists which ensured it of quick progress in the competition field. It also acquired the services of Walter Hargreaves (Professor of French Horn and Cornet at the Royal Marine School of Music) as its Musical Director which also helped it to become one of the top and most consistent bands. It has always done well in the National Championships at both regional and national levels and won the Edinburgh Festival Championship in 1972. It qualified for the Open Championship in 1973 and gained second place in 1974 and 1976. In 1973 they won the title of Wills' British and European Band. They were the West of England Champions for 1974 and Granada Band of the Year. Originally financed by the Stanshawe Estate in the town of Yate near Bristol, they acquired the patronage of the Sun Life Insurance Society Ltd in 1978. In the same year Roy Newsome took over as professional conductor. Resident conductor is Brian Howard.

Selected LP recordings

Langford in Concert—RCA PL25185 (79)†. *Carnival Day; Scarborough Fair; Caller Herrin'; The Seventies Set; Softly awakes my heart; The Boy From Menaem—Salute to the Six; Cushie Butterfield; Après un rêve; A West Country Fantasy; Widdicombe Fair; Metropolis* (Langford, or arr Langford). c Roy Newsome & Brian Howard

*Oliver Cromwell—Two Ten TT001 (78)†. *Rosslyn March* (Ball); *Prestbury Park* (Lane); *Tuba Tapestry* (Brand); *The Prizewinners* (Sparke); *Oliver Cromwell* (Geehl) **23**; *Fantasy for Tuba* (Arnold); *Rock of Ages* (Redhead, arr Hargreaves). (John Fletcher—tuba). c Walter Hargreaves

Sounds of Brass, Vol.22—Decca SB322 (76), cass KBSC322†. *The Thieving Magpie—Overture* (Rossini, arr Wright); *Hava Nagila* (arr Siebert); *Berceuse de Jocelyn* (Godard, arr Ball); *Symphony No.5—Themes* (Tchaikovsky, arr Ball); *Gold and Silver Waltz* (Lehár); *The Bartered Bride—Polka* (Smetana, arr Wright); *Grandfather's Clock* (Doughty); *The Frogs of Aristophanes—Overture* (Bantock, arr F. Wright) **52**. c Walter Hargreaves

*Spectrum—Saydisc SDLB262 (75) (77). *Spectrum* (Vinter); *Variations on a Ninth* (Vinter) **64**; *Academic Festival Overture* (Brahms, arr D. Wright); *Suite Gothique* (Boellmann, arr Ball). c Walter Hargreaves

Thoresby Colliery Welfare Band (1948)

Founded at the Thoresby Colliery in Edwinstowe, Notts, in 1948. Progressed from fourth to second section contest status over the next few years. In 1967 William Lippeatt (formerly of Grimethorpe) became Musical Director and several important wins followed: 1968—Teesside International Eisteddfod; 1969—Belle Vue Grand Shield and Midland Region Contest at Leicester. Qualified for National Finals and were upgraded to championship class; 1970—fifth in British Open. They have made many broadcasts. In 1973 the band received the sponsorship of DOSCO Engineering Ltd. In 1975 became Midland Area Champions and sixth in the World Championships. They are known by their supporters as the *Stars of Sherwood.*

Tredegar Town Band (1876)

Tredegar Workmen's band was formed in 1876 following a meeting of townspeople who decided to place the 'Tredegar Band on a regular basis'. Presumably an ad hoc band had been prior existence for the local ironmaster had organised his own works band to play at social functions in the 1840s and there are several contemporary references to a Tredegar Ironworks band playing at community events. For much of its 103-year history it has played in adversity, with local miners and steelworkers forming the core of the band, and struggling to play in a variety of settings as unlikely as an engine-shed, a loft, a colliery stables and a nissen hut. Even so, it managed some years of distinction, and as early as 1903 had persuaded a Northern musician, Eli Shaw, to come down as conductor. The band played at the Crystal Palace about 1926 though it has no record of how well it did. Its fortunes took a steady upturn from the 1970s. It won the second section of the Great Britain Championships and consolidated its progress subsequently in the championship section, aided by some shrewd professional coaching, especially from Roy Newsome who has enjoyed a friendly relationship with the Band Society for some years.

It won the Belle Vue Spring Shield in 1975, securing an invitation to the Autumn 'Open' Championships the same year, and since securing two sevenths and an 11th position in the three appearances there to date. They were sixth-placed in the Great Britain Finals in 1977 and were finalists again in 1978, when they also secured a fifth-place in the new European Championship the following day. In 1978 they won, for the second time in their history, the title of Champion Band of Wales by securing four 'firsts' in the six domestic Welsh contests held during the year. Since 1970 they have developed a Junior Band of young people under 18 and from it they have secured a number of fine players. The Junior Band made considerable progress in its own right and in 1974, and again in 1975, won the Butlin's Youth Championship of Great Britain at the Royal Albert Hall. It is interesting to note that players from those 'double' years went on to considerable distinction, a dozen or so of them graduating to the Town Band and others going on to bands like Cory, Grimethorpe and Fodens. The present conductor—the seventh in the 103 years of the Society is W. David Thomas, appointed in January, 1978, and a Rhondda-born Welshman living near Bristol, formerly principal cornettist with the Stanshawe Band.

Selected LP recordings

Tredegar Town Band:
Bound in Brass†—*Men of Harlech* (German); *New World Fantasy* (Langford); *Iona; All through the night* (arr Langford); *Entry of The Gladiators* (Fucik); *Marching Trumpets* (Seymour); *Divertimento* (Kelly). c W. David Thomas

Tredegar Junior Band:
Sounds of Brass, Vol.20—Decca SB320 (75). *Patterns for Brass Band* (Gregson); *Watching the wheat* (arr Geehl); *Spanish Eyes* (Kaempfert, arr Bryce); *Ceramic City Festival* (Johnson); *Jamie's Patrol* (Dacre); *Tredegar Castle* (Newsome); *La Golondrina* (Serradell, arr Siebert); *Comrades in Arms* (Adam); *Moon River* (Mancini, arr Duthoit); *Torch of Freedom* (Ball). c Tudor Williams

Versatile Brass (James Shepherd)

During the ten years that James Shepherd was the principal cornettist with the Black Dyke Mills Band he conceived the idea of a well balanced and adventurous ensemble of some ten or 12 brass musicians who could introduce brass music on television, radio, in the concert hall and on recordings. He believed that virtuosity, versatility and entertainment value would attract a following and in 1972 he formed his Versatile Brass ensemble and they quickly became a popular attraction throughout Britain and on the Continent. The group is made up of musicians exclusive to its needs and its music is both progressive and novel. Their present conductor is Ray Woodfield who also arranges for the group. A recent addition has been a bass guitar for their more popular items.

Selected LP recordings
Sounds of Brass, Vol.14—Decca SB314 (74)†. *Song of the Volga Boatmen* (arr Woodfield); *Antiphony No.1* (Schutz, arr Heaton); *Hejre Kati* (Hubay, arr Mendez); *The Typewriter* (Anderson); *Three Dance Episodes for Brass Octet and Percussion* (Gregson); *The Milliardaire* (Gomez; Stone); *Radetzkiana* (Strauss, arr Paige); *Andante and Scherzo* (Fletcher); *Rondo No.3* (Mozart, arr Owenson); *Polka—Ein Schnaps* (Baker; Stone); *Carnival of Venice* (Arban); *Barbie* (Laine). c Dennis Wilby

Sounds of Brass, Vol.21—Decca SB321 (75)†. *Fives and Threes* (Golland); *Breezy Bach* (arr Moore); *Bach Goes to Town* (Templeton); *The sun whose rays* (Sullivan, arr Woodfield):; *African Wedding* (Paige; Stone); *The Music of Michel Legrand* (arr Charleson); *Spanish Eyes* (Kaempfert, arr Bryce); *Sweet Gingerbread Man* (Legrand; Berman); *Match of the Day* (Stoller); *Trumpetitistics* (Relton); *Chevalier d'Honneur* (Relton); *Divertimento for Brass—March* (Kelly); *Orfeo* (Monteverdi, arr Golland); *Burlesque* (Duck, arr Walker). c Ray Woodfield

Sounds of Brass, Vol.31—Decca SB331 (78)†. *Impact* (Woodfield); *My favourite things* (Rodgers); *Mexican Hat Dance* (Mendez); *Three Dance Miniatures* (Hedges, arr Walker; *Varied Mood* (Woodfield); *Bye Bye Blues* (Hamm; Bennett); *Cossack Ride & Slavonic Dance* (Baron; Woodfield); *Carpenteria; Chanson Suisse* (arr Woodfield); *By the time I get to Phoenix* (Webb); *Prelude and Escapade* (Bulla); *The Trouble With the Tuba Is* (Relton); *Conversation in Brass* (Wiggins). c Ray Woodfield

Sounds of Brass, Vol.37 (Strike up the Band)—Decca SB337, cass KBSC337 (79)†. *Strike Up the Band* (Gershwin, arr Woodfield); *Cavatina* (Meyers); *Czardas* (Monti, arr Renton); *Gymnopedie No.1* (Satie, arr Walker); *Violin Concerto—Finale* (Mendelssohn, arr Hopkinson); *The Harmonious Brassmen* (Hopkinson); *Gayaneh—Sabre Dance* (Khachaturian, arr Walker); *Send in the*

clowns (Sondheim, arr Charleson); *Rondeau* (Mouret, arr Bryce); *Humoresque* (Tchaikovsky, arr Walker); *Caprice* (Woodfield); *A Portrait of Gershwin* (arr Woodfield). c Frank Renton

*Whole in One (Direct Cut Disc)—Penhyde Press (78). *Toccata; Black Velvet; Canonic Study No.1—Allegro* (Telemann); *Divertimento for Wind—Minuetto and Rondo* (Haydn); *Miniature Suite—two movements* (D. Wright); *Hunter's Moon; Havah Nagilah; King's Hunting Jigg; Plink, Plank, Plunk; Mossley Festival Parade.*

The Virtuosi Brass Band of Great Britain (1973)
This first-class recording group was brought together in 1973 and has now produced nine LPs under conductors such as Eric Ball, Harry Mortimer, James Scott and Maurice Handford. It has brought together 28 of Britains' finest brass band instrumentalists drawn from many established championship bands with James Shepherd as principal cornet and leader. They meet on the average twice a year to produce these excellent LPs which are highly valued for their interesting repertoire and skilful playing.

Selected LP recordings
*The Virtuosi Brass Band, Vol.1—Virtuosi VR7301 (73). *Epic Symphony* (Fletcher) **26, 51**; *Rhapsody in Brass* (Goffin); *Air from Suite in D* (Bach, arr D. Wright); *Prelude to a Comedy* (Ball); *Zampa—Overture* (Hérold, arr W. Rimmer). c Eric Ball

The Virtuosi Brass Band, Vol.2—Virtuosi VR7302 (74)†. *The Middy* (Alford); *The Cossack* (W. Rimmer); *B.B. & C.F.* (Hume); *Castell Coch* (Powell); *Punchinello* (W. Rimmer); *The Standard of St. George* (Alford); *Washington Grays* (Grafulla); *The Cornish Cavalier* (Moyle). c Eric Ball

The Virtuosi Brass Band, Vol.3—Virtuosi VR7303 (74)†. *Comedy Overture* (Ireland) **34**; *Music for Brass—Scherzo* (D. Wright); *Samum—Symphonic Foxtrot* (Robrecht); *Rosamunde—Entr'acte Act 3* (Schubert, arr Ball); *Ballet Egyptien* (Luigi, arr D. Rimmer). c Eric Ball

The Virtuosi Brass Band, Vol.4—Virtuosi VR7404 (75)†. *Scherzophrenia* (Bryce); *Fugue in E 'St. Anne'* (Bach, arr Ball); *Lorenzo* (Keighley) **28, 64**; *Eight Bells* (Osgood); *Oliver Cromwell* (Geehl) **23, 41, 46**. c Eric Ball

*The Virtuosi Brass Band, Vol.5—Virtuosi VR7405 (75)†. *La Reine de Saba* (Gounod, arr Greenwood); *I wish you love* (Trenet, arr Waterworth); *A Moorside Suite* (Holst) **28**; *Russlan and Ludmilla—Overture* (Glinka, arr Hargreaves); *Deux Grotesques* (Picon, arr Dawson); *Rondoletto for Two Euphoniums* (Bryce); *David of the White Rock* (arr Willcocks); *Royal Border Bridge, 1850* (Butterworth). c James Scott

The Virtuosi Brass Band, Vol.6—Virtuosi VR7506 (76)†. *Festival Overture* (Shostakovitch, arr Cornthwaite); *The Watermill* (Binge); *Kenilworth* (Bliss) **36**; *Aida—Grand March* (Verdi, arr D. Wright); *La Traviata—Prelude* (Verdi, arr D. Rimmer); *Relay* (Golland); *Fingal's Cave* (Mendelssohn, arr Thompson). c Harry Mortimer

The Virtuosi Brass Band, Vol.7—Virtuosi VR7507 (76)†. *Second Suite in F* (Holst arr Herbert); *Nimrod* (Elgar, arr D. Wright); *Imperial March* (Elgar, arr Ball); *The Dream of Gerontius—Angel's Farewell* (Elgar, arr Ball); *Three Figures* (Howells) **60**. c Maurice Handford

*The Virtuosi Brass Band, Vol.8—Virtuosi VR7608 (77)†. *Le Roi d'Ys—Overture* (Lalo, arr F. Wright) **59, 71**; *Solemn Melody* (Davies, arr Hume); *Rusalka's Song to the Moon* (Dvorák, arr Corbett); *Le Cygne* (Saint-Saens, arr Mott); *Blackfriars* (Cundell, arr F. Wright) **55**; *Nabucco—Lament of the Captive Jews* (Verdi); *Tyrolean Tubas* (Clarke); *Tannhauser—Grand March* (Wagner, arr Hawkins). c Harry Mortimer

The Virtuosi Brass Band, Vol.9—Virtuosi VR7609 (78)†. *Four Preludes for Tuba and Brass Band* (Greenwood); *Jesu, joy of man's desiring* (Bach, arr Ball); *September Fantasy* (Ball); *Ruler of the Spirits* (Weber, arr Halliwell); *Les Francs Juges* (Berlioz, arr F. Wright) 61; *Stardust* (Carmichael); *Steadfast and True* (Teike); *Two Guitars*. c Stanley Boddington

The Virtuosi Brass Band—Philips SONO25BS (76). *La Reine de Saba* (Gounod, arr Greenwood); *Samum* (Robrecht); *Rondoletto* (Bryce); *Air from Suite in D* (Bach, arr D. Wright); *The Standard of St. George* (Alford); *Round the Clock* (Osgood); *I wish you love* (Trenet, arr Smith); *Prelude to a Comedy* (Ball); *Rosamunde—Entr'acte Act 3* (Schubert, arr Ball); *Ballet Egyptien* (Luigini, arr D. Rimmer). c Eric Ball, James Scott & Harry Mortimer

The Webb Ivory Newhall Band
(Newhall Band)

The history of the Newhall Band can be traced back to the early 1900s when it was just a village band that was gradually moulded into a permanent unit. It remained a lower section band until 1970, the year it won the second section Midland Area Championship. Successes followed at Buxton, Cleethorpes, Mansfield, Nottingham and London where the Band became the second Section National Brass Band Champions (1970). They were promoted to championship status in 1971. The Band has had successes at Belle Vue, Cardiff, Edinburgh, Lansing and Bagnall as well as on the Continent, recently winning first Prize at the Edinburgh Festival Contest and being one of the bands representing the Midlands at the 1978 National Finals. In January 1978 the band accepted a sponsorship from the Webb Ivory Company and became known as the Webb Ivory Newhall Band. It remains a totally amateur band with some of its members travelling over 100 miles to attend twice weekly rehearsals in Burton-on-Trent. The musicians are from all trades and professions and under their Musical Director Ernest Woodhouse have now become one of the leading Concert Bands. They have regularly broadcast and take part in six major championships each year.

Selected LP recording

From Bandstand to Concert Hall—Grosvenor GRS1075 (79)†. *Concert Prelude* (Sparke); *Springtime* (Heath); *Wellington March* (Zehle); *Scherzo* (Boekel); *The Highlander* (Sutton); *Early one morning* (arr Seymour); *Camptown Races* (Foster, arr Harvey); *Dumbo's Dance* (Gardner); *Funiculi Funicula* (Denza, arr Siebert); *Appreciation* (Powell); *My love is like a red, red rose* (arr Langford); *Clair de lune* (Debussy, arr Mott); *Honest Toil* (W. Rimmer). c Ernest Woodhouse

Wingates Temperance Band
(1873)

The band was formed in 1873 by the Westhoughton Independent Methodist as a drum and fife band, changing shortly after to brass instrumentation. It reached the Belle Vue Championship by 1904 and thereafter went from success to success achieving the unique double by winning both the National

The Webb Ivory Newhall Band.

and the Open championships in 1906 and 1907. The band has won the British Open seven times (1906, 1907, 1918, 1921, 1923, 1939, 1975) and the National again in 1931 and 1971, and has been placed on in-numerable occasions. They can claim to have won every major title in the contest world. Their Musical Directors have included such famous names as William Halliwell, William Rimmer and Harold Moss.

Selected LP recordings

Fireworks and Sparklers—Grosvenor GRS1045 (76)†. *Epic Theme* (Golland); *The Lost Chord* (Sullivan, arr Langford); *Fireworks* (Howarth) **75**; *The Thunderer* (Sousa, arr H. Mortimer); *Thais—Meditation* (Massenet, arr Golland); *Winter Dreams* (Hughes); *Capriccio Espagnol—Finale* (Rimsky-Korsakov, arr Golland). c Richard Evans

Flourishing Brass—Polydor 2460 246 (75). *The Pathfinders* (Lockyer, arr Beckingham); *Berenice—Minuet* (Handel, arr Hawkins); *John Peel* (arr F. Mortimer); *Jamaican Rumba* (Benjamin, arr Spurgin); *Three Dale Dances* (Wood); *Merry Musicians* (Greenwood);

The Caliph of Bagdad—Overture (Boieldieu, arr Rimmer); *Bell Bird Polka* (Barsotti); *Sea Dogs—Concert Overture* (Johnstone). c John Harrison

Listen to the Band, No.1—The World Famous Wingates Temperance Band—Music for Pleasure MFP1099 (67). *Slaidburn* (W. Rimmer); *Skye Boat Song* (Lawson, arr Rimmer); *Kim* (Street): *España* (Chabrier, arr Rimmer); *Music for the Royal Fireworks* (Handel, arr Wright); *Tantalusqualen—Overture* (Suppé); *Three Blind Mice* (Douglas); *Belmont* (arr Boddington); *Weber's Last Waltz* (Weber, arr Rimmer); *Black Knight* (Rimmer). c Hugh Parry

The National Championship—Pye GSGL10482 (72). *Victors Return; Serenade Espagnole; Festival music* (Ball); *Bandology* (Osterling); *Rhapsody in Blue* (Gershwin); *4th Horn Concerto—Rondo* (Mozart) *American Patrol* (Meachum); *Una voce poco fa* (Rossini) Also:

Brass from Wingate—Pye GSGL10461.

Songs of Joy and Peace—Polydor 2928 009.

Sounds of Brass, Vol 38—Decca SB338, cass KBSC338 (79)†.

Wingates Temperance Band—Fanfare SIT60047.

Yorkshire Imperial Metals Band
(Yorkshire Copper Works Band)
(1936)

The band was formed in 1936 at the instigation of the then Managing Director of the Yorkshire Copper Works, Mr Kenneth Fraser, at Stourton. It soon became a prominent band under the musical direction of the late William Halliwell and was in the championship grade by 1938, qualifying for the British Open in 1939 and was frequently heard on the radio. The band's fortunes fluctuated until the early 1960s when they began to make their mark in competitions and in 1961 they won the first BBC competition for brass bands. Trevor Walmsley became their musical director in 1965 and their subsequent successes included: Triple Winners Edinburgh International Music Festival 1966; British Open runners-up 1966; Yorkshire Champions 1968 and 1970; winners of the Teesside International Music Festival 1970; North Region Champions 1970; winners North East Area 1969 and 1971. They won the British Open at Belle Vue in 1970 and 1971. The crowning triumph came in 1978 when they won the National Championship with their performance of the music from Sir Arthur Bliss's *Checkmate* ballet. A band of dedicated amateurs entirely drawn from the employees of Yorkshire Imperial Metals, they are unique in that much of the metal tubing used in the manufacture of their instruments is made in the works. They are very active as a concert band and have been seen on Yorkshire TV's *Stars on Sunday*. Their present Musical Director is Dennis Carr.

Selected LP recordings
The Band of Yorkshire Imperial Metals—Two Ten TT002 (78)†. *Glendene* (J. Carr); *Napoli* (Bellstedt, arr Brand); *Peasant's Song* (Grieg arr Street); *Scena Sinfonica* (Geehl) **52**; *Concert Prelude* (Sparke); *Rhapsody for E flat Soprano Cornet* (Eaves); *Portsmouth* (trad arr Brand); *Dolly Suite—Berceuse* (Fauré, arr Sparke); *Strand-on-the-Green* (Platts). c Denis Carr

Brass International—Pye TB3001 (75). *Valdres March; Frolic for Trombones* (Heath); *Yesterday* (Lennon & McCartney); *Night on a Bare Mountain* (Mussorgsky); *If I were*

King (Adam); *Malaguena* (Lecuona); *Eye Level; Post Horn Galop* (Koenig); *McArthur Park*. c Trevor Walmsley

*Checkmate—Two Ten TT003 (78)†. *County Palatine* (Johnstone); *Two of the Tops* (J. Carr); *Serenade* (Bourgeois); *Tam o' Shanter's Ride* (D. Wright); *Yorkshire Imperial Metals* (S. Wood); *Fantasy for Euphonium & Brass Band* (Sparke); *Sleeping Beauty Panorama* (Tchaikovsky, arr Brand); *Checkmate—Dances* (Bliss, arr Ball) **78**. c Denis Carr

Highlights in Brass—Pye GSGL10488 (72) (74). *Prelude for an Occasion* (Gregson); *Festival Music—Overture, Romance and Impromptu* (Ball) **56**; *Bandology* (Osterling); *Rhapsody in Blue* (Gershwin, arr Huckridge); *Horn Concerto No.4—Rondo* (Mozart, *American Patrol* (Miller); *The Barber of Seville—Una voce poco fa* (Rossini). c Trevor Walmsley

Sounds of Brass, Vol.2—Decca SB302 (72)†. *Yeomen of the Guard—Overture* (Sullivan, arr Muscraft); *Pageantry* (Howells) **37**; *The Severn Suite—Fugue* (Elgar); *The Tops* (Powell); *España* (Chabrier, arr D. Wright); *South Rampart Street Parade* (Haggart; Bauduc; Crosby); *The Stripper* (Rose, arr Walker). c Trevor Walmsley

Sounds of Brass, Vol.6—Decca SB306 (73)†. *Yorkshire Imperial March* (Wood); *Trumpet Concerto in F minor—1st Movt.* (Boeme, arr Walker); *La Bohème—Musetta's Waltz* (Puccini); *Carnival of Venice* (Steiger); *Napoli* (Bekksted, arr Owenson); *Indian Summer* (Herbert, arr Hespe); *Mélodie et Caprice* (Hespe); *Willow Echoes* (Simon); *Meditation for Brass* (Beresford-Field). c Trevor Walmsley

Sounds of Yorkshire Imperial Metals—Silverline DJSL034. *Orpheus in the Underworld—Overture* (Offenbach, arr F. Wright); *The Paragon* (Sutton); *Recitative and Romance* (Heath); *Watching the Wheat* (trad arr Geehl); *Imperial Echoes* (Safaroni); *Little Suite No.1* (Arnold); *Lt Kije—Troika* (Prokofiev); *Colonel Bogey on Parade* (Alford) c Denis Carr

*Superstar Brass—Pye TBX3008 (73). *Florentiner March* (Fucik); *El Cumbanchero; Holiday for Trombones; Summertime* (Gershwin); *The Silken Ladder* (Rossini); *Procession of the Sardar* (Ippolitor-Ivanov); *The Typewriter* (Anderson); *Largo al factotum* (Rossini); *Godspell—Jesus Christ Superstar*

Medley (Webber). c Trevor Walmsley
Yorkshire Brass—CBS 62937 (67), Embassy 31012. *Kenilworth—March* (Bliss); *Somewhere a voice is calling* (Tate); *The Wee MacGregor Patrol* (Amers); *Adieu* (Beethoven); *Phil the Fluter's Ball* (French, arr Langford); *A Downland Suite—Elegy* (Ireland); *Traffic Tangle* (Howe); *The Sunshine of your smile* (Raye); *Round Tower* (Hutchings); *Resurgam* (Ball) **50**. c Trevor Walmsley

Other bands and recordings

A) Individual bands

Bacup Band (1858-71)
Winners of the British Open 1864, 1865, 1869 and 1870.

Batley Old Band
Winners of the British Open in 1890.

Bickershaw Colliery Band
Winners of the British Open in 1940, 1943 and 1946.

Burton Constructional (Newhall) Band
Top Brass—Pye TB3006 (76). *Australasian March* (W. Rimmer); *The girl I left behind me* (arr Langford); *The Star* (Catelinet); *Jolson Memories* (arr Young); *La Mantella* (Zutano, arr D. Rimmer); *The Elephant March* (Hume); *Silver threads among the gold* (Danks, arr Allison); *Mancini Magic* (arr Street); *Prelude and Fugue* (Bach, arr Brugman); *Hasta la vista* (Wallebom, arr Langstrand & Howe). c Ernest Woodhouse

Camborne (Compair Holman) Town Band
Sounds Great—Rainbow Sound RSR101S (74). *Challenge March* (Broadbent); *Saxhorn Polka* (Jakeway); *L'Arlésienne—Agnus Dei* (Bizet, arr Wright); *Whims* (Schumann); *The Wedding* (Preito); *Cornish Cavalier* (Moyle); *Robert Farnon for Brass* (arr Street); *If with all your heart* (Mendelssohn); *Great Soul* (Palmer); *High on a hill* (Moorhouse; Rees; Bradley, arr Siebert); *Pirates of Penzance—Overture* (Sullivan, arr Sargent). c Derek Johnston

Cammell Laird Works Band
Brass Prom—Reality RY109, SRY1009 (67). *Lohengrin—Prelude Act 3* (Wagner, arr D. Wright); *Carmen—Arogonaise & Finale* (Bizet, arr D. Wright); *Swan Lake—Dance of the Swans & Csardas* (Tchaikovsky, arr D. Wright); *Espana* (Chabrier, arr D. Wright); *Thunder and Lightning Polka* (Strauss, arr D. Wright); *Sylvia—Procession of Bacchus* (Delibes, arr D. Wright); *Casse Noisette* (Tchaikovsky, arr D. Wright); *The Grenadiers* (Waldteufel, arr D. Wright); *The Bartered Bride—Overture* (Smetana, arr D. Wright). c Denis Wright

Cammell Laird Band
Cammell Laird Band—Fontana STL5531 (70). *Fanfare and Soliloquy* (Sharpe); *Copa Cobana* (Stephens); *Thundercrest* (Osterling, arr Wright); *Lucy Long* (Godfrey, arr Herbert); *French Military March* (Saint-Saens); *Scherzo* (Boekel); *Tyrolean Tubas* (Clark); *Seventy-Six Trombones* (Willson, arr Duthoit); *Chit-Chat Polka* (Strauss, arr Pope); *Marche Slave* (Tchaikovsky, arr Davies). c James Scott

Carlisle St Stephens Band (1908)
Winners of the National Championship in 1927 and 1929.

Cinderford Band
Forest Festival Brass—Grosvenor GRS1070 (78)†.

Crossfield's (Perfection) Soap Works Band
Winners of the National Championship in 1911.

Crossley Carpet Works Band (Halifax)
Championship Brass—Paxton LPT1013 (63). *La Forza del Destino—Overture* (Verdi, arr F. Wright) **62**; *Marche Militaire* (Schubert, arr W. Rimmer); *Glastonbury Overture* (D. Wright). c John Harrison
Top Brass—Pye GGL0395, GSGL10395 (67). *The Cavalier* (Harrison); *Pop goes the weasel* (Hawkins); *The Jester* (Greenwood); *Rule Britannia—Overture* (Arne, arr W. Rimmer); *One Note Bugler* (Scull); *Hymn to Music* (Buck); *Cornets to the Fore* (Owenson); *Tannhauser—Grand March* (Wagner, arr D. Wright). c John Harrison

Dalmellington Main Band
Doone Valley Brass—Neptune NA103 (77).

Denton Original Band (1817)
Winners of the National Championship in 1900.

Dodworth Colliery Band
Entertaining Brass—Response RES200 (79)†.

E. Haswell Band
H.G. & The Eltaswell Band—Pye NSPL18610 (79)†.

Ferodo Works Band
Championship Brass—Paxton LPT1011 (62). *Sinfonietta* (Leidzen) *55*. (see also The Fairey band). c George Hespe

Music for Brass—Paxton (EP) PEP123. *Galopade* (Palmer); *Kinderscout* (Hespe). (See also All Star Brass). c George Hespe

Hebburn Colliery Band
Winners of the National Championship in 1904.

Hendon Band (1957)
The Hendon Way—Pye TB3011 (77).

Horwich RMI Band
Winners of the National Championship in 1922.

Irwell Springs Band
Winners of the National Championship in 1905, 1908 and 1913.

Kilmarnock Band
Kilmarnock Concert Brass

Lee Mount Band
Winners of the National Championship in 1901.

The Lewis Merthyr Band
Voices and Brass: A Winter Celebration —Pye TB3018 (79). *Fantasia on Welsh Hymn Tunes* (Thomas); *Silent Night* (arr L. Williams); *A Christmas Medley* (arr Carter); *A Christmas Fantasy* (Langford); *Laudamus* (Owen, arr Prothero); *Alleluia* (Mozart, arr Mortimer); *When a Child is Born* (Zacar; Jay, arr Golland); *O Praise the Lord with One Consent* (Handel, arr Woodgate); *Christmas Swing-Along* (arr Ashmore); *A Christmas Overture* (arr Golland) with Helen Lewis & The Cwmbran Male Choir—c Huw Davies. c Nigel Seaman

Leyland Motors Band
Sounds of Brass, Vol.26—Decca SB326 (76)†. *Royal Tiger March* (Moss); *Chal Romano—Overture* (Ketelbey, arr Moss); *Trumpet Concerto—excerpts* (Haydn, arr Wright); *Le Domino Noir—Overture* (Auber,

arr W. Rimmer); *Suite Gothique* (Boellmann); *Variations on a Welsh Melody* (W. Rimmer); *Overdale* (Moss). c Michael T. Cotter

Leyland Vehicles Band
Travelling With Leyland—RCA PL25175 (79)†.

London Brass Players
Harry Mortimer & The London Brass Players—State ETMP7 (79)†. *Heritage* (Langford); *Honest* (Price; Jackman); *The Beast of Black Mountain* (Jackman); *Happy Ending* (Wallens); *Journey's End* (Shakespeare); *Nights of Gladness* (Ancliffe); *The Old Haunted Colliery* (Scott); *Jubilee Hoe Down* (Clarke); *Hanford Heights* (Davies); *Free As Air* (Kelly); *Music for a Pageant* (Fonteyn); *Barwick Green* (Wood). c Harry Mortimer

Luton Band (Luton Red Cross Band)
Winners of the National Championship in 1923.

Splendour in Brass—Polydor 2928 004.

Markham Main Colliery Band
Mineworkers' National Champions 1904 & 1965.

Markham Main Colliery Band—Pye GGL0426, GSGL10426 (68). *Viennese Ladies—March* (Lehár); *Peasant's Song* (Grieg); *Spanish Dance No.1* (Moskowski); *Yesterday* (Lennon & McCartney); *The Three Musketeers—Suite* (Hespe) *53*; *Hungarian Dance* (Messager); *Just Jane* (Street); *Ritual Fire Dance* (Falla); *Moon River* (Mancini); *Jeepers creepers* (Warren); *Fiddler on the Roof* (Bock). c Allan Street

Top Brass—Pye GGL10394, GSGL10394 (67). *The Australasian* (W. Rimmer); *High Heels* (Street); *Alpine Polka* (Round); *Water Music—Suite* (Handel); *L'Arlesienne— Farandole* (Bizet); *Arabella* (Chester); *Hymn to St. Francis* (arr Street); *Three Sketches* (Street). c Allan Street

Marsden Colliery Band
Winners of the National Championship in 1925.

National Youth Brass Band of Great Britain (1952)
National Youth Band—Pye GGL0428, GSGL10428 (68). *French Military March* (Saint-Saens); *Voices of Youth—Suite* (Gregson); *Capriccio Italien* (Tchaikovsky); *Scherzo for Band* (Boekel); *Air from Suite in D*

(Bach); *Entertainments for Brass Band* (Vinter). c Geoffrey Brand
Top Brass—Pye GGL0403, GSGL10403 (68). *Lohengrin—Prelude Act 3* (Wagner, arr D. Wright); *William Tell—Ballet Music* (Rossini); *Chanson Triste* (Tchaikovsky); *Little Suite for Brass* (Arnold); *The Spirit of Pageantry* (Fletcher); *Introduction & Allegro Spiritoso* (Senaillé, arr D. Wright); *Rhapsody No.2 on Negro Spirituals* (Ball). c Geoffrey Brand

Ransome Hoffmann Pollard Works Band (1937)
Rolling Brass—Pye 'Marble Arch' MALS1418 (71). *Ridgehill* (Sykes); *King Cotton* (Sousa); *Wendine* (Masters); *The Cossack* (W. Rimmer); *Ravenswood* (W. Rimmer); *Punchinello* (W. Rimmer); *The Australasian* (W. Rimmer); *Castel Coch* (Powell); *Raby* (Allen); *The Whistling Cockney* (Burgess); *Drum Majorette* (Steck). c Dennis Masters
Sounds of Brass, Vol.3—Decca SB303 (73)†. *An Epic Symphony—Heroic March* (Fletcher); *The Grenadiers* (Waldteufel); *The Caledonian* (Allison); *Casino Dances* (Gung'l); *Messiah—Hallelujah Chorus* (Handel); *Nibelungen March* (Wagner, arr Grant); *Capriccio Italien* (Tchaikovsky); *Les Francs Juges—Overture* (Berlioz, arr F. Wright) **61**. c Dennis Masters

Redbridge Brass (1966)
The Redbridge Phenomenon—Grosvenor GRS1018. *March Prelude* (Gregson); *The Prince of Denmark's March* (Clarke); *The Washington Post* (Sousa); *Pennine Way* (Johnstone); *March of the Clowns* (Picon); *Amparita Roca* (Texidor); *Washington D.C.* (Kelly); *Bandology* (Osterling); *Sospan Fach* (arr Jacob); *Flying Feathers* (Osgood); *March with a Beat* (Hanmer). c John Ridgeon

Royal Doulton Band (1973)
Clayhanger—Pye TBX3005. *Clayhanger Theme* (Hill); *The Falcons* (Williams); *To a wild rose* (MacDowell, arr Ball); *Trumpets Wild* (Walters); *Instant Concerto* (Walters); *March of the Toys* (Herbert); *Pendyne March* (Martyn); *The Rosary* (Nevin); *The Entertainer* (Joplin, arr Hanmer); *Work Song* (Adderly; Brown); *Paint Your Wagon—Selection* (Loewe). c Edward Gray
Also:
Brass Aria—Pye TBX3014 (77).
Royal Doulton Band—Pye (78)†.

Rushden Temperance Band (1875)

St. Austell Band
White Heritage—Polydor 2928 012.

Saint Dennis Band (1836)
The Best in the West—Polydor 2485 010 (71). *Cornish Floral Dance Patrol* (arr Moyle); *Watching the wheat* (arr Wiggins); *Jolson Memories* (arr Young); *Thornton* (Moyle); *Rufford Abbey* (D. Rimmer); *Roll Away Bet* (Hume); *Berceuse de Jocelyn* (Godard, arr Beckingham); *Brass Band Blues* (Gould); *Sandy and Jock* (Sutton); *A Psalm for All Nations* (Ball). c E.J. Williams
Cornish Festival Brass—Pye TB3009 (76). *Restormel* (Moyle); *Cornish Rock* (Moyle); *Golden Rain* (D. Rimmer); *Cornish Festival Overture* (Ball); *Centaur* (Broadbent); *To a wild rose* (MacDowell, arr Ball); *Frolic for Trombone* (Heath); *Angel Voices* (arr Jordan); *From the New World* (Dvorák, arr D. Rimmer). c E.J. Williams

Shaw Band
Winners of the National Championship in 1909.

Solna Brass (Stockholm)
Concerto—Grosvenor GRS1031 (75). *Promenade—Overture* (Bryce); *Music for the Royal Nuptials* (Roman); *Four Fancies* (Maurer, arr Gay); *Cornet Concerto* (D. Wright) (soloist: Bram Gay). c Per Ohlsson

Solna Brass—RCA PL25147 (78)†. *Serenade for Strings—March* (Wiren, arr Fröden); *Norwegian Dance No.2* (Grieg, arr Ryan); *Maple Leaf Rag* (Joplin, arr Bryce); *Valse Triste* (Sibelius, arr Fröden); *Spanish Gypsy Dance* (Marquina, arr Dawson); *Old Fäbodpsalm* (Lindberg, arr Stern); *Under the Blue and Yellow Flag* (Widquist, arr Fröden); *Trombone Concerto* (Rimsky-Korsakov, arr Langford); *Mock Morris* (Grainger, arr Wright); *Swedish Rhapsody No.2* (Leidzen). c Lars-Gunnar Björklund

Stalybridge Band (1890)
Stalybridge Brass—Grosvenor GRS1055 (77)†. *Entry of the Gladiators* (Fucik, arr Langford); *Golliwog's Cakewalk* (Debussy, arr Ball); *We've only just begun* (Nichols; Williams, arr Ralton); *Copa Cobana* (Stephens); *Robert le Diable—Overture* (Meyerbeer, arr Moreton); *Cossack Patrol* (Knipper, arr Langford); *The Little Rhapsody in Blue* (Gershwin, arr Thompson); *Trumpets Wild* (Schumann, arr Walters); *En-*

tertainments—*Elegy* (Vinter); *Colonel Bogey on Parade* (Alford). c Les Hine

Templemore Band (1937)
Tullis Russell Mills Band (1920)
50th Anniversary—Tullis Russell SSLX326 (70). *Traditional Christmas Carols; Trumpet Fiesta* (Phillips); *Jamie's Patrol* (Dacre); *Viennese Ladies—Overture* (Lehár); *St. Clement; Phil the Fluter's Ball* (French, arr Langford); *Trumpet Tune and Air* (Purcell, arr Wright); *National Symphony—Shrine of Scotland* (D. Rimmer); *Spanish Gypsy Dance* (Marquina, arr Dawson); *Rhapsody on Negro Spirituals* (Ball); *Cossack March* (W. Rimmer). c Duncan S. Campbell

The Watney Silver Band (1937)
Originally West London Silver Band & Borough of Barnes Band.
Festival Band Series, Vol.2—Saga EROS8129. *Marching Trumpets* (Seymour); *The Sound of Music—Edelweiss* (Rodgers); *Tabarinage* (Docker); *Trombola* (Bryce); *Semiramide—Overture* (Rossini, arr Hawkins); *Sounds of Sousa* (arr Hanmer); *Mellow Mood* (Sansom); *La Mascarada* (Siebert); *The Lazy Trumpeter* (Siebert); *The Cock o' the North* (arr Bryce); *Little Suite No.2—Galop* (Arnold). c Albert Meek
The Watney Silver Band—Music for Pleasure MFP1303 (69). *Fanfare—Watneys* (Meek); *Best Foot Forward* (Tomlinson); *Round the Clock* (Osgood); *Trombones to the Fore* (Scull, arr Pope); *Il Bacio* (Arditi, arr Bidgood); *Poet and Peasant—Overture* (Suppé); *The Arcadians—Overture* (Monckton; Talbot, arr Wood); *The Red Barrel* (Meek); *Caramba* (Brandez); *The Rover's Return* (Siebert); *Chi-Chi* (Walker, arr Brand); *Merry Mancunians* (Langford). c Albert Meek

Whitburn Burgh Band
Whitburn Brass—Neptune NA112 (79)†.

William Davis Construction Group Band
Constructive Brass—Grosvenor GRS1048 (77)†. *HMS Pinafore—Overture* (Sullivan, arr Martyn); *Send in the clowns* (Sondheim, arr Bartram); *Three Dale Dances* (Wood); *Way Out West* (Crookes); *Wellington March* (Zehle); *Napoli* (Del Staiger); *Norwegian Dance No.2* (Grieg, arr Ryan); *Divertimento* (Kelly). c John Berryman

B) Various—massed bands, recording bands, collections, etc

All Star (Concert) Brass Band—Paxton (45) PEP101. *Hora Tzigane* (Rayner); *Nine Busy Fingers* (Woods); *Cornet Carillon* (Binge); *Diabolero* (Picon). c Harry Mortimer
All Star (Concert) Brass Band—Paxton (45) PEP102. *Magic Lanterns* (Field, Hanley); *Pageantry* (Russell); *Trombones on the Spree* (Field); *Three Jolly Sailormen* (Siebert). c Harry Mortimer
All Star (Concert) Brass Band—Paxton (45) PEP103. *Lazy Trumpeter* (Siebert); *Tombola* (Alexander); *Hungarian March* (Berlioz); *Lohengrin—Prelude Act 3* (Wagner, arr Wright). c Harry Mortimer & Eric Ball
All Star (Concert) Brass Band—Paxton (45) PEP104. *Ichabod* (Tchaikovsky); *Blaenwern & Crimond* (arr Boddington); *Slavonic Dance* (Dvořák); *Gay Cavalier* (Beaver). c Harry Mortimer
All Star (Concert) Brass Band—Paxton (45) PEP107. *Polished Brass* (Siebert); *Sousa on Parade* (Sousa); *Mac & Mort* (Mortimer); *Valour and Victory* (Scull). c Harry Mortimer
All Star (Concert) Brass Band—Paxton (45) PEP108. *Egmont Overture* (Beethoven); *Donnybrook Fair* (Lucas); *Welsh Fantasy* (Price). c Harry Mortimer
All Star (Concert) Brass Band—Paxton (45) PEP109. *Indian Summer—Suite* (Ball); *Hindoo Song* (Rimsky-Korsakov); *Sleigh Ride* (Anderson). c Harry Mortimer
All Star (Concert) Brass Band—Paxton (45) PEP110. *To a wild rose* (MacDowell, arr Ball); *L'Arlesienne Suite—Farandole & Minuet* (Bizet); *All in the April evening* (Roberton); *Gypsy Wedding Dance* (Siebert). c Harry Mortimer
All Star (Concert) Brass Band—Paxton (45) PEP117. *Robert le Diable—Overture* (Meyerbeer); *Fair Maid of Perth—Romance* (Bizet); *Watching the wheat* (arr Geehl). c Harry Mortimer
All Star (Concert) Brass Band—Paxton (45) PEP123. *Trombones to the Fore* (Scull); *Warriors Three* (Siebert) (see also Ferodo Works Band). c Harry Mortimer
All Star (Concert) Brass Band—Paxton (45) PEP124. *The Explorers* (Yorke); *Bolero Brillante* (Geehl); *Fantasy on National Airs*

(Wright). c Harry Mortimer

The Big Brass Band—Decca LK4963, PFS4143 (68) SPA464 (79)†. *BB and CF* (Hume); *Bugler's Holiday* (Anderson); *In a Monastery Garden* (Ketelbey); *Swing Along* (Siebert); *Puppet on a String* (Martin, arr Coulter); *Passing of the Regiments* (arr Winter); *1812 Overture* (Tchaikovsky, arr D. Wright); *Santa Lucia* (Denza, arr Siebert); *Seventy-Six Trombones* (Willson); *España* (Waldteufel, arr D. Rimmer); *Abide with me* (Lyte). c Harry Mortimer

Brass on the March—Columbia TW0138 (66). (BMC Concert Band; Fairey Band; Fodens Motor Works Band) *Under the Double Eagle* (Wagner); *Le Rêve Passé* (Helmer); *With Sword and Lance* (Starke); *The Thin Red Line* (Alford); *Fame and Glory* (Matt); *El Abanico* (Javaloyes); *Old Comrades* (Teikel); *National Emblem* (Bagley); *The Phantom Brigade* (Alford); *Niebelungen* (Wagner, arr Grant); *Voice of the Guns* (Alford); *On the Quarter Deck* (Alford). c Harry Mortimer

Bright as Brass, Vol.2—Decca LK4363, SKL4109 (60). (Fodens Motor Works Band; Fairey Band; Morris Motors Band) *Le Prophète—Coronation March* (Meyerbeer, arr Reynolds); *The Pirates of Penzance—Overture* (Sullivan, arr D. Rimmer); *Shepherd's Hey* (Grainger, arr D. Wright); *Alpine Rumba* (Haysom, arr Gay); *Donkey Serenade* (Friml, arr Denham); *Lilac Time—Selection* (Schubert-Clutsam, arr Hume); *Marche Slave* (Tchaikovsky, arr Davies); *Tyrolean Tango* (Stewart, arr Brand); *Trombones to the Fore* (Scull, arr Pope); *Lord Nuffield March* (Zbridger); *Navy Mixture* (Seymour); *Royal Air Force March-Past* (Walford-Davies). c Harry Mortimer

Fantasy in Brass—Columbia 33SX1471, SCX3461 (63). (Fairey Band; Fodens Motor Works Band; GUS Band; Morris Motors) *Summit March* (Seymour); *The Faithful Hussar* (Frantzen); *Slavonic Rhapsody No.1* (Friedemann); *Post Horn Galop* (Koenig); *When Johnny comes marching home* (arr Howe); *Farewell Waltz* (Binge); *Sousa on Parade* (Sousa, arr Palmer); *Sandpaper Ballet* (Anderson); *Iolanthe—Overture* (Sullivan, arr Sargent); *Stardust* (Carmichael); *Praise my soul, the King of Heaven* (Goss). c Harry Mortimer

Favourite Overtures for Brass—Columbia TW0225 (69). (Men O' Brass: Fairey Band; Fodens Motor Works Band; BMC

Band) *The Mikado—Overture* (Sullivan, arr Sargent); *Fra Diavolo—Overture* (Auber); *Ruy Blas—Overture* (Mendelssohn, arr Langford); *Morning, Noon and Night in Vienna—Overture* (Suppé); *William Tell—Overture* (Rossini). c Harry Mortimer

Festival Brass (W.D. & H.O. Wills, 1970)—HMV CSD3675 (70). (Morris Motors; Ransome & Marles; Yorkshire Imperial; Cambourne) *Opening Fanfare* (Moreton); *Bramwyn* (Carr); *Light Cavalry—Overture* (Suppé); *Londonderry Air* (arr Coleman); *March of the Pacemakers* (Langford); *Trombones to the Fore* (Scull); *Liebestraume* (Liszt, arr Coleman); *Embassy Suite—Finale* (Street); *Lustspiel* (Keler-Bela, arr Martyn); *Marche Slave* (Tchaikovsky). c Harry Mortimer

A Festival of Massed Bands—Rediffusion 15-69 (78). (City of Coventry; GUS (Footwear); Ransome Hoffman and Pollard; Yorkshire Imperial Metals; Trumpets of Royal Marines School of Music; Luton Girls Choir; etc) *Supreme Command—Fanfare* (Dunn); *Crown Imperial* (Walton, arr F. Wright); *Ruy Blas—Overture* (Mendelssohn, arr Langford); *Carmen—Prelude* (Bizet, arr Martyn); *Messiah—Hallelujah Chorus* (Handel, arr Ball); *The Mountbatten March* (Dunn); *Jesu, joy of man's desiring* (Bach) *New World Fantasy* (arr Langford); *Little Lisa* (Warr); *Carmen—Gypsy Chorus* (Bizet, arr Martyn); *Onward Christian Soldiers* (Sullivan). c Harry Mortimer & Sir Vivian Dunn

Fireman's Galop—Columbia TWOX1033 (75). (Men O' Brass: Fairey Band; Fodens Motor Works; City of Coventry) *Thunderbirds* (Gray, arr Siebert); *HMS Pinafore—Overture* (Sullivan, arr Martyn); *Orpheus in the Underworld—Can-Can* (Offenbach, arr Woodfield); *Colditz March* (Farnon); *Match of the Day* (Stoller); *Who do you think you are kidding, Mr. Hitler* (Perry; Taverner); *Tricky Trombones* (Helyer); *633 Squadron* (Goodwin, arr Bryce); *The Rover's Return* (Siebert); *Tango Taquin* (Barratt; Siebert); *The Three Trumpeters* (Agostini, arr Bainum); *New World Fantasy* (arr Langford); *Fireman's Galop* (Hertel, arr Siebert). c Harry Mortimer

A Lifetime of Music—EMI NTS145 (78). (All Star Brass) *Mephistopheles* (Douglas); *The Arcadians—Overture* (Monckton; Talbot, arr Wood); *Passing by* (E. Purcell, arr F. Wright); *Air and Variations on Grand-*

father's Clock (arr Doughty); *Sandon* (arr Newsome); *Death or Glory* (Hall); *Marche Militaire* (Schubert, arr Sargent); *The Tops* (Powell); *March of the Manikins* (Fletcher); *No, No Nanette & Tea for Two* (Youmans, arr Hume); *Love will find a way* (Fraser-Simson, arr Hume); *She will say her say & Robbers' Chorus* (Norton, arr Hume); *L'Arlesienne—Farandole* (Bizet, arr D. Wright). c Harry Mortimer

Marching with the Grand Massed Bands—Columbia 33SX1652, SCX3520 (64). (Fairey Band; Fodens Motor Works; BMC) *Blaze Away* (Holzmann); *El Abanico* (Javaloyes); *Marching Sergeants King Cotton* (Sousa); *March of the Slide Trombone; Trafalgar; The Churchill March; Imperial Echoes* (Safroni, arr Hume); *Quand Madelon* (Robert); *El Capitan* (Sousa); *Bright and Early; Entry of the Gladiators* (Fucik); *Out of the Blue* (Bath); *Broad Highway*. c Harry Mortimer

Massed Brass Band Festival Concert From Belle Vue—Columbia TW0240 (69). (BMC; Fairey; Fodens; Grimethorpe; CWS (Manchester); Rossendale Male Voice Choir; and Ian Wallace) *Famous British Marches* (arr Langford); *Largo* (Handel, arr Seymour); *Post Horn Galop* (Koenig, arr Mortimer); *Drake's Drum* (Stanford, arr Harris); *TUC Centenary March* (Vinter); *Orpheus in the Underworld—Galop* (Offenbach, arr F. Wright); *Life Divine* (Jenkins) **21**; *Waltzing with Strauss* (arr Seymour); *Faust—Soldiers Chorus* (Gounod, arr Mortimer); *Thunderbirds March* (Gray, arr Siebert); *Jerusalem* (Parry, arr D. Wright). c Harry Mortimer

Massed Brass from the Royal Albert Hall (Wills 1971)—HMV CSD3697 (71). (Grimethorpe; GUS; Morris Motors; Yorkshire Imperial Metals) *Radetzky March* (Strauss I, arr Ryan); *Academic Festival Overture* (Brahms, arr Wright); *French Military March* (Saint-Saens); *Berenice—Minuet* (Handel, arr Mortimer); *Ride of the Valkyries* (Wagner, arr Thompson); *The Mikado—Overture* (Sullivan, arr Seymour); *To a wild rose* (MacDowell, arr Martyn); *Mors et Vita—Judex* (Gounod, arr Seymour); *Trumpet Voluntary* (Clarke, arr Gay); *Agnus Dei* (Bizet, arr Smith-Masters); *Finlandia* (Sibelius, arr Bidgood). c Harry Mortimer

Massed Brass Spectacular (Men O' Brass)—Columbia TW0185 (67). *Colonel Bogey on Parade* (Alford); *Trumpet Voluntary*

(Clarke, arr Gay); *Thunder and Lightning Polka* (Strauss, arr Wright); *Pomp and Circumstance March No.2* (Elgar, arr Hume); *Praise to the Holiest* (arr Siebert); *The Lost Chord* (Sullivan, arr Langford); *Men o' Brass Fanfare* (Hespe); *Royal Standard March* (Chesterton); *Wee MacGregor Patrol* (Amers); *Onward Christian Soldiers* (Sullivan, arr Siebert); *Aida—Grand March* (Verdi, arr Wright); *Messiah—Hallelujah Chorus* (Handel, arr Langford). c Harry Mortimer

Massed Brass Bands, Vol.1—Decca LK4279, SKL4013 (59). *Fanfare* (Seymour); *Iolanthe—March of the Peers* (Sullivan, arr Rimmer); *Flanagan's Mare* (Stanton, arr Gay); *Slavonic Rhapsody* (Friedmann, arr Wright); *A Trumpet Piece for a Ceremonial Occasion* (Scull, arr Wright); *The Holy City* (Adams); *Swashbuckler March* (Moreton); *Trombones on Broadway* (Barsotti); *Chit Chat Polka* (Strauss, arr Pope); *Faust—The Soldiers' Chorus* (Gounod); *Zamorra* (Seymour); *Napoleon Galop* (Martyn); *Colonel Bogey* (Alford); *William Tell—Overture* (Rossini, arr Hawkins). c Harry Mortimer

Massed Brass Bands, Vol.2—Decca LK4278, SKL4056 (59). *Fanfare* (Seymour); *Pendine* (Martin); *Marching Trumpets* (Seymour); *2nd Rhapsody on Negro Spirituals* (Ball); *Brass Band Blues* (Gould); *Czech Polka* (Strauss); *Tannhausser—Grand March* (Wagner, arr Rimmer); *Orpheus in the Underworld—Overture* (Offenbach); *Watching the Wheat* (arr Geehl); *Three of a Kind* (Helyer); *Serenade* (Heykens); *Spanish Harlequin* (Haysom). c Harry Mortimer

Massed Brass Bands, Vol.3—Decca LK4342, SKL4089 (60). *Fanfare* (Mortimer); *Ruy Blas—Overture* (Mendelssohn, arr Langford); *Perpetuum Mobile* (Strauss); *John Peel* (arr Mortimer); *Trumpet Voluntary* (Clarke, arr Gay); *The Yeomen of the Guard—Overture* (Sullivan, arr Sargent); *Finlandia* (Sibelius, arr Bidgood); *Whispering Brass* (Haysom, arr Gay); *Swedish Rhapsody* (Alfven); *Elizabethan Serenade* (Binge); *Merrie England—Selection* (German); *Sunset* (Lear). c Harry Mortimer

Men o' Brass—Columbia 33SX1752 (65), TW0101 (66) EMI NT335 (76). (Fairey Band, Fodens Motor Works, BMC) *Marche Militaire* (Schubert, arr Sargent); *Iolanthe—Overture* (Sullivan, arr Sargent); *Yeomen of the Guard—Overture* (Sullivan, arr Sargent);

Polonaise, Op.40, No.2 (Chopin, arr Sargent); *Prelude, Op.28, No.15* (Chopin, arr Sargent); *Fantasia, K608* (Mozart, arr Sargent). c Sir Malcolm Sargent

Men o' Brass—HMV CSD3691 (71). (Fairey Band, Fodens Motor Works, BMC) *Fanfare* (Hespe); *Men o' Brass* (Scull); *Masaniello—Overture* (Auber); *Three Jolly Sailormen* (Siebert); *A Victorian Rhapsody* (Jacob); *Deep Harmony* (Parker); *Semper Sousa* (arr Seymour); *When the Saints go marching in* (arr Langford); *Grandfather's Clock* (arr Doughty): *España—Waltz* (Waldteufel); *A Hunting Medley* (arr H. Mortimer); *March Brilliant* (Hume); *Hymns of Praise* (Seymour). c Harry Mortimer

Men o' Brass and Voices—HMV CSD3691 (71). (BMC Band, Fairey Band, Fodens, London Philharmonic Choir; Owen Brannigan) *Tribute to Sir Malcolm Sargent* (Dunn); *The Barber of Seville—Overture* (Rossini, arr Seymour); *The Long Day Closes* (Sullivan, arr Seymour); *Fantasy on British Sea Songs* (arr Langford); *The Old Superb* (Stanford, arr Harris); *The Damnation of Faust—Hungarian March* (Berlioz, arr Catelinet); *HMS Pinafore—Overture* (Sullivan, arr Sargent); *1812 Overture* (Tchaikovsky, arr D. Wright); *God Save the Queen* (arr Hespe). c Harry Mortimer & Sir Vivian Dunn

Semper Sousa—Columbia TW0385 (72). (Men o' Brass: Fairey, Fodens, City of Coventry) *Semper Sousa* (arr Seymour); *Picador March; The Corcoran Cadets; The Directorate; Fairest of the Fair; Beau Ideal; King Cotton; The Freelance; National Fencibles; Our Flirtations; The Occidental; El Capitan* (Sousa). c Harry Mortimer

Sousa the Great—Columbia SX6004, TW0113 (66). (BMC Band, Fairey, Fodens) *Stars and Stripes Forever; Washington Post; The Liberty Bell; Manhattan Beach; The Crusader; The Gladiator; The Belle of Chicago; The Invincible Eagle; The Thunderer; The Grid Iron Club; High School Cadets; Semper Fidelis; Hands Across the Sea* (Sousa). c Harry Mortimer

Stars in Brass—Columbia 33SX1530, SCX3484 (63). *Hungarian March* (Berlioz); *Tyrolean Tubas* (Clark); *Pique Dame—Overture* (Suppé); *Waltzing Trumpets* (Stephens); *Prelude to Revelry* (Jacob); *Le Père la Victoire* (Ganne); *Marching with Sullivan on Parade* (Sullivan); *The Sleigh Ride* (Anderson); *The Headless Horseman*

(Goodwin); *Kenilworth Suite* (Bliss) **36**; *Trumpet Fiesta* (Phillips); *Evening Hymn and Last Post* (arr Tulip). c Harry Mortimer

Other general collections

*The Best of Brass—World Records SM501/5 (78)†. (All Star Brass; Men o' Brass; Massed Brass; GUS; Fairey; Parc & Dare; Cory; Black Dyke Mills; Hammond's Sauce Works; etc)

Brass Spectacular (Golden Hour)—Pye GH608 (75)†. (Various Bands from the Pye label)

Festival of Championship Brass—Decca SPA, cass K28K32 (76). (Black Dyke Mills; Fairey; GUS; Yorkshire Imperial Metals; Brighouse & Rastrick; City of Coventry; Grimethorpe Colliery; Tredegar Junior; etc)

Festival of Famous Brass Bands—Boulevard BD3007 (79)†. (Watney; Luton; Grimethorpe Colliery; Fodens)

Golden Hour of Brass Bands—Pye GH521 (73)†. (Various bands from the Pye label)

Golden Hour of Top Brass—Pye GH641 (77)†. (Various Bands from the Pye label)

40 Brass band Favourites—Pickwick PDL8008 (2), cass PLDC8008 (79)†. (Fairey; City of Coventry; Leyland Vehicles; Sun Life Stanshawe; Grimethorpe Colliery; Solna Brass; Black Dyke Mills; City of London; GUS; Wingates Temperance; Yorkshire Imperial Metals)

Themes in Brass (Golden Hour)—Pye GH662 (78)†. (Various bands from the Pye label)

20 Brass Band Favourites—Pickwick PLE7015 (77)†. (Brighouse & Rastrick; Black Dyke Mills; Grimethorpe Colliery; Royal Doulton; Hendon; Excelsior Ropes Works; Yorkshire Imperial Metals; Fodens; Carlton Main Frickley)

22 Brass Band Favourites—Music for Pleasure MFP504360 (79)†. (Various bands from the EMI labels)

The Very Best of Brass—Columbia TWOX1048 (76)†. (Black Dyke Mills; GUS; BMC Concert Band; Fodens; All Star; Fairey; City of Coventry; Parc & Dare

The Very Best of Brass, Vol.2—Columbia TWOX1056 (77)†. (Fairey; Fodens; City of Coventry; Men O' Brass; Hammond's Sauce Works; Parc & Dare; GUS)

The World of Brass Bands—Decca PA20,

SPA20, cass KCSP20 (69)†. (Fodens; Fairey; Morris Motors)

The World of Brass Bands, Vol.2—Decca PA68, SPA68, cass KCSP68 (71)†. (Fodens; Fairey; Morris Motors; etc)

The World of Brass Bands, Vol.3—Decca SPA306 (73), cass KCSP306†. (Fodens; Fairey; Morris Motors)

The World of Brass Bands, Vol.4—Decca SPA413, (78), cass KCSP413†. (Black Dyke Mills; Brighouse & Rastrick; City of Coventry; Fairey; Manchester CWS; Yorkshire Imperial Metals)

The World of Brass Bands, Vol.5—Decca SPA533 (79), cass KCSP464†. (Philip Jones Brass; Fodens; Fairey; Ever Ready; Leyland; Desford; Brighouse & Rastrick)

C) Championship recordings

National Brass Band Festival, 1967—Pye NPL18200, NSPL18200 (68). (Brighouse & Rastrick; City of Coventry; Grimethorpe; GUS; Hanwell) *Crown Imperial* (Bliss); *Waltz Memories* (Schubert); *Facilita* (arr H. Mortimer); *Bandology* (Osterling); *Radetzky March* (Strauss I, arr Hartmann); *La Traviata—Prelude* (Verdi, arr D. Rimmer); *1812 Overture* (Tchaikovsky, arr D. Wright). c Sir Arthur Bliss, Eric Ball, Frank Wright, W.B. Hargreaves

National Brass Band Festival, 1968—Pye NPL18260, NSPL18260 (69). (Grimethorpe; Wingates Temperance; CWS; Luton; Shaftesbury Crusade) *The Impresario—Overture* (Cimarosa, arr Ball); *3rd Rhapsody on Negro Spirituals* (Ball); *The Mastersingers—Prelude* (Wagner, arr F. Wright) **68**; *The Thundercrest* (Osterling, arr F. Wright); *Music for the Royal Fireworks—Suite* (Handel, arr D. Wright); *Thunder and Lightning* (Strauss, arr F. Wright); *The Sceptered Isle—March* (Tomlinson); *Pomp and Circumstance March No.1* (Elgar, arr Hume). c Eric Ball, Frank Wright, Vilem Tausky

National Brass Band Festival, 1969—Pye GSGL10445 (70).

National Brass Festival, Royal Albert Hall, 1972—Decca SKL5143 (73). (Black Dyke Mills; Fairey; GUS; Yorkshire Imperial Metals; Yorkshire Celebration Choir) *Flourish for Brass* (Walters); *Lohengrin—Prelude Act 3* (Wagner, arr F. Wright); *Zadok the Priest—Coronation Hymn* (Handel, arr Brand); *Rhapsody in Blue* (Gershwin, arr Huckridge); *Cornet Cascade* (Docker); *Marche Joyeuse* (Chabrier, arr F. Wright); *The Force of Destiny—Overture* (Verdi, arr F. Wright); *La Traviata—Prelude Act 1* (Verdi, arr D. Rimmer); *Sea Song Suite* (arr Jacob). c George Hurst, Geoffrey Brand, Trevor Walmsley, Roy Newsome

National Brass Festival, Royal Albert Hall, 1973—Decca SKL5171 (74). (Brighouse & Rastrick; City of Coventry; Grimethorpe; GUS) *Colonel Bogey on Parade* (Alford); *Two Blind Men of Toledo* (Méhul, arr D. Wright); *Tournament for Brass* (Ball); *Radetzky March* (Strauss I, arr Ryan); *The Plantagenets* (Gregson); *Presenting the Brass* (Howarth); *Waltz No.1* (Shostakovitch). c Geoffrey Brand, Eric Ball, Walter Hargreaves

National Brass Festival, Albert Hall, 1974—Decca SPA369 (75)†. (Black Dyke Mills; Brighouse & Rastrick; Cory; City of Coventry) *Ruy Blas—Overture* (Mendelssohn, arr Langford); *Little Serenade* (Tomlinson); *Cornet Concerto* (Tomlinson); *Torch of Freedom* (Ball); *Trombonioso* (Binge); *The Mastersingers—Prelude Act 3* (Wagner, arr F. Wright) **68**; c Sir Charles Groves, Ernest Tomlinson.

National Brass Festival, Albert Hall, 1975—Pye TB3004 (76)†. (Brighouse & Rastrick; Cory; Fairey; Yorkshire Imperial Metals) *Colditz March* (Farnon, arr Langford); *Concorde March* (Farnon, arr Street); *Westminster Waltz* (Farnon, arr Brand); *Belle of the Ball* (Anderson, arr Tomlinson); *Rhapsody for Trombone and Brass Band* (Langford); *Cavalleria Rusticana—Intermezzo* (Mascagni); *Tombstone, Arizona* (Wood); *The Girl with the Flaxen Hair* (Debussy, arr Brand); *The Trojans—March* (Berlioz, arr Robinson); c Robert Farnon, Geoffrey Brand, H. Arthur Kenney

National Brass Festival, Albert Hall, 1976—RCA LSA3285 (77). (Brighouse & Rastrick; CWS; GUS; Yorkshire Imperial Metals; Versatile Brass) *The Wayfarer—Sinfonietta* (Ball) **76**; *Danza Alegre* (Burke); *Carnival of Venice* (arr Del Steiger); *La Bamba* (Woodfield); *I only have eyes for you* (Warren, arr Woodfield); *Rhapsody on American Gospel Songs* (Ball); *Salute to the Six* (Langford); *Crown Imperial* (Walton, arr F. Wright); etc. c Bryden Thomson, Eric Ball, James Shepherd.

National Brass Festival, Albert Hall,

1977—RCA PL25118 (78)†. (Grimethorpe Colliery; Wingates Temperance: Stanshawe Colliery; Yorkshire Imperial Metals) *Orb and Sceptre* (Walton, arr Ball); *Greensleeves* (arr Howarth); *Berne March* (arr Howarth); *Concerto No.2 for Brass Band—Finale* (Bourgeois); *Lohengrin—Prelude Act 3* (Wagner, arr D. Wright); *Life Divine* (Jenkins) **21**; *Trumpet Voluntary* (Bennett arr Howarth); *Concerto for Trumpet* (James, arr Howarth); *Russlan and Ludmilla—Overture* (Glinka, arr Hargreaves). c Elgar Howarth, Harry Mortimer.

National Brass Festival, Albert Hall, 1978—RCA PL25192 (79)†. (Carlton; Ever Ready; Besses; Solna; Black Dyke; Great Universal) *October Festival* (Ball); *Caribbean Cameo* (trad arr Sharpe); *Serenade—Alla Marcia* (Wiren, arr Fröden); *Rhapsody in Brass* (Goffin); *European Fantasy* (Langford); *Lincolnshire Poacher* (arr Langford); *In the Hall of the Mountain King* (Grieg, arr Smith); *The Corsair—Overture* (Berlioz, arr Brand); *Marche Slave* (Tchaikovsky, arr Davis)

D) Other brass recordings

Hallé Brass Consort
Hallé Brass Consort—Pye GGC14114,

GSGC14114 (68). *Quintet for Two Trumpets, Horn, Trombone and Tuba* (Arnold); *Quintet for Brass* (Gregson); *Music Hall Suite for Brass Quintet* (Horovitz); *Rounds for Brass Quintet* McCabe).

Philip Jones Brass Ensemble
Divertimento—Argo ZRG851 (77)†. *4 Pieces* (Maurer); *Sleeping Beauty—Waltz* (Tchaikovsky, arr Fletcher); *Quartet in the Form of a Sonata* (Simon); *Étude Charac-teristique* (Arban, arr Howarth); *Fanfare* (Bennett); *Fantasy for Trombone* (Arnold); *Pasce Tuos* (Dufay, arr Howarth); *Four Outings* (Previn).

Easy Winners—Argo ZRG895, cass KZRC895 (77)†. *Kraken* (Hazell); *Tuba Serenade* (Mozart, arr Fletcher); *Ragtime Dance* (Joplin, arr Iveson); *Black Sam* (Hazell); *Frère Jacques* (Iveson); *Borage* (Hazell); *The Easy Winners* (Joplin, arr Iveson); *Tico Tico* (Abreu; Oliveira; Drake, arr Iveson); *Mr Jums* (Hazell); *Czardas* (Monti, arr James); *Le Petit Nègre* (Debussy, arr Emerson); *Of Knights and Castles* (Premru); *Le Bateau sur Léman* (Premru); *Blues March* (Premu).

Just Brass—Argo ZRG655, (70)†. *Brass Quintet* (Arnold); *Suite for Brass Septet*

The Philip Jones Brass Ensemble (The Decca Record Company Ltd).

(Dodgson); *Divertimento* (Salzedo); *Symphony for Brass* (Ewald).

PJBE Plays—Argo ZRG813 (75)†. *Divertimento* (Addison); *Sonata for Brass* (Dodgson); *Theme and Variations* (Gardner); *Commedia IV* (Bennett)

Modern Brass—Argo ZRG906 (79)†. *Symphony for Brass Instruments, Op.123* (Arnold); *Capriccio for Brass* (Salzedo); *Music from Harter Fell* (Premru).

Also:

Baroque Brass—Argo ZRG898†.

Classics for Brass—Argo ZRG731 (73)†.

Fanfare—Argo ZRG870 (78)†.

Golden Brass—Argo ZRG717†.

Philip Jones Brass Ensemble—Claves DPS600†.

*Pictures at an Exhibition (Mussorgsky) —Argo ZRG885†.

Renaissance Brass—Argo ZRG823†.

Strings and Brass—Argo ZRG644†.

Voices and Brass—Argo ZRG576†.

World of Brass—Decca SPA464†.

Locke Brass Consort

Jubilant Brass—RCA RL25081 (77)†.

Locke Brass Consort—Unicorn RHS339 (77)†.

Locke Brass Consort—Unicorn RHS349 (78)†.

Gerard Schwarz (etc)

Cousins—Nonesuch H-71341 (77).

James Watson (trumpet)

Trumpet Man (with orchestra—Columbia SCX6589 (79)†.

Lyndon Howard Baglin (euphonium)

Lyndon Baglin: Showcase for the Euphonium—Saydisc SDL269 (78)†.

Foursome for Brass—Saydisc SDL254.

Bibliography

Play the Music, Play! by Major Brindley Boon (Salvationist Publishing, London, 1966) [Salvation Army Bands].

Brass Bands in the 20th Century edited by Violet & Geoffrey Brand (Egon Publishers, Letchworth, 1979).

The Bandsman's Everything Within edited by Kenneth Cook (Hinrichsen, London, 1950).

Oh! Listen to the Band edited by Kenneth Cook (Hinrichsen, London, 1950).

Brass Bands of Yorkshire by T.L. Cooper (Dalesman, Yorks, 1974).

The Standard Directory of Brass and Military Bands edited by Leo Croke (Musical Distributors, London, 1939).

The Brass Band by Harold C. Hind (Boosey & Hawkes, London, 1934; reprint 1952).

Brass in Your School by Ian Lawrence (Oxford University Press, London, 1973).

That the Medals and the Baton be Put on View: the Story of a Village Band, 1875-1975 by Henry Livings (David & Charles, Newton Abbot, 1973) [The Dobcross Band].

Talks With Bandsmen: Popular Handbook for Brass Instrumentalists by A.R. Rose (Rider, London, 1895).

The Brass Band Movement by John F. Russell & J.H. Elliott (Dent, London, 1936).

A Practical Guide to Instruments for the Brass band by Edrich Siebert (Studio Music, London, 1976).

Brass Bands by Arthur R. Taylor (Granada Publishing, London, 1979).

Scoring for Brass bands by Denis Wright (Duckworth, Colne).

Brass Band Tuning by Denis Wright (Wright & Round, Liverpool, 1933).

The Amateur Band Teacher's Guide and Bandsman's Adviser by Denis Wright & Enoch Round (Brass Band News, Gloucester, 1889).

Brass Today edited by Frank Wright (Bessen, London, 1957).

Famous Bands of the British Empire by A.E. Zealey & J. Ord Hume (Hull, London, 1926).